INTERNATIONALIZATION OF HIGHER EDUCATION

Internationalization of Higher Education

Access and Quality

Edited by
Lokanath Mishra

SHIPRA

ISBN: 978-81-7541-688-8

First Published in India in 2013

Internationalization of Higher Education: Access and Quality

Published by:
SHIPRA PUBLICATIONS
H.O.: LG 18-19, Pankaj Central Market, Patparganj,
Delhi-110092, Tel: 91-11-2223 5152, 2223 6152
Br.Off.: 4617/18, Ansari Road, Darya Ganj,
New Delhi-110002, Tel: 9650028065, 9810522367
E-mail: info@shiprapublications.com
www.shiprapublications.com

Foreword

Education is a continuous process, an endless or the lifelong practice, to make the life of man worthy, prosperous and meaningful. True education brings out what a human being already has within. It fills him with enthusiasm and dynamism, and calls for action to pave the way to progress and achieving the goal in an atmosphere surcharged with cooperation and coordination with a sole purpose of the wellbeing of one and all. Education urges for doing something concrete in accordance with the universal principle of unity. Therefore, education plays the vital role in man's life, for the all-round development of his personality and the welfare of humanity as a whole.

Further, higher education plays an indispensible role in the making of life—developing human mind and body, personality in full. On the strength of study, research, observation and analysis it creates a broad outlook in man. Thus, the role of higher education in man's life becomes more important in comparison to primary and secondary levels of learning. Side-by-side in its ongoing process higher level of education faces more challenges also. For, the responsibility of the community of teachers and educators associated with it multiplies many folds, and if it is discharged well through their continuous and prejudice-free efforts, they, in fact, contribute significantly towards this end and, therefore, perform their duty towards the society, national and the world.

It is a matter of satisfaction and pleasure that Dr. Lokanath Mishra, a known educator and currently the Principal of Vivek College of Education in the city of Bijnor [Uttar Pradesh] has prepared an edited work under the title, *Internationalization of Higher Education.* For this, he has put immense labour and thus through his endeavor he has rendered a commendable service to the world of higher education. It is indeed a welcome addition to the realm of higher education. I congratulate the author and the contributors for their valuable and timely effort and wish the work a grand success.

Padma Shri Professor Dr. Ravindra Kumar
Former Vice Chancellor, Meerut University

Preface

The humble piece of work has witnessed the light of the goddess MAA MANGALA. I bow my head to her mercy. Internationalization, like globalization is a concept with different interpretations. Internationalization of higher education can be viewed either from a national policy perspective or institutional perspective. Internationalization can be viewed as "an intentional national response to globalization" used to facilitate understanding of the global environment and ways of interaction in it or "as a systematic, sustained effort by government to make higher education institutions more responsive to the challenges of 'globalization' of the economy and society". Transnational education is commonly defined as "All types of higher education study programs or sets of courses of study, or educational services (including those of distance education) in which the learners are located in a country different from the one where the awarding institution is based". Such programs may belong to the education system of a State different from the State in which it operates, or may operate independently of any national education system.

I am extremely beholden to my wife Mrs. Reeta Mishra and all the family members who have been a pillar of strength of my work. The editor is highly indebted to his research guide Prof. Santanu Kumar Swain, Faculty of Education, BHU; Dr Ravindra Kumar , Ex-Vice Chancellor of CCS University, Meerut; Prof. Ajaz Mashi, Jamia Millia Islamia, New Delhi; Prof. K.C. Kapoor, Vice-Chancellor of Rajeev Gandhi Central University, Arunachal Pradesh; Prof. Nima Venkata Rao and Dr. B.C. Das, Asst. Professor, Banasthali University for providing the guidance for developing the book.

I look forward to suggestions from all the readers for further improving the subject content as well as presentation of the book.

Contents

PART III
Quality in Higher Education

List of Abbreviations

AC & EC	Academic Council and Executive Council
AICTE	All India Council for Technical Education
API	Academic Performance Indicator
ASC	Academic Staff College
ASIST	Assistance for Strengthening Infrastructure in Science and Technology
ASIHSS	Assistance for Strengthening Infrastructure in Humanities and Social Sciences
CAS	Centers for Advanced Studies
CBCS	Choice-based Credit System
CDC	College Development Council
CEC	Consortium for Educational Communication
CEDC	Community Education Development Cell
CPE	Colleges with Potential for Excellence
CTE	College of Teacher Education
DEC	Distance Education Council
DHEI	Diversity in Higher Education Index
DIET	District Institute of Education and Training
DISE	District Information System for Education
EBD	Educationally Backward District
EER	Eligible Enrolment Rate
EHEI	Equity in Higher Education Index
ENCORE	Enhance Scholarly Faculty Resources
EOC	Establishment of Equal Opportunity Cell
FDC	Faculty Development Centre
FDP	Faculty Development Programme
FYP	Five-Year Plan
GER	Gross Enrolment Ratio
GoI	Government of India
IASE	Institute of Advanced Study in Education

ICT	: Information and Communication Technology
IIIT	: Indian Institute of Information Technology
IISER	: Indian Institute of Science Education and Research
IIM	: Indian Institute of Management
IIT	: Indian Institute of Technology
IMF	: Instrumentation Maintenance Facility
IQAC	: Internal Quality Assurance Cell
ISEC	: International Standards for Educational Classification
IT	: Information Technology
ITI	: Industrial Training Institute
IUC	: Inter-University Centre
JRF	: Junior Research Fellowship
MIS	: Management Information System
MHRD	: Ministry of Human Resource Development
MoU	: Memoranda of Understanding
MRP	: Major Research Project
NAAC	: National Assessment and Accreditation Council
NCHER	: National Commission on Higher Education and Research
NCTE	: National Council for Teacher Education
NE	: North-Eastern
NET	: National Eligibility Test
NGO	: Non-Government Organization
NIFT	: National Institute of Fashion Technology
NIT	: National Institute of Technology
NKC	: National Knowledge Commission
NKN	: National Knowledge Network
NMC	: National Monitoring Cell
NMEICT	: National Mission on Education through Information and Communication Technology
NPE	: National Policy on Education
NSS	: National Sample Survey
NSSO	: National Sample Survey Organization
NUEPA	: National University of Educational Planning and Administration
OBC	: Other Backward Classes
ODL	: Open and Distance Learning
PBAS	: Performance Based Appraisal System
PIHEAD	: Promotion of Indian Higher Education Abroad
PPP	: Public Private Partnership
RA	: Research Associateship

RUSA	: Rashtriya Uchch Shiksha Abhiyan
SAM	: Sensitization / Awareness / Motivation
SAP	: Special Assistance Programme
SC	: Scheduled Caste
SCERT	: State Council of Educational Research and Training
SPA	: School of Planning and Architecture
SSA	: Sarva Shiksha Abhiyan
ST	: Scheduled Tribe
UG/PG	: Undergraduate / Postgraduate
UGC	: University Grants Commission

1

Internationalization of Higher Education: Global Trends

Kartar Singh

Internationalization of Higher Education is globally one of the current topics of discussion. Author explains the meaning of Internationalization, Higher Education and Internationalization of Higher Education. A difference between Internationalization of Higher Education and Globalization of Higher Education is also explained. Different modes and models of Internationalization of Higher Education which are globally operating are described. Features of Internationalization of Higher Education in India, reasons along with rational are discussed. At last, different approaches and benefits of Internationalization of Higher Education are highlighted.

MEANING OF INTERNATIONALIZATION, HIGHER EDUCATION AND INTERNATIONALIZATION OF HIGHER EDUCATION AND GLOBALIZATION VERSUS INTERNATIONALIZATION

Internationalization

The prefix "inter" of "Internationalization" comes from a Latin word which originally means "between, mutual" and others. When a "nation" is taken as a country, "international" can be interpreted as "between or among countries", and its verb form "internationalize" can be translated as "making relations, effects or scopes international," or specifically, "bringing under international control or protection". It would be easy to say that "internationalism", "internationalize" and "Internationalization "all derive from "international". Consequently, none of "internationalize" form "Internationalization" which means the "action or process" of internationalizing. More precisely, "Internationalization" places emphasis on transferring into other nations or especially in international society beyond the boundary of the nation, accepting relationships among nations, impacts on and from other nations, or mutual influences and relationships at a national level.

Higher Education

Education beyond the class 12th is known as higher education. Higher education has become increasingly international in the past two decades as more and more students choose to study abroad or enroll in foreign educational programmes and institutions in their home country. It is happening because of that a large number of students have been passing class 12th and it is being difficult for their home country to absorb this increasing number of students in the existing higher education system.

Internationalization of Higher Education

The Internationalization of higher education is basically the process of presenting exchange activities in education and research of various kinds among universities and institutions in different countries. Full-fledged international exchange in higher education is typically regarded as an activity in the higher education sector; developed on the premise of the existence of a nation after modern states were established in Europe. UNESCO (2006) has given the following definition of the Internationalization of education. "It is Higher education that takes place in situations where the teacher, student, programme, institution or provider and course materials cross-national jurisdictional borders. Cross-border education may include higher education by public or private and not-for-profit/ for-profit providers. It encompasses a wide range of modalities in a continuum from face-to-face (taking various forms from students traveling abroad and campuses abroad) to distance learning (using technologies and including e-learning)."The purpose, content and pattern of the exchange vary across the ages. For example, international exchange, which was a fundamental human exchange consisting mainly of students, teachers and scholars up until the 1970s, has drastically changed to include joint research activities, curricular exchange, mutual accreditation of programmes and degrees among universities beyond national borders as well as the affiliation or linkage of universities since the 1980s and especially the 1990s. The current Internationalization of higher education mainly comprises: (i) human exchange, mainly of students, teachers and researchers; (ii) the exchange and accreditation of programmes, courses and degrees, including the sharing of curriculums and especially the development of transnational programmes, and (iii) research project activities, including the organization of international conferences and joint research, mainly for presenting research results and academic exchange.

Internationalization of Higher Education is seen as one of the ways a country responds to the impact of globalization. Knight (1993) describes Internationalization of Higher Education as "the process of integrating an international/intercultural dimension into the teaching, research and service functions of the institution". There are several key concepts in this definition that the idea of Internationalization being a dynamic process and not a set of isolated activities, integration or infusion that contributes to the sustainability of the international dimension. In this way, this definition refers to the primary and universal functions of an institution of higher education, namely, teaching research and service to society. Vender Wende (1997) "any systematic sustained efforts aimed at making higher education responsive to the requirements and challenges related to the globalization of societies, economy and labour markets". On the basis of this definition it can be said that the Internationalization is not merely an aim itself, but an important resource in the development of higher education towards firstly, a system in line with international standards, secondly, one open and responsive to its global environment.

Globalization and Internationalization

It is also important to differentiate globalization and Internationalization, when trying to understand the Internationalization of higher education. The term globalization has been used since the latter half of the 1960s. There has been a drastic rise of globalization in the fields of economy and culture for last two decades. Jane Knight from (1994) "a process of integrating an international and cultural dimension into the teaching, research and service functions of the institution." Scott (2006) observes that both Internationalization and globalization are complex phenomena with many strands, and concludes that "the distinction between Internationalization and globalization, although suggestive, cannot be regarded as categorical. They overlap, and are intertwined, in all kinds of ways." Teichler (2004) notes that "globalization initially seemed to be defined as the totality of substantial changes in the context and inner life of higher education, related to growing inter-relationships between different parts of the world whereby national borders are blurred or even seem to vanish." But according to him, in recent years the term 'globalization' is substituted for internationalization in the public debate on higher education, resulting at the same time in a shift of meanings: "the term tends to be used for any supra-regional phenomenon related top higher education and/or anything on a global scale related to higher education characterized by market and competition." Altbach, Reisberg and Rumbley (2009: 7) state that "Globalization, a key reality in the 21st century, has already profoundly influenced higher education. We define globalization as the reality shaped by an increasingly integrated world economy, new information and communications technology, the emergence of an international knowledge network, the role of the English language, and other forces beyond the control of academic institutions. Internationalization is defined as the variety of policies and programmes that universities and governments implement to respond to Globalization." Knight (2008) acknowledges the need for constant updating of the meaning of internationalization of higher education, as "the international dimension of higher education has been steadily increasing in importance, scope, and complexity." As new realities and challenges of the current environment she mentions globalization and the emergence of the knowledge economy, regionalization, information and communication technologies, new providers, alternate funding sources, borderless issues, lifelong learning, and the growth in the numbers and diversity of actors.

Globalization and Internationalization are related but not the same thing. Globalization is the context of economic and academic trends that are part of the reality of the 21st century. Internationalization includes the policies and practices undertaken by academic systems and institutions – and even individual – to cope with the global academic environment. Globalization as the economic, political, and societal forces is pushing 21st century higher education towards greater international involvement. Global capital has, for the first time, heavily invested in knowledge industries worldwide, including higher education and advanced training. This investment reflects the emergence of the "knowledge society," the rise of the service sector, and the dependence of many societies on knowledge products and highly educated personnel for economic growth. The results of globalization include the integration of research, the use of English as the lingua Franca for scientific communication, the growing international labour market for scholars and scientists, the growth of communications firms and of multinational and technology publishing, and the use of information technology. Information technology facilitates communication; permits efficient storage, selection, and dissemination of knowledge; and allows providers to offer academic programmes through e-learning. The essay delineates academic programmes, institutions, innovations, and practices created to cope with globalization and to reap its benefits. Globalization may be unalterable, but Internationalization involves many choices. Globalization tends to concentrate wealth, knowledge, and power in those already possessing these elements. International academic mobility similarly favours well-developed education systems and institutions, thereby compounding existing inequalities. Initiatives and programmes, coming largely from the developed countries, focus on the developing countries. Developed countries own most knowledge, knowledge products, and information technology infrastructure, though their activities are increasing, especially in Asia and Africa. Internationalization is a two-way street – students move largely from Asia to Europe, for example – and serves important needs in the developing world. But the Europe largely controls the process. The cross-border movement of students and of higher education programmes and institutions – big business for universities and other providers – the growing international market for academic and scientific personnel, curricular Internationalization, and the commercialization of international higher education, especially the growing influence of the for-profit higher education sector. World Trade Organization (WTO) member countries implement the agreement; focus on facilitating academic mobility via:

Cross-border supply – This mode may include distance education (e-learning) and franchising courses or degrees. It does not necessarily require the physical movement of the consumer or provider.

Consumption abroad – The consumer moves to the country of the provider. This mode includes traditional student mobility.

Commerce presence – The service provider establishes facilities in another country including branch campuses and joint ventures with local institutions.

Presence of natural persons – This mode includes persons, including professors and researchers, who temporarily travel to another country to provide educational services.

Rationale of Internationalization of Higher Education – There are a number of different rationales for wanting to integrate an international dimension into higher education. Warner (1992) examines the various assumptions and imperatives that derive the Internationalization agenda at different universities. He proposed following three different models:

Competitive Model – He wanted to introduce international content into curricula and other elements of campus life is chiefly a means to make students, the institution and the country more competitive in the global economic marketplace.

Liberal Model – He identified the primary goal of the Internationalization as self-development in a changing world and global education in human relations and citizenship.

Social Transformation Model – He suggested that the most important goal of Internationalization is to give students a deeper awareness of international and intercultural issues related to equity and justice, and to give them the tools to work actively and critically towards social transformation.

Knight (1997) clusters the possible rationales for Internationalization into following four groups:

Political Rational – It relates to issues concerning the country's position and role as a nation in the world for security, peace, stability etc.

Economic Rational – It refers to objectives related to either the long-term economic effects, where Internationalization of higher education is seen as a contribution to the skilled human resources needed for international competitiveness of the nation and where foreign graduates are seen as keys to the country's trade relations or the direct economic benefits like institutional income.

Academic Rational – It includes objectives related to the aims and functions of higher education. It is often assumed that by enhancing the international dimension of teaching, research and service there is value added to the quality of a higher education system. This premise is clearly based on the assumption that Internationalization is considered to be central to the mission of the institution. Linked to the notion of enhancing the quality of education is the idea that Internationalization is often a positive change agent for institutional building.

Cultural and Social Rational – It concentrates on the role and place of the country's own culture and language and on the importance of understanding foreign languages and culture.

INTERNATIONALIZATION OF HIGHER EDUCATION AT GLOBAL LEVEL

Laureate (formerly Sylvan Learning Systems) and the Apollo Group (the parent company of the University of Phoenix, now the largest private university in the United States) – entered the international market by establishing new institutions, purchasing existing institutions, and partnering with firms or educational institutions in other countries. Many countries also host new private universities with overseas links, some in the for-profit sector. Many universities use American, British, German, or other foreign curricula; many teaching English, and some are accredited in other countries. Many universities are located in countries where governments cut public funding and encouraged international ventures – Australia and the United Kingdom, for example. Most initiatives – including branch campuses, franchised degree programmes, and partnerships with local institutions – are focused on developing and middle-income countries. Many countries recruit international students to earn profits by charging high fees – including Australia, Canada, the United Kingdom, and the United States. The proportion of young people demanding and obtaining access worldwide expanded dramatically with the advent of mass higher education. Demand is rapidly increasing, even in countries still enrolling less than 20 per cent of the age group, such as India, China, and much of Africa. Many international higher education services – focused on profits – provide access to students in countries lacking the domestic capacity to meet the demand. Access can take many forms: branch campuses, franchised foreign academic programmes or degrees, or independent institutions based on foreign academic models.

DEVELOPING-COUNTRY INTERNATIONALIZATION

Developing countries host a significant number of international students. Developing countries seek to attract foreign students to their universities to improve the quality and cultural composition of the student body, gain prestige, and earn income. India and the Philippines, for example, are significant host countries for students from other developing countries. India hosts more than 8,000 students from abroad, 95 per cent of developing countries (Bhalla, 2005). China, Malaysia, and India are developing strategies to attract students and to export educational programmes and institutions.

INDIVIDUAL INTERNATIONALIZATION

Individuals make many key decisions concerning destinations and fields of study. Students, though constrained by immigration regulations, decide whether they will return home following their academic work or stay at home and enroll in the programmes offered by foreign education providers. Most of the world's more than 2 million international students are self-funded, that is, they and their families pay for their own academic work. Students are therefore the largest source of funds for international education – not governments, academic institutions.

India's higher education sector imports and exports programmes and services at an unprecedented pace. One initiative is the partnership between the Caparo Group – a U.K. firm with interests in steel, engineering, and hotels – and Carnegie Mellon University (United States) to set up a new campus in India. Asia Pacific Vietnam is an emerging center of activity. RMIT from Australia owns 100 per cent of a branch campus, whereas Troy State

University from the United States established a foreign branch, the International College of IT and Management. The number of active partnerships between local and foreign institutions is steadily expanding. For instance, the University of Hue in Vietnam recently developed a franchised and joint degree bachelor's programme in tourism with the University of Hawaii. Hanoi University of Technology is currently offering master's and bachelor's degrees with higher education institutions from Belgium (1), France (8), Germany (1), Singapore (2), and the United States (1). The Vietnamese government recently announced the development of the International University in Vietnam – another initiative to increase national capacity for higher education. Half the university teaching staff will be Vietnamese, and the other half will be from foreign universities. Foreign institutional involvement will build on and expand from the current links of Ho Chi Minh City National University. Australia, China, Egypt, and the United States are increasing cross-border education in Thailand. The Egyptian Al-Azhar University and Jinan University of China plan to open a branch campus, whereas Swinburne University of Technology (Australia) has operated a branch campus since 1998, though it is changing its focus to industry training only. Troy State University has a teaching site in Bangkok for its MBA programme; students can transfer to the United States depending on funds and visa requirements. The Thai-German Graduate School of Engineering, 13 Australian universities, and nine U.K. universities also operate in Thailand. The University of New South Wales (Australia) will establish the first 100 per cent foreign-owned higher education institution in Singapore after receiving government approval. The university plans to offer undergraduate and graduate programmes and to develop a strong research capacity. Other respected foreign institutions offer education and training programmes in Singapore through joint ventures, exchanges, and branch campuses, including the University Of Chicago Graduate School Of Business, Shanghai Jiaotong University, Stanford University, the German Technische Universidad München, and the Technische Universities Eindhoven (the Netherlands). Singapore institutions, in turn, are noteworthy exporters. The National University of Singapore and Fudan University developed a joint MBA, aimed at Chinese and Singapore students. The National University is also embarking on a new graduate school initiative for Chinese students to be located in Suzhou Graduate Town, part of the Suzhou Industrial Park. Raffles LaSalle Limited is a publicly traded Singapore company that provides programmes in fashion and design in many Asian countries. It is described as a remarkable instance of international partnership, combining a Singapore firm with branches in Australia, China, Malaysia and Thailand, accreditation from an Australian state and a Canadian province, degrees from an Australian and a UK university, and a number of in-county university and college partners.

INTERNATIONALIZATION OF HIGHER EDUCATION IN INDIA

The Association of Indian Universities arranged a Round Table on

'Internationalization of Indian Higher Education' at the University of Mysore. They discussed the mechanisms to promote Internationalization of Indian Higher Education at select Indian universities. They adopted the following 'Mysore Statement'. The Mysore Statement contains:

Accepting that Internationalization of higher education is a fact of life in the new 'knowledge era',

Realizing that Internationalization would lead to an improvement in the quality of education, promote Indian culture abroad, produce understanding and yield financial benefits,

Recognizing that partnership and networking are essential for to enrich the teaching learning and to improve quality of research,

Believing that it is necessary to act in earnest immediately, Resolved the government, academic institutions and the Association of Indian Universities take necessary steps to promote Indian higher education internationally.

After the deliberations, they recommended following actions to the Government:

Take suitable action to promote Indian culture abroad. This needs setting up a Committee for promoting Indian Education Abroad.

Allow Indian Universities to open offshore campus abroad. Amend the University Grants Commission Act 1956 and the Acts of other statutory councils to include a specific provision allowing universities to open offshore campuses and export Indian education through the distance.

Simplify the procedures about registration, entry test need, the issue of 'No Objection Certificate' and the issue and extension of visas.

Indian Embassies and High Commissions abroad must play a role in providing information about higher education available in India. They should help in the conduct of fairs, entrance examinations and student recruitment.

Frame an open-door policy for financing students.

They recommended the creation of a central website to strengthen the information base and spread of information.

Government and other statutory bodies' should grant greater autonomy and flexibility to universities to admit foreign students and to enter collaborative arrangements with foreign institutions.

Create a Task Force including representatives of different bodies like the University Grant Commission, All India Council for Technical education and the Medical Council of India for admitting students to different professional programmes.

The government should consider extending financing for international education. This will enable institutions providing financial aid to Indian students going abroad, to foreign students coming to India and to educational institutions wishing to develop infrastructures for international education.

There should be a suitable means to watch the standard of education given by foreign universities. The committee recommended following actions for considerations of Academic Institutions:

Universities and other academic institutions that enroll large number of international students must have enough facilities to provide needed environment. Evaluate strengths in different disciplines of education and identify areas that would attract international students at different levels. Simplify the procedure for admitting international students.

Indian academic institutions should set up partnerships and develop networks with foreign universities in both the developed and the developing countries.

It is better if the academic environment of the partnering university is similar to that of Indian universities. Updating and Internationalization of the curriculum will get highest priority.

Students from non-English speaking countries often have an inadequate knowledge of the English language. Arrangement for conducting special English classes for them is necessary. Indian universities should develop special short-term programmes for students from developing countries who would like to visit India to learn more about its culture and heritage, natural possessions, diversity, languages or indigenous technologies.

STREAMS AND MODALITIES OF INTERNATIONALIZATION OF HIGHER EDUCATION

The streams of Internationalization of higher education have two major dimensions. One dimension is merely domestic which refers to the international and intercultural dimensions of without ever leaving their home country. The second dimension refers to the mobility of the participants across national borders. It is also called cross-border education, and this type of education growing rapidly, particularly at the higher education level. According to a UNESCO (2006) report, cross-border mobility of the programmes is "a movement of individual education or training courses and programmes across national boundaries through face-to-face, distance or a combination of these. Foreign country provider or the affiliated domestic partner or both of them jointly award credits for the course." Franchising, double or joint degrees and various articulation models are popular methods of international programme mobility. A short description of each follows:

Franchise: This is an arrangement whereby a reputed institution allows another institution in another country to deliver programmes in that country. The more a reputed organization usually awards the qualification. Partners customize their arrangements for teaching, management, assessment, profit sharing and awarding of qualification each franchise.

Double/joint Degree: In these arrangements, institutions in different countries offer a programme jointly for which a student receives a qualification from each organization. Institutions customize arrangements for the programme provision and the basis for awarding the qualifications for each arrangement.

Articulation: Articulation arrangements between institutions of different countries allow students to gain credit for courses offered by all the providers.

This allows students to gain credit for work done by a provider other than the provider awarding the qualification.

Distance Education: In this arrangement, institutions deliver a programme to students in different countries through distance and online. It may include some face-to-face support for students through domestic study centers. The main reason of these collaborations is to improve acceptability of the programmes and their creditworthiness. Who awards the degree is important depending on the reputation of the institution. Recognition of qualification for employment or further study is the most important reason. Given that several types of programme delivery in these collaborations, there are questions about the ownerships of intellectual property rights associated to course design and materials, responsibilities of partners in academic, staffing, recruitment, evaluation, financial and administrative matters. From an academic point, these dimensions in higher education affect the country's higher education institutions intellectual enrichment, and stimulate teaching and research. From the cultural angle, it helps to understand the cultures of other cultures.

REASONS OF INTERNATIONALIZATION OF HIGHER EDUCATION

Demand for Internationalization and Initiatives

Trends of Higher Education in India

Higher Education in India has expanded many folds in the last few decades. The number of universities has increased from 20 in 1947 to 634 in 2011. The growth in capacity of higher education has improved enrollment ratio from less than 1 per cent in 1950 to around 12.4 per cent in 2011. Since independence of the country in 1947, the higher education has grown 33 folds in a number of institutions making availability of education to the masses. The education providers include public nonprofit, private nonprofit and private for-profit institutions and have a mixture of public and private institutions. There is no boundary between public and private institutions as many public universities now look for private financing and charge a tuition or service charge. On the other hand, private institutions are eligible for public funds and engage in social nonprofit actions. The expansion of public universities has been slow and skewed at regional distribution. Many Universities, managed by the state governments have many affiliating colleges and academic matters are not properly managed. Thus despite noticeable growth in the number of state run universities there is scope rather need for expansion in the number of institutions. Since 1990, private higher education institutes have started emerging. These are business houses that provide education programmes or services for profit purposes. They impart education and training programmes than undertaking research and scholarly pursuits. Examples of some these new providers are Aptech and NIIT. These new providers are either campus based or virtual universities and they coexist with traditional education providers.

Global Trends in Higher Education

There are 2364 universities in USA, 104 universities in the UK, 330 universities in Germany. USA has the largest system of higher education in the world. The student enrollment ratio in higher education in USA is 86 per cent and in France is 55 per cent. According to UNESCO (2006) report, the need for international education will increase from 1.8 million international students in 2000 to 7.2 million international students in 2025. This rise creates huge challenges as well as opportunities. Though exact figures cannot be correctly estimated, it is obvious there will be a rise in the programmes and institutions across national boundaries. To meet this rising demand, institutions across the globe have introduced several steps. We produce some of the Initiatives below.

- Phoenix University has become the largest private university in the U.S. (owned and managed by the Apollo Group company) and delivering courses in Puerto Rico, Netherlands, Mexico and Canada. Other Apollo institutions are offering courses in Brazil, India and China.
- The Netherlands Business School opened a branch campus in Nigeria.
- Harvard University is improving campuses in Cyprus and the United Arab Emirates.
- Jinan University will be the first Chinese university to open a branch outside China.
- Laureate Education picked up higher education organizations in Chile, Mexico, Panama, Costa Rica, Spain, Switzerland and France.
- Dubai has developed a "Knowledge Village" in the Dubai Technology and Media Free Zone.
- The London School of Economics, Manipal Academy of Higher Education (India) and the University of Wollongong (Australia) are offering courses using franchising agreements and branch campuses.
- The University of Westminster (UK) has formed partnership with Kingdom University of Bahrain and developing similar arrangements with institutions in Nigeria, Uzbekistan and Kazakhstan.

The examples confirm that globalization and global partnership between institutions are going to increase in coming years.

Increasing academic and professional requirements of graduates. It reflects the demands of the globalization of societies, economy and labour markets and thus higher education must provide an adequate preparation for that. These requirements include not only academic and professional knowledge, but also multilingualism, and social and intercultural skills and attitudes. The level of specialization in research and the size of investments that are indispensable to certain fields of research and development require collaborative efforts and intensive international co-operation.

The recruitment of foreign students has become a significant factor for institutional income and of national economic interest. It has been the desire of the institutions to generate additional revenues through Internationalization of higher education.

The use of new information and communication technologies in the delivery of education.

Involvement of private sectors in education. It has been observed that earning money is a key motive for all Internationalization projects in the profit sectors.

Economic Competitiveness

Economic growth and investment in the future economy. It has been needed to build a more educated workforce, generally in emerging economies. Environmental interdependence.

Influence of international trade.

Desire to promote mutual understanding in one to another country.

The migration of skilled workers in a globalized economy.

These above mentioned reasons demonstrate the fact that higher education has now become a real part of the globalization process.

APPROACHES OF INTERNATIONALIZATION OF HIGHER EDUCATION

It refers to the stances adopted by persons in leadership positions towards the promotion and implementation of programmes aimed at Internationalization.

The activity approach: This promotes activities such as curriculum, student, faculty exchange, technical assistance and international students.

The competency approach: This emphasizes the development of skills, knowledge, attitudes and values in students, faculty and staff. The focus of this approach is how the generation and transfer of knowledge help to develop competencies in the personification of the higher education institution so that they become more internationally knowledgeable and intercultural skilled. Thus, in this approach, the development of internationalized curricula and programmes is a means towards developing the appropriate competencies in the students, staff and faculty.

The authors' approach: This emphasizes creating a culture that values and supports international/intercultural perspectives and initiatives. This approach acknowledges that the intercultural dimension is fundamental to any institution of higher learning, and believes that without a strong belief system and supportive culture, the international dimension of an institution will never be realized.

The process approach: This stresses integration or infusion of an international/intercultural dimension into teaching, research and service through a combination of a wide range of activities, policies and procedures.

ADVANTAGES OF INTERNATIONALIZATION OF HIGHER EDUCATION

- Improved quality of teaching and learning as well as research.

- Better preparation of students as national and global citizens and as productive members of the workforce.
- Access to students to programmes that are unavailable or scare in their home countries.
- Ehanced opportunities for faculty improvement.

ADVANTAGES OF INTERNATIONALIZATION TO INDIA

India has many advantages of continuing its Internationalization of education. Some of the advantages are discussed below. As in the US, India also has a large and diverse higher education system. It is the third largest after the US and China with 10 million students continuing study in about 16,000 institutions. This large higher education infrastructure serves to all the needs of the country. Formal programme or training is available in almost all sectors needed for development, ranging from ancient philosophy to the advances in information-technology. The types of courses offered are comparable to courses available internationally. Though the quality and soundness of the system as a whole may not be the best, there is no dearth of good institutions. Many institutions in India enjoy the premium status like Indian Institutes of Technology (IITs), Indian Institutes of Management (IIMs), and a few other universities with a global brand value. The increasing number students from the families of Non-Resident Indians (NRIs) who seek admission in the leading Indian institutions are a sign of comparability of the quality of education. The cost of education in India is also fairly low.

India has the advantages of medium of instructions in which education is passed on. Most of the higher education institutes use English as the medium of instruction. Some of the Indian institutes like Center for English and Foreign Languages in Hyderabad, have set up offshore campuses. Learning English throughout their educational career enables Indian nationals to take up teaching and research assignments across the world at all levels. India also has no university postsecondary institutions that provide specialized training for the diverse needs of the country. There are a many private and corporate institutions like NIIT and APTECH. These institutes work as ancillary educational providers and are quite successful. Availability of seats in higher education institutes is also high in India. The competition may be fierce in entering the top institutes but that does not mean the admission capacity is limited. In fact, since the arrival of national private providers in the education sector, India has more 'seats' than there are takers. Because of the growth of private providers, in Engineering and Technology related areas, every year, there are many 'vacancies' in the capacity for want of seekers. This problem is even more severe in the liberal arts and science institutions. Another problem in India is the lowest annual rate of growth in demand for higher education from the society. The countries of the Asia Pacific region, it is stabilized at 2-3 per cent level over the past decade and it is 5 per cent in India. How to continue this growth, if there is not enough number of eligible students is the major concern. The top American universities have complex motives for entering the Indian market. Many of them are genuinely interested in Internationalization, and see India as an important destination for economic growth in the 21st century. They wish to expand it in one of the world's major higher education markets and may use their Indian outposts to recruit bright Indian students, and academic staff, to come to the United States.

CHALLENGES TO INTERNATIONALIZATION OF HIGHER EDUCATION

Recognition: The recognition of international degrees is also important in facilitating periods of study abroad and for allowing students holding foreign degrees to work in their own country.

Cost: The cost of higher education of foreign institutions is very high which is not affordable to a larger group of the population of India.

Infrastructure: The institutes which have been established in other countries lacking proper required infrastructure.

Medium of Instruction: The foreign established institutes are providing education in English medium; this can be suitable only for a class of society and not to all.

Curriculum: The curriculum which is followed in foreign established institutes may not fulfill local need of a country.

Precautions: Despite many advantages, the country must deal Internationalization issue cautiously. Now Indian government is preparing to allow entry of foreign education providers in the higher education and about 50 foreign universities have evinced interest in setting up campuses in India. The interested universities, mostly from the US, the UK and Australia, have approached the Ministry of Human Resource Development (MHRD). The Foreign Education Providers Bill, a proposed legislation to allow the entry of foreign universities in India. The bill is applicable to deemed universities and private aided or unaided professional educational institutions affiliated to a university. Further, it defines a 'Foreign Education Provider' as a university or an Institution accredited and established under a foreign law and notified as an institution deemed to be a university by Central Government. The Bill controls the Admission structure of both aided and unaided professional educational institutions. Foreign Education Providers will need to seek a status of a Deemed University before they can start operating in India and no foreign institution, which is not categorized as a Foreign Education Provider, can operate in India. Currently foreign universities are not allowed to offer degree courses in India, although it allows 100 per cent foreign investment in education sector. Now, nearly 150 foreign institutes offer courses with Indian university under at winning arrangement – part of the course in India, the remaining abroad – that is allowed by the education department. A panel set up by the government to draw up a reform road map for the higher education sector recommended that only the top 200 foreign universities be allowed to enter the country. Another report, Renovation and Rejuvenation of Higher Education in India, suggests that only the best foreign universities be allowed to work in the higher education sector to avoid unreliable operators.

Currently, it is not possible for nonprofit companies under Article 25 of the Companies Registration Act – like industry associations – to set up an institution and get university status. Educational institutions in India can be set up only by trusts, societies and charitable companies, but the profits cannot be taken out of the institution and have to be reinvested. These controls not only hamper expansion, it also encourages promoters to resort to unethical accounting practices to take out profits. India is one of the world's largest markets for foreign universities. The country has a significant unmet demand for higher education access. Currently only 10 per cent of the age group receives university education, which is half the rate in China and well below the rate in most developing countries. Thus, foreign institutions have a huge opportunity for profitable growth in the Indian market. Why do foreign universities and education companies would enter the Indian market, the goal is clear – everyone wants to extract profits – mostly by offering programmes in fields that are in high demand. Foreign providers are not interested in investing in high-cost academic infrastructures and research. They wish to maximize the profit minimizing the investment. Some countries, including the United Kingdom and Australia, have a national policy to earn profits from higher education exports. The British Council and similar organizations help British educational institutions to increase their export potentials. Developing countries are now seen as a market for higher education and foreign universities from other countries are trying to increase their market share. As the demand for opening the higher education sector in India is increasing, providing a suitable regulatory framework for international education providers is important. The effective regulatory mechanism is necessary to ensure quality higher education. India's main contribution to global higher education is mainly through the export of students, many of whom don't return leading to high brain drain. Higher education is not purely a commodity to be bought and sold on the international market. Higher education represents an essential part of a nation's priority and a key to future prosperity. It may also be noted that most of the prestigious institutions of America are not in the international market to sell education for profit. It is the "for-profit organizations" of the USA who are active and most of them are not reputed ones.

CONCLUSION

The concept of the Internationalization of higher education has gradually changed through the ages, and its perception and definition differs from nation and region. Accordingly, determining the definition of the Internationalization of higher education from historical and comparative perspectives is an extremely important challenge to be met. Higher Education in India has expanded many folds in the last few decades. With the expansion in state funded institutions, private operators are also being allowed to supplement education. The road ahead for India is related to the creation of quality Higher Education Institutions to meet the challenge. The Government resources for higher education are not enough and investments in this sector from private and foreign sources are welcome. India needs to have a policy towards private higher education including foreign universities desirous of setting up a campus in India or entering joint ventures. The Foreign Education Providers Bill, a proposed legislation to allow the entry of foreign universities in India, is yet to be implemented. It was also felt that foreign universities must not be allowed to encourage in gross commercialization of higher education. Only universities of repute are allowed entry and such universities should be required to set up their full-fledged campuses in India. India needs to examine its policies on allowing foreign institutions into the country. Why foreign institutions are interested to enter the country? What is the status of the foreign institution in their country? Are they capable of offering the same quality in India as it does at their own country? Will the foreign institution be able to continue its offerings in India over time, etc.? India's ability to emerge as an economic powerhouse will depend on the enough availability of highly skilled human resources, which in turn needs up gradation in the education system to international standard.

REFERENCES

Altbach, P.G. and Knight, J. (2007), The Internationalization of Higher Education: Motivations and Realities, pp. 290-305, in *Journal of Studies in International Education,* Sage Publication.

International Association of Universities, *Newsletter*, July 2001, Vol. 7, No. 3.

Knight, J. (2003), Internationalization of Higher Education: Practices and Priorities. International Association of Universities Survey Report.

Knight, J. (2006), Higher Education Crossing Borders: A Guide to the Implications of the General Agreement on Trade in Services (GATS) for Cross-border Education. UNESCO.

Knight, J., (2008), *Higher Education in Turmoil.* Sense Publishers.

Qiang, Z. (2003), Internationalization of Higher Education: Towards a Conceptual Framework, pp. 248-270, in *Policy Futures in Education,* Vol. 1, No. 2, Ontario Institute for Studies in education, University of Toronto, Canada.

2

Internationalization of Higher Education in India: Emerging Trends and Strategies

Faiza Altaf

Internationalization is a revolutionary development in Higher Education. The overall demand for higher and adult education, and professionally related courses, is increasing in most countries. There are several reasons for this – changing demographics, the increased number of secondary schools pass-outs, wish for continual learning, and the growth of the information technology. While demand is growing, the ability of the traditional institutions to satisfy this need is questionable. We need to prepare students to perform successfully in the complex, global environment. Globalization and Internationalization are related but not the same thing. Globalization is the context of economic and academic trends that are part of the reality of the 21st century. Internationalization includes the policies and practices undertaken by academic systems and institutions – and even individuals – to cope with the global academic environment. (Altbach & Knight)

UNESCO (2006) has given the following definition of the Internationalization of education.

> "It is Higher education that takes place in situations where the teacher, student, programme, institution or provider and course materials cross-national jurisdictional borders. Cross-border education may include higher education by public or private and not-for-profit/ for-profit providers. It encompasses a wide range of modalities in a continuum from face-to-face (taking various forms from students traveling abroad and campuses abroad) to distance learning (using technologies and including e-learning)."

Internationalization is therefore 'a process of integrating an international perspective into the education'. It needs an institutional vision to motivate people to change the whole to think globally and collaboratively. It is a way towards an ever-changing, diverse external environment that focused on global environment.

STREAMS OF INTERNATIONALIZATION OF HIGHER EDUCATION

The streams of Internationalization of higher education have two major dimensions. One dimension is merely domestic which refers to the international and intercultural dimensions of without ever leaving their home country. The second dimension refers to the mobility of the participants across national borders. It is also called cross-border education, and this type of education growing rapidly, particularly at the higher education level. According to a UNESCO (2006) report, cross-border mobility of the programmes is "a movement of individual education or training courses and programmes across national boundaries through face-to-face, distance or a combination of these. Foreign country provider or the affiliated domestic partner or both of them jointly award credits for the course." Franchising, double or joint degrees and various articulation models are popular methods of international programme mobility. A short description of each follows:

(a) Franchise: This is an arrangement whereby a reputed institution allows another institution in another country to deliver programmes in that country. The more a reputed organization usually awards the qualification. Partners customize their arrangements for teaching, management, assessment, profit sharing and awarding of qualification each franchise.

(b) Double/Joint Degree: In these arrangements, institutions in different countries offer a programme jointly for which a student receives a qualification from each organization. Institutions customize arrangements for the programme provision and the basis for awarding the qualifications for each arrangement.

(c) Articulation: Articulation arrangements between institutions of different countries allow students to gain credit for courses offered by all the providers. This allows students to gain credit for work done by a provider other than the provider awarding the qualification.

(d) Distance Education: In this arrangement, institutions deliver a programme to students in different countries through distance and online. It may include some face-to-face support for students through domestic study centers. The main reason of these collaborations is to improve acceptability of the programmes and their creditworthiness. Who awards the degree is important depending on the reputation of the institution. Recognition of qualification for ownerships of intellectual property rights associated to course design and materials, responsibilities of partners in academic, staffing, recruitment, evaluation, financial and administrative matters. From an academic point, these dimensions in higher education affect the country's higher education institutions intellectual enrichment, and stimulate teaching and research. From the cultural angle, it helps to understand the cultures of other cultures.

DEMAND FOR INTERNATIONALIZATION AND INITIATIVES

According to UNESCO (2006) report, the need for international education will increase from 1.8 million international students in 2000 to 7.2 million international students in 2025. This rise creates huge challenges as well as opportunities. Though exact figures cannot be correctly estimated, it is obvious there will be a rise in the programmes and institutions across national boundaries. Study abroad brings several advantages to students, universities, countries, and Academe. However, across countries with incongruent pre university education structures, some students are denied admission to foreign universities, due to gaps in their admissibility. Some institutions offer university bridging programmes, to enhance the admissibility of these students to the required level. Nonetheless, the efficacy of these programmes, in closing the competence gap between their attendees and conventional enrollees, is the subject of much controversy – albeit neither their proponents nor critics have provided empirical evidence to support their side of the argument. To meet this rising demand, institutions across the globe have introduced several steps. Some of the Initiatives are below.

1. Phoenix University has become the largest private university in the U.S. (owned and managed by the Apollo Group company) and delivering courses in Puerto Rico, Netherlands, Mexico and Canada. Other Apollo institutions are offering courses in Brazil, India and China.
2. The Netherlands Business School opened a branch campus in Nigeria.
3. Harvard University is improving campuses in Cyprus and the United Arab Emirates.
4.) Jinan University will be the first Chinese university to open a branch outside China.
5. Laureate Education picked up higher education organizations in Chile, Mexico, Panama, Costa Rica, Spain, Switzerland and France.
6. Dubai has developed a "Knowledge Village" in the Dubai Technology and Media Free Zone.
7. The London School of Economics, Manipal Academy of Higher Education (India) and the University of Wollongong (Australia) are offering courses using franchising agreements and branch campuses.
8. The University of Westminster (UK) has formed partnership with Kingdom University of Bahrain and developing similar arrangements with institutions in Nigeria, Uzbekistan and Kazakhstan.

The examples confirm that globalization and global partnership between institutions are going to increase in coming years.

INTERNATIONALIZATION OF HIGHER EDUCATION IN INDIA

It was found that campus Internationalization requires a deep understanding and appreciation of the institutional context (Elizabeth). The Association of Indian Universities arranged a Round Table on 'Internationalization of Indian Higher Education' at the University of Mysore. They discussed the mechanisms to promote Internationalization of Indian Higher Education at select Indian universities. They adopted the following 'Mysore Statement'.

(*Source:* International Association of Universities Newsletter July 2001 Volume 7, No. 3)

The Mysore Statement contains:

- Accepting that Internationalization of higher education is a fact of life in the new 'knowledge era',
- Realizing that Internationalization would lead to an improvement in the quality of education, promote Indian culture abroad, produce understanding and yield financial benefits,
- Recognizing that partnership and networking are essential for to enrich the teaching learning and to improve quality of research,
- Believing that it is necessary to act in earnest immediately,
- Resolved the government, academic institutions and the Association of Indian Universities take necessary steps to promote Indian higher education internationally. They recommended following actions. After the deliberations, they recommended following actions to the Government
- Take suitable action to promote Indian culture abroad. This needs setting up a Committee for promoting Indian Education Abroad.
- Allow Indian Universities to open offshore campus abroad. Amend the University Grants Commission Act 1956 and the Acts of other statutory councils to include a specific provision allowing universities to open offshore campuses and export Indian education through the distance.
- Simplify the procedures about registration, entry test need, the issue of 'No Objection Certificate' and the issue and extension of visas.
- Indian Embassies and High Commissions abroad must play a role in providing information about higher education available in India. They should help in the conduct of fairs, entrance examinations and student recruitment.
- From an open-door policy for financing students.
- They recommended the creation of a central website to strengthen the information base and spread of information.
- Government and other statutory bodies' should grant greater autonomy and flexibility to universities to admit foreign students and to enter collaborative arrangements with foreign institutions.
- Create a Task Force including representatives of different bodies like the University Grants Commission, All India Council for Technical education and the Medical Council of India for admitting students to different professional programmes.
- The government should consider extending financing for international education. This will enable institutions providing financial aid to Indian students going abroad, to foreign students coming to India and to educational institutions wishing to develop infrastructures for international education.

- There should be a suitable means to watch the standard of education given by foreign universities. The committee recommended following actions for considerations of Academic Institutions:
- Universities and other academic institutions that enroll large number of international students must have enough facilities to provide needed environment.
- Evaluate strengths in different disciplines of education and identify areas that would attract international students at different levels.
- Simplify the procedure for admitting international students.
- Indian academic institutions should set up partnerships and develop networks with foreign universities in both the developed and the developing countries.
- It is better if the academic environment of the partnering university is similar to that of Indian universities.
- Updating and Internationalization of the curriculum will get highest priority.
- Students from non-English speaking countries often have an inadequate knowledge of the English language. Arrangement for conducting special English classes for them is necessary.
- Indian universities should develop special short-term programmes for students from developing countries who would like to visit India to learn more about its culture and heritage, natural possessions, diversity, languages or indigenous technologies.

ADVANTAGES OF INTERNATIONALIZATION IN INDIA

India has many advantages of continuing its Internationalization of education. Some of the advantages are discussed below:

It was found that campus Internationalization requires a deep understanding and appreciation of the institutional context. As in the US, India also has a large and diverse higher education system. It is the third largest after the US and China with 10 million students continuing study in about 16,000 institutions. This large higher education infrastructure serves to all the needs of the country. Formal programme or training is available in almost all sectors needed for development, ranging from ancient philosophy to the advances in information-technology. The types of courses offered are comparable to courses available internationally. Though the quality and soundness of the system as a whole may not be the best, there is no dearth of good institutions. Many institutions in India enjoy the premium status like Indian Institutes of Technology (IITs), Indian Institutes of Management (IIMs), and a few other universities with a global brand value.

The increasing number students from the families of Non Resident Indians (NRIs) who seek admission in the leading Indian institutions are a sign of comparability of the quality of education. The cost of education in India is also fairly low. India has the advantages of medium of instructions in which education is passed on. Most of the higher education institutes use

English as the medium of instruction. Some of the Indian institutes like Center for English and Foreign Languages in Hyderabad, have set up offshore campuses. Learning English throughout their educational career enables Indian nationals to take up teaching and research assignments across the world at all levels. India also has no university postsecondary institutions that provide specialized training for the diverse needs of the country. There are many private and corporate institutions like NIIT and APTECH. These institutes work as ancillary educational providers and are quite successful. Availability of seats in higher education institutes is also high in India. The competition may be fierce in entering the top institutes but that does not mean the admission capacity is limited. In fact, since the arrival of national private providers in the education sector, India has more 'seats' than there are takers. Because of the growth of private providers, in Engineering and Technology related areas, every year, there are many 'vacancies' in the capacity for want of seekers.

This problem is even more severe in the liberal arts and science institutions. Another problem in India is the lowest annual rate of growth in demand for higher education from the society. The countries of the Asia Pacific region, it is stabilized at 2-3 per cent level over the past decade and it is 5 per cent in India. How to continue this growth, if there is not enough number of eligible students is the major concern. The top American universities have complex motives for entering the Indian market. Many of them are genuinely interested in Internationalization, and see India as an important destination for economic growth in the 21st century. They wish to expand it in one of the world's major higher education markets and may use their Indian outposts to recruit bright Indian students, and academic staff, to come to the United States.

CONCLUSION

Higher Education in India has expanded many folds in the last few decades. With the expansion in state funded institutions, private operators are also being allowed to supplement education. The road ahead for India is related to the creation of quality Higher Education Institutions to meet the challenge. The Government resources for higher education are not enough and investments in this sector from private and foreign sources are welcome. India needs to have a policy towards private higher education including foreign universities desirous of setting up a campus in India or entering joint ventures. The Foreign Education Providers Bill, a proposed legislation to allow the entry of foreign universities in India, is yet to be implemented. It was also felt that foreign universities must not be allowed to encourage in gross commercialization of higher education. Only universities of repute are allowed entry and such universities should be required to set up their full-fledged campuses in India. India needs to examine its policies on allowing foreign institutions into the country. Why foreign institutions are interested to enter the country? What is the status of the foreign institution in their country? Are they capable of offering the same quality in India as it does at their own country? Will the foreign institution be able to continue its offerings in India over time, etc.? India's ability to emerge as an economic powerhouse will depend on the enough availability of highly skilled human resources, which in turn needs up gradation in the education system to international standard.

REFERENCES

Altbach, P.G. and Knight, J. http://jsi.sagepub.com/content/11/3-4/290 retrieved on 10 October 2012

Bruner, J. (1960). *The Process of Education.* Cambridge, MA: Harvard University

Elizabeth, J.C. http://jsi.sagepub.com/content/11/3-4/290 retrieved on 10 October 2012.

IAU Newsletter. (2001). Internationalization of Indian Higher Education. International Association of Universities *Newsletter*, Vol. 7, No. 3.

Mitra, Subrata Kumar (2010). *Asian Social Science*, Vol. 6, No. 6.

3

Future Scenario of Internationalization of Higher Education

L. Mishra

Internationalization has become one of the most ubiquitous terms in 21st century systems of higher education. While the term "Internationalization" means different things to different people in different contexts (Knight 2003), the current global enthusiasm for internationalizing higher education has stemmed from a number of factors.

Internationalization is generally defined as increasing cross border activities amidst persistence of borders and universities are increasingly required to provide an education that fosters global knowledge, skills and languages in order to perform professionally and socially in an international and multicultural environment.

The most comprehensive definition is found in Knight (1999) "Internationalization of higher education is the process of integrating an international/intercultural dimension into the teaching, research and service functions of the institution.

As per the term Internationalization, it has been employed regarding several themes (Teichler 2007: 10-11) as the physical mobility, prevalently of students, but also of academic staff and occasionally administrative staff and it is included in programmes aiming to promote Internationalization. Various programmes for the support of student mobility were established with the hope, that cognitive enhancement would be accompanied with attitudinal change: growing "global understanding", more favourable views of the partner country, a growing empathy with other cultures, etc.

Internationalization is often confused with globalization (Altbach, 2004). We define globalization as the economic, political, and societal forces pushing 21st century higher education toward greater international involvement. Global capital has, for the first time, heavily invested in knowledge industries worldwide, including higher education and advanced training. This investment reflects the emergence of the "knowledge society," the rise of the service sector, and the dependence of many societies on knowledge products and highly educated personnel for economic growth.

WHY INTERNATIONALIZATION

There are various reasons for internalization of higher education Worldwide, the top five reasons for internationalizing an institution in order of importance are,

(1) to improve student preparedness;
(2) internationalize the curriculum;
(3) enhance the international profile of the institution;
(4) strengthen research; and
(5) knowledge production; and diversify its faculty and staff.

INTERNATIONALIZATION AND INTERCULTURAL KNOWLEDGE

The primarily concern is with learning, viewing Internationalization in higher education as an opportunity to develop curriculum objectives concerned with (flows of) intercultural phenomena.

The advancement of human knowledge that is based on common bonds of humanity is arguably a global enterprise. Universities are, therefore, by nature of their commitment to advancing human knowledge, international institutions. This view has the potential of opening up the development of intercultural knowledge in higher education. Above all, there is a need to develop international education objectives, in particular abilities and competencies in various types of education within higher education, giving them a clear and visible position within the curricula. If the goal is for the student to become inter culturally knowledgeable, developing cross cultural knowledge, skills and abilities, then these aims also need to be more distinctly emphasized in curricula, and become a central part of all higher education contexts. In order to create competence and knowledge innovation, as well as an emerging internationalized culture and competence-based understanding, it would be necessary to support the students' development of competencies related to learning from a cross-cultural perspective.

INTERNATIONAL STUDENT FLOWS

The unprecedented growth of activities of universities in international level in volume, scope, and complexity during the past two decades range from traditional study-abroad programmes, allowing students to learn about other cultures, by providing access to higher education in countries where local institutions cannot meet the demand. Other activities stress upgrading the international perspectives and skills of students, enhancing foreign language programmes, and providing cross cultural understanding. The results of globalization include the integration of research, the use of English as the lingua Franca for scientific communication, the growing international labour market for scholars and scientists, the growth of communications firms and of multinational and technology publishing, and the use of information technology (IT). IT facilitates communication; permits efficient storage, selection, and dissemination of knowledge; and allows providers to offer academic programmes through e-learning. The essay delineates academic programmes, institutions, innovations, and practices created to cope with globalization and to reap its benefits. Globalization may be unalterable, but Internationalization involves many choices. Globalization tends to concentrate wealth, knowledge, and power in those already possessing these elements. International academic mobility similarly favours well-developed education systems and institutions, thereby compounding existing inequalities. Initiatives and programmes, coming largely from the north, are focused on the south. Northern institutions and corporations own most knowledge, knowledge products, and IT infrastructure, though south-to-south activities are increasing, especially in Asia and Africa. Internationalization is a two-way street – students move largely from south to north, for example – and serves important needs in the developing world. But the north largely controls the process. We focus on the cross-border movement of students and of higher education programmes and institutions – big business for universities and other providers – the growing international market for academic and scientific personnel, curricular Internationalization, and the commercialization of international higher education, especially the growing influence of the for-profit higher education sector.

When asked about the most important benefits of Internationalization, the top three reasons at the global level listed in order of relevance were:

- increasing international awareness of students;
- strengthening research and knowledge production; and
- fostering international cooperation and solidarity.

PROFITS

Earning money is a key motive for all Internationalization projects in the for profit sector and for some traditional non-profit universities with financial problems. Non-profit higher education providers entered the international market by establishing new institutions, purchasing existing institutions, and partnering with firms or educational institutions in other countries. Many countries also host new private universities with overseas links, some in the for-profit sector. Many universities use American, British, German, or other foreign curricula; many teach in English, and some are accredited in other countries. Traditional non-profit universities also entered the international market. Their main need for Internationalization, are not financial. Instead, they wish to enhance research and knowledge capacity and to increase cultural understanding. Many universities are located in countries where governments cut public funding and encouraged international ventures – Australia and the United Kingdom, for example. Most initiatives – including branch campuses, franchised degree programmes, and partnerships with local institutions – are focused on developing and middle-income countries. Many countries recruit international students to earn profits by charging high fees – including Australia, Canada, the United Kingdom, and the United States. International graduate students also provide research and teaching services for modest compensation. International students also spend significant amounts of money in the host countries. It is also difficult to calculate the impact of international activities on engaging academic institutions and firms, but again the amount is large and rapidly growing.

ACCESS PROVISION AND DEMAND ABSORPTION

The proportion of young people demanding and obtaining access worldwide expanded dramatically with the advent of mass higher education. Demand is rapidly increasing, even in countries still enrolling less than 20 per cent of the age group, such as India, China, and much of Africa. Many international higher education services focused on profits – provide access to students in countries lacking the domestic capacity to meet the demand. Access can take many forms: branch campuses, franchised foreign academic programmes or degrees, or independent institutions based on foreign academic models.

QUALITY ASSURANCE AND RECOGNITION

The first issue is, is the institutions, companies, and networks that deliver cross border courses or programmes registered, licensed, or recognized by the sending and the receiving countries? Many countries – lacking capacity or political will – do not have the regulatory systems to register or evaluate out-of-country providers. Regulatory frameworks for quality assurance or accreditation, even when they exist, usually do not apply to providers outside the national education system. This loophole permits bona fide and rogue foreign providers to avoid compliance with national regulations in many countries and makes monitoring their activities difficult. The accreditation process is becoming internationalized and commercialized.

THE FUTURE OF INTERNATIONALIZATION

A recent phenomenon in the debate on the future of Internationalization of higher education appears to be the inclination to put new broad labels on the term, such as mainstreaming, comprehensive, holistic, integrated and deep Internationalization. Internationalism will remain a central force in higher education, though its contours are unclear.

- Political realities and national security. Terrorism may affect international higher education. Tightened visa requirements in the United States and other countries, security restrictions on the subjects that can be studied, and fear of terrorism expressed by potential international students may affect cross-border student flows.
- Government policies and the cost of study: Policies concerning the cost of tuition and fees for visas and other documents may affect international initiatives.
- Expanded domestic capacity. Interest in studying abroad or in enrolling in international programmes may decline as countries increase access to higher education, especially to master's and doctoral programmes.
- English. The growing use of English as a medium of research and instruction, especially at the graduate level, may stimulate interest in international programmes, offered by universities in English.

- The Internationalization of the curriculum. Students may find international programmes useful as a curricula move toward models developed in the United States and other industrialized countries.
- E-learning. International acceptance of degrees will lead to an expanded role for distance education, though it is unclear whether international e-learning degrees will become more widespread or domestic e-learning programmes – often located in developing or middle-income countries – will continue to dominate.
- The private sector. Private higher education is the fastest-growing segment of higher education worldwide, though only a small part of this sector is international. It is not clear if private higher education providers will find the international market sufficiently profitable – though some expansion seems likely. We advocate a reorientation towards outcomes and impacts and away from a purely input and output approach. Instead of bragging about the number of students going abroad and hosting of international fee paying students, the number of courses in English and the abstract claim of making students global citizens, we want to focus on learning outcomes. How can we make sure that students receive the right learning outcomes that make them ready for a world that is more and more inter-cultural and internationally connected? What does that mean for faculty development? What are the implications for the assessment of students? How can instruments such as study abroad, international classrooms, teaching in another language, recruitment of international students and cross-border delivery, contribute to that process?

In other words: how can we make sure that all students and not only the small elite of already internationally-oriented students and faculty receive the basic intercultural and international skills and knowledge they need in current society? Is it possible to look at new ways of Internationalization such as virtual exchange? Can we learn from experiences with internationalizing secondary education and build on them? Or are we sticking to the classic concepts of cross-border mobility? In recent years we have seen good practices of new approaches to Internationalization; we should embrace them and incorporate them. Without denying the importance and good work of international offices, Internationalization has to move out of these offices and become part of curriculum development, quality assurance, faculty development.

CONCLUSION

These are the motives for the growth in international higher education and the landscape of programmes and institutions. International higher education will provide substantial access in some countries and will be a "niche market" in others. We are at a crossroads – today's emerging programmes and practices must ensure that international higher education benefits the public and not simply be a profit center.

REFERENCES

Altbach, P.G. (2002). Knowledge and education as international commodities. *International Higher Education*, 28, 2-5.

Altbach, P.G. (2004). Globalization and the university: Myths and realities in an

Bhalla, V. (2005). International students in Indian universities. *Internationalization Higher Education*, 41, 8-9.

Knight, Jane (2010). Internationalization of higher education, http://ceps.pef.uni-lj.si/dejavnosti/sp/2011-06-02/Internac.%20HE%20-%20motivations%20and%20realities%20Altback,%20Knight%2007.pdf

Unequal World. In National Education Association (Ed.), *The NEA 2005 Almanac of Higher Education* (pp. 63-74). Washington, DC: National Education Association.

4

Increasing and Widening Access to Higher Education in India

B.N. Kamble

'Internationalization' is a term widely used to describe the international dimension of higher education – although it is often used in general. The Internationalization of higher education is widely viewed as valuable that include increasing communication and respect between people of different cultures, advancing the purposes of learning and scholarship, facilitating international relations and enhancing leadership in a global community. Globalization and Internationalization are viewed as distinct concepts, globalization is one aspect of the context within which higher education operates, and which renders consideration of the international dimension of higher education important. However, Internationalization of higher education does not mean a blurring of the boundaries between state, market and higher education institutions (HEIs) as globalization does.

"Universal" higher education clearly does not mean that everyone obtains a higher education degree or a place of study. The higher education purposes include preparation for the labour market; preparation for life as active citizens in democratic societies; personal development and the development and maintenance of a broad, advanced knowledge base. The concept of quality education comprises access to learning for all; developing each learner's personality, talents, and abilities; equipping learners with self-confidence and competences; promoting democracy and human rights; passing on cultural values but also enabling learners to decide on their own values and providing a secure learning environment.

The paper is based on a selective review of the literature with the aim to focus on the Internationalization of higher education increasing and widening access to higher education in India, the paper is organized in five sections. This chapter will discuss the Altbach's centre-periphery hypothesis and Dale's mechanisms of external effects to study with reference to the Internationalization of higher education increasing and widening access to higher education in India. The paper concludes that there is an urgent need for a suitable regulatory framework regarding the foreign higher education providers in India.

PARTNERSHIPS BETWEEN FOREIGN AND INDIAN EDUCATION PROVIDERS

After the Uruguay Round negotiations in 1995 the General Agreement on Trade and Services (GATS), a treaty of the World Trade Organization (WTO), has been entered into force. GATS were created to extend the multilateral trading systems to services. The signing of this agreement has had important implications for nations and their service delivery. The list of sectors addressed is vast and includes the sector education. The GATS, treating knowledge as a commodity that should be freely traded, has transformed the idea of education from a public good to a service of which profit can be made. This shift to profit making and market - drive has lead to a new era of power and influence.

Theoretical Framework: The GATS, treating knowledge as a commodity that should be freely traded, has transformed the idea of education from a public good to a service of which profit can be made. This shift to profit making and market-drive has lead to a new era of power and influence. The legal status of learning centers is difficult under current legislation. Therefore it is important that this type of partnership and its status become part of further legislation in the future. The franchisee an Indian institution is allowed to execute a programme in the name of a foreign partner with the foreign curriculum and evaluation methods.

Types of Programmes: The institutions are offering professional programmes to their students in subjects such as hospitality management, business administration, beauty and fashion, which are in general most often offered at private institutions than at public institutions. In addition, due to the lack of recognition and accreditation, they are not in the position to offer academic programmes such as bachelor's and master's programmes.

Cooperation between Partners: The cooperation between Indian and foreign education providers are discussed by applying Altbach's centre-periphery hypothesis and Dale's mechanisms of external effect.

Applying Altbach's Centre-Periphery Hypothesis: The Altbach's center periphery hypothesis with regard to higher education and globalization, it is clear that due to India's size it might be seen as a counter to some and the higher education system is lacking in many fields such as meeting the demands of the prospective student population. Altbach's hypothesis focuses on the relationship between the developed and emerging nations but there are also relationships between emerging nations occurring. In the context the Indian institutions have ties with Altbach's traditional centers in the developed nations and institutions in Asia and the Middle East. Through the contacts with partner institutions in these parts of the world both can benefit and learn from each other's experience.

Applying Dale's Mechanisms of External Effects: Dale mechanisms is looking clear as an indicator, first, relationships are voluntary. The number of institutions needs to set up a partnership with a foreign partner because of difficulties in attracting students, a good reputation, however, no institution is forced to set up a partnership with a foreign institution. The second indicator is the explicitness of the process. All processes around partnerships are explicit and clear between partners. The responsibilities and tasks of both partners were clearly determined. The areas influence the institutions involved do have an impact on the national level, especially on the Indian national level for the influence the higher education system.

The mechanism of installing interdependence to Altbach's centre-periphery hypothesis is stating that interdependence. The Indian institutions learn from their partners and the partnerships give their quality a boost, they are not dependent on their partner for their functioning and existence, (World Bank, 2000: 24-27).

Definitions and Modes of Supply

Definition: In the services sectoral classification of WTO, education services are mentioned along with five subsections. These subsections with corresponding central product classification numbers are (i) primary education services (921); (ii) secondary education services (922); (iii) higher education services (923); (iv) adult education services (924) and (v) others (929).

Modes of Supply: The four modes of supply of educational services are referred to in GATS negotiations as set out in the Article I: 2. The modes are essentially defined on the basis of the origin of service supplier and the consumer, and the degree and type of territorial presence, which they have at the moment the service is delivered.

The agreement covers four modes of supply:

- cross-border supply,
- Consumption abroad,
- Commercial presence, and
- Presence of a natural person.

Mode I – Cross border supply: In this type of education service, cross border supply covers all services provided through distance or through telecommunications or the mail and through services

Embodied in exporting goods (I am being, services supplied in or by a physical medium, such as a computer diskette or drawings). In such cases, the service supplier is not present within the territory of the member where the service is delivered.

Mode II – Consumption abroad: This mode of supply is often referred to as "movement of the consumer". The essential feature of the model is that the service is delivered outside the territory of the member making commitment.

Mode III – Commercial presence: It refers to the actual presence of foreign investors in a host country. This model covers not only the presence of juridical persons in the strict legal sense,

But also that of legal entities, which share some of the same characteristics.

Mode IV – Presence of natural persons: This model covers natural persons who are themselves service suppliers as well as natural persons who are employees of service suppliers, (Bhushan Sudhanshu, 2004).

According to the Association of Universities and Colleges of Canada (AUCC, 2011), many other countries are projecting increase in university enrollment and participation rates over the coming decade, some more strongly than others. Emerging economies like China, India and Brazil anticipate very strong increases in enrollment. Already these countries, along with the U.S., have the largest total number of higher education students. However, their participation rates trail far behind developed nations. As their economies expand, there is a strong potential for rapid enrollment growth, which will likely exceed domestic capacity for students, and in turn, will create international student demand.

INCREASING AND WIDENING ACCESS TO HIGHER EDUCATION IN INDIA: NUMBER OF INSTITUTIONS AND ENROLLMENT IN INDIA

More than 5,000 colleges have been added in the last one year alone. India has the largest higher education system in the world with respect to the number of institutions Higher education enrollment has grown at a healthy pace, with 3.6 million students being added over the last four years India's higher education system is the world's third largest with respect to student enrollment, next only to China and the USA.

The Indian higher education system has exhibited impressive growth over the last decade to become one of the world's largest systems of higher education. The number of institutions has grown at a Compounded Annual Growth Rate (CAGR) of 11 per cent while student enrollment has grown at a CAGR of 6 per cent. Geographically, the Central region has experienced the highest increase in number of institutions, while the Southern region has exhibited the highest increase in student enrollment. The Gross Enrollment Ratio (GER) currently stands at about 13.8 per cent, with West India has the highest GER of 25.7 per cent. Over the last decade, the number of universities in the country has grown at a CAGR of 7.5 per cent as against the 4.7 per cent growth observed since 1951-2001. The number of colleges has grown at a CAGR of 11 per cent in the period 2001-2011 as against 6.1 per cent in the period 1951-2001.

Currently, North India has 9,834 institutions (31%), South has 9,970 (32%), West has 4,307 (14%), East has 2,946 (9%) and Central has 4,261 institutions (14%) Central India recorded the highest growth in a number of institutions. However, enrollment over the same period increased by only 3.7 per cent. While South India added about 800 colleges from 2009 to 2010 (10.5% growth), enrollment increased by 15.5 per cent, the highest amongst the regions.

The Planning Commission has set a target of achieving a GER of 15 per cent by 2011-12 (end of the 11th Five-Year Plan) and 21 per cent by 2016-17 (end of 12th Five-Year Plan).

The Ministry of Human Resource Development has set a target of achieving 30 per cent GER by 2020.

However, at the current growth rate (3.3% over 2000-10), the GER is projected to fall short of all the targets. To achieve the 30 per cent target GER by 2020, the CAGR needs to be pushed up from the current 3.3 per cent to 8 per cent. With a GER of 13.8 per cent and enrollment of 14.6 million, access to higher education in India is currently restricted to a limited population. There is wide disparity in the Higher Education GERs across states, urban and rural areas, gender, and communities. Examples:

1. *Interstate disparity*: 31.9 per cent in Delhi vs. 8.3 per cent in Assam
2. *Urban-rural divide*: 23.8 per cent in urban areas vs. 7.5 per cent in rural areas
3. *Differences across communities*: 6.6 per cent for SCs, 6.5 per cent for STs, 8.7 per cent for OBCs, and 17.2 per cent for others
4. *Gender disparity*: 10.6 per cent for female vs.14.4 per cent for male
5. *Faculty shortage*: 45 per cent of the positions for professors, 51 per cent positions for readers, and 53 per cent positions for lecturers were vacant in Indian universities in 2007-08.
6. *Poor academic standards*: The system is plagued with outdated curricula and ill-equipped libraries (average 9 books per student vs. 53 in IIT Bombay)
7. *Unaccredited institutions*: As of March 2011, only 161 universities and 4,371 colleges had been accredited by NAAC

Table 1: International Students in Indian Universities (Continent Wise)

No.	Continents	2002-03	2003-04	2004-05	2005-06	2006-07	2007-08
1.	Asia	—	—	9849	10493	13400	15437
2.	Africa	—	—	2005	2403	13616	3796
3.	America	—	—	593	654	776	626
4.	Europe	—	—	178	206	238	309
5.	Australia	—	—	55	71	69	81
6.	Miscellaneous	—	—	587	629	592	957
	Total	**10936**	**11934**	**13267**	**14456**	**28691**	**21206**

Source: Various Documents of University Grants Commission (UGC) and Association of Indian Universities (AIU) 2009-2010.

The share of unaided private institutions in the higher education sector has increased considerably over the last few years. Majority of institutions offering programmes in professional disciplines such as engineering, pharmacy, and hotel management have been established by the private sector. As of 2006-07, private sector participation ranged from 50 per cent to 95 per cent of the total number of institutions for various professional courses. There has also been a rapid growth in the percentage of students enrolled in unaided private higher education institutions.

INCREASING AND WIDENING ACCESS: HIGHER EDUCATION INTERNATIONALIZATION IN INDIA

Universities and institutions of higher education in India have manifested a substantial growth in international students opting India as a knowledge hub in recent decade. There are numerous ways of internalization of higher education; formal agreements through Memorandum of Understanding (MoU) have been a common mechanism for international collaboration, the presence of international students in universities and institutions of higher education impacts upon teaching, curriculum development, cultural interaction, etc., international research collaboration either through formal agreements or personal contacts, faculty exchange, borrowing for best practice in teaching and academic management and through curriculum change or adoption.

Graph 1: Percentages (%)

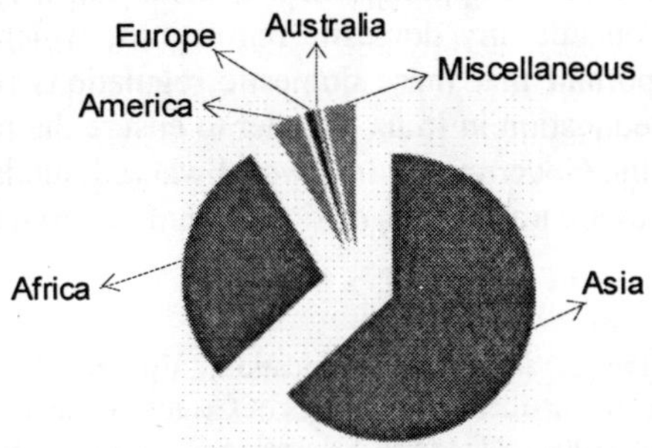

Table 1 shows, 'the trends of international students' inflow, it appears that a typical growth has been taking place by increasing number of international students in Indian universities and other institutions of higher education whereas a sharp growth has also been registered from 2005-06 onwards by sudden increase of international students, (Table 1 and 2). Among all the international students, most popular education they choose for are undergraduate and post-graduate especially in science/technology and other professional courses, but even at research level, as evidences reveal, a sufficient number of international students have opted for research studies and this number is increasing as well. Liberalization, privatization and globalization (LPG) movement since early 1990s has manipulated entire sectors particularly the higher education and as a result internationalization

Table 2: Top Ten Universities with International Students (2007-08)

No.	Name of The University	Male (%)	Female (%)	Total	% Total
1.	University of Pune	73.31	26.69	3,807	36.63
2.	University of Mysore	65.47	34.53	1,312	12.63
3.	Manipal University	43.80	56.20	1,226	11.80
4.	University of Delhi	58.36	41.64	1,131	10.88
5.	Osmania University	81.96	18.04	682	6.56
6.	Alagappa University	50.70	49.30	568	5.47
7.	Jamia Hamdard University	66.21	33.79	509	4.90
8.	Bharti Vidyapeeth, Pune	72.67	27.33	494	4.75
9.	Aligarh Muslim University	82.19	17.81	365	3.51
10.	Banaras Hindu University	74.16	25.84	298	2.87
	Total			**10,392**	**100.00**

Source: Various Documents of UGC and AIU (2009-2010).

dynamic phenomenon of this era. Especially in the 21st century, movement of international students not only from Asian and African continent but also from Australian, European and American continents were registered at a great extent.

5. CONCLUSION

It has become clear that there is an urgent need for a suitable regulatory framework regarding the presence and activities of foreign education providers active in India's higher education system. Whether or not their presence and activities are appreciated, it is clear that they are active and at the moment fall outside any domestic regulations, which is worrisome. In addition it is important that these domestic regulations reflect a long term vision for higher education in India in order to ensure the possible meeting of objectives set by the Government. In a world where boundaries are becoming vaguer and services are traded, it is difficult to hold on to national objectives.

REFERENCES

AUCC (2011), "Trends in Higher Education, Volume 1 – Enrolment," The Association of Universities and Colleges of Canada, Ottawa.

Bhushan Sudhanshu (2004), 'Trade in Education Services under GATS Implications for Higher Education in India,' *Economic and Political Weekly* June 5, 2004, 2395-2402.

Ernst and Young Pvt. Ltd (2011), "Private sector participation in Indian higher education FICCI Higher Education Summit," Federation of Indian Chamber of Commerce and industry, Higher Education Network, (FICCI-HEN) and Ernst and Young Pvt. Ltd., Kolkata

Kamble, Mohit (2012), Higher Education In India: After 2001 Scenario", A Research Paper on "Higher Education in India: After 2001 Scenario", for UGC Sponsored National Seminar on "Economics and Quality of Higher Education in the Context of Changing Nature of Labour Market", Organized Secretary, Department of Economics, Pravara Rural Education Society's Arts, Commerce, and Science College, Satral, Dist. Ahmednagar, Maharashtra, India, March 31 and April 01, 2012, published in a conference volume with ISBN: 978-93-81948-15-6, edited by Russell Onkar and Talule D., (2012), "Perspectives on Education and Employment," Chinmay Prakashan, Aurangabad, Maharashtra, pp. 108-116.

Tinkling, Teresa, Sheila Riddell and Alastair Wilson (2002), "Wider Access For Disabled Students?", Disabled Students and Multiple Policy Initiatives in Higher Education: Working Paper 1, June 2002, Centre for Educational Sociology, University of Edinburgh.

Weerts, Kim (2009), "Education and Development Working Paper 10, India's confrontation with Foreign Higher Education Providers," IS Academe-Quality Education alumni, University of Amsterdam.

World Bank (2000), "Higher Education in Developing Countries, Peril and Promise", the Task Force on Higher Education and Society, Washington.

www.economist.com

www.ey.com

www.india.gov.in

www.indiabudget.nic.it

www.planningcommission.nic.in

www.ugc.ac.in

5

Impact of Globalization on Higher Education

Zakiya Rafat

In the present borderless information society, education needs to be able to respond to additional demands of a rapidly globalizing world by raising awareness of environmental, peace, cultural and social diversity, increased competitiveness, and the concept of a global village. Such education is to a knowledge or information society what secondary education was in an industrial economy. Education prepares the individual to connect – and live in harmony – with the environment around him. Globalization has changed the size, nature and quality of that environment. The challenge of higher education, therefore, is to reform, create and develop systems that prepare the individual to work in a borderless economy and live in a global society. In other words, our educational institutions need to produce global citizens.

Defining 'Globalization' is commonly used as a way of describing the spread and connectedness of production, communication and technologies across the world. Globalization also refers to the efforts of the International Monetary Fund (IMF), the World Bank and others create a global free market for goods and services. Globalization in the sense of connectivity in economic and cultural life across the world has been growing for centuries. However the speed of communication and exchange, the complexity and size of the networks involved, and the sheer volume of trade, interaction and risk can be labeled as 'globalization'.

Globalization involves the diffusion of ideas, practices and technologies. It is something more than Internationalization. It isn't simply modernization or westernization. It certainly isn't just the liberalization of markets. Anthony Giddens (1990: 64) has described globalization as 'the intensification of worldwide social relations which link distant localities in such a way that local happenings are shaped by events occurring many miles away and vice versa'. This involves a change in the way geography is understood and localness is experienced. Although it offers an opportunity, it brings considerable risks, for example those linked to technological change.

CHARACTERISTICS OF GLOBALIZATION

In economic terms, a rise in internationalized advertising and consumption patterns, a reduction in barriers to the free flow of goods, workers, and investments across national borders, and correspondingly, new pressures on the roles of worker and consumer society.

In political terms, a certain loss of nation-state sovereignty, or at least the erosion of national autonomy, and, correspondingly, a weakening of the notion of the "citizen".

In cultural terms, a tension between the ways in which globalization brings forth more standardization and cultural homogeneity, while also bringing more fragmentation through the rise of locally oriented movements due to the desire of preserving one's identity. Sometimes this merger, between the global and the local is termed "the global." In educational terms, there is a growing understanding that globalization, is reflected in an educational agenda that privileges, if not directly imposes, particular policies for the evaluation, financing, assessment, standards, teacher training, curriculum, instruction, and testing.

GLOBALIZATION AND EDUCATION

Globalization is a process, which has affected many areas of human life, one of those being educated. In the twentieth century, many developing countries have experienced growth in the educational facilities available to them due to the entry of institutions from the West. Some believe that this process is an invaluable opportunity for the people of the developing countries to raise their skills and standards of education. Others fear that it is merely a modern version of cultural imperialism that will lead to the creation of a universal, ultimately Western society. One aspect of the globalization of education has been the creation of 'twinning projects' between one Western and one non-Western university. Through Globalization of education, which is being knowledge transfer from the Western countries into developing countries, is intended to improve the skills and capabilities of the people receiving it.

Globalization has created an information based society. Educational scenario is rapidly changing because of globalization. The developments in technology and communication systems have brought about changes in the teaching and learning systems across the world. New ideas, change in values and knowledge, have changed the roles of students and teachers too. Education is now expected to shape children, the future citizens of the world into global citizens', with a broad range of skills and knowledge. As such it is the need of the hour to include subjects which reflect this global outlook and provide individuals with a better chance of employment, which in turn leads to a better lifestyle, power and status.

Education is undergoing constant changes under the effects of globalization. The effects of Globalization on education bring rapid developments in technology and communications are foreseeing changes within school systems across the world as ideas, values and knowledge, changing the roles of students and teachers, and producing a shift in society from industrialization towards an information-based society. It reflects the effect on culture and brings about a new form of cultural imperialism. It brings rapid developments in technology and communications are foreseeing changes within school systems across the world as ideas, values and knowledge. The rise of a global society, driven by technology and communication developments are shaping children, the future citizens of the world into 'global citizens', intelligent people with a broad range of skills and knowledge to apply to a competitive, information based society. The future of countries often lies within their ability to compete in a global market where industrial based economies are giving way to knowledge based industries, realizing the importance of "knowledge, skills and the intellectual capacity to meet the challenges of accelerated change and uncertainty".

Technological advancements have introduced technology in the classrooms which have changed the way education is being delivered to the students. There is reliance on electronic sources such as the emergence of video conferencing and communication and information based technology, the Internet, with a massive network of computers located throughout the world, to deliver the material. The rapid growth of television services, and influence of this media of mass communication, has also contributed to preparing a knowledgeable person. As a result, the barriers of distance are being broken down at a rapid rate, due to this key aspect of globalization. There is no need to be physically present in an educational institution in order to learn. Impact of Globalization The spread of education internationally, as a result of globalization, has affected cultures worldwide. The capitalist society is gradually becoming global with a strong emphasis on free trade. Educational institutions are becoming more market oriented, focusing their energy more on creating funds rather than providing sufficient education for students.

Due to this increasing free trade around the globe – to end protection in many sectors so that there is more competition and privatization, education is increasingly being drawn into this global capitalist competition. The Internationalization of education has become one of the key themes of educational policy and planning in the 1990s and the integration of worldwide capital and labour markets; educators are being forced to respond to a new set of challenges. The Internationalization of education, particularly higher education, is a growing phenomenon. Universities and colleges around the world are increasingly becoming forced to compete in the global capitalist market and engage in entrepreneurial activity to sustain themselves in an increasingly 'uncertain world'.

IMPORTANCE OF GLOBAL EDUCATION

A global education should teach about issues that cross national boundaries, and interconnected systems on ecological, cultural, economical, political and technological. Such a programme can draw upon expertise in many areas such as humanities, social science and environmental science. In the present borderless information society, education needs to respond to the demands of a rapidly globalizing world. This can be done by raising awareness of environmental, peace, cultural and social diversity, increased competitiveness, and the concept of a global village. Such education is the requirement of the knowledge or information society. Education prepares the individual to connect – and live in harmony – with the environment around him. Globalization has changed the size, nature and quality of that environment. The challenge of higher education, therefore, is to reform, create and develop systems that prepare the individual to work in a borderless economy and live in a global society. In other words, our educational institutions need to produce global citizens.

Education is becoming a lifelong learning and training process, developing transferable skills and knowledge that can be applied to competitive markets where knowledge and information is being traded as a commodity. The introduction of technology into the classroom is changing the nature of delivering education to students is gradually giving way to a new form of electronic literacy, more programmes and education materials are made available in electronic form, teachers are preparing materials in electronic form; and students are generating papers, assignments and projects in electronic form". Video projection screens, books with storage device servers and CD ROMs as well as the emergence of on-line digital libraries are now replacing blackboards. Even exams and grades are gradually becoming available through electronic means and notebooks are starting to give way to laptops. Also, students can be examined through computer managed learning systems and do tutorial exercises on a computer rather than in a classroom.

Such developments in education portray that there has been a shift from industrial to information-based societies. Subsequently, the technology is forcing a change in the education environment towards a reliance on electronic sources to deliver material. With such changes and the emergence of video conferencing and the Internet, the barriers of distance are being broken down at a rapid rate, due to the key aspect of globalization. Children and adults can now learn in a variety of ways and no longer have to be physically present in an educational institution in order to learn, a definite advantage of flexible delivery systems. It allows for the exploration of new areas of learning and thinking. The rapid growth of television services, with their immense influence as media of mass communication, has been very relevant in the technological shift.

Other large contributions to this shift include the transistor and space satellites. Communication and information based technology over the years is the Internet, which is a massive network of computers located throughout the world. These computers maintain libraries of text, images, computer software, and other forms of data that can be accessed by anyone, anywhere, at any time.

This implementation of technology and communication to be successful and to educate a society, both the students and teachers need to be technologically literate. Communication technology is offering new challenges for students of all abilities as they can discuss issues of concern with their fellow students from around the world, thus developing communication and interpersonal skills, fostering a mutual understanding across countries and cultures.

Developments in the delivery of education are allowed for individuals to explore new areas of learning and thinking that could not be done with pen and paper. They are discovering knowledge through inquiry and experimentation rather than memorizing facts in a teacher dominated classroom setting. In fact, students no longer need to be physically present to learn as education material is becoming readily available over the Internet, through video conferencing, and tape recordings. Institutions are now turning towards the use of the Internet to deliver courses to students.

A shift in education is becoming evident where more responsibility is being placed on the individual for his or her learning, instead of solely on the teacher. Subsequently, the teachers themselves also need to be highly technologically literate, needing the competence and confidence to prepare students for a global information society.

Education is undergoing constant changes under the effects of globalization. The effects of globalization on education bring rapid developments in technology and communications are foreseeing changes within learning systems across the world as ideas, values and knowledge, changing the roles of students and teachers, and producing a shift in society from industrialization towards an information-based society. It reflects the effect on culture and brings about a new form of cultural imperialism. The rise of new cultural imperialism is shaping children, the future citizens of the world into 'global citizens', intelligent people with a broad range of skills and knowledge to apply to a competitive, information based society. Globalization and technological advancements are delivering and increasing access to the world and subsequently subjects should reflect this global outlook.

PROBLEMS AND LIMITATIONS IN GLOBALIZATION

Globalization of higher education creates both challenges and opportunities. Education will be the answer to many problems raised by globalization. Educational goals are seen to be an area of great concern in the era of globalization. It is here that universities play a crucially important role, for creating a better society. It is impossible to ignore the local universities 'need to reflect on the impact of globalization. Universities providing a high quality education in the globalised world must focus on internationalism and cross-cultural communication. Education should not become a means of westernizing the world but it should treat each unique culture and society with respect, realizing that global education is not only learning about the West, but also studying different cultures of the world, using different approaches, ways of teaching and different media.

One of the major consequences of the globalization of education has been commoditization and the corporatization of institutions of higher learning. It is said that the for-profit education market in the United States is worth more than $500 billion in revenue for the involved corporate. More than one thousand state schools have been handed over to corporations to be run as businesses. But there is a fundamental problem with the way business models have been applied to the delivery of education and other public goods.

Unthinking adoption of the private sector model prevents the development of a meaningful approach to management in the public services in general or to the social services in particular based on their distinctive purposes, conditions and objectives.

There is another, more serious, problem with the corporatization of education. Corporations operate on the principles of cost reduction and profit maximization. These require introducing standardization and the packaging of product in compact, measurable, byte-like, configuration. Applied to education, these approaches would possibly negate its basic fabric and purpose. Education has always encouraged and represents openness, inquiry, diversity, research and limitless learning. Corporatization of education would make it elitist – the one provided by corporations for the masses and the poor who cannot afford going to the traditional institutions of learning, and the other for the rich and the affluent.

Another major problem with the global education system is accessed. Many people in the developing world are still illiterate. According to a statistical analysis by UNESCO, literacy rates (percentage of people aged 15 and above who can read and write in their native language) in countries of Southern Asia in 1995 were quite low.

While third world states encourage their citizens to seek more education, severe limitations in delivering basic services are a problem. A lack of infrastructure and funding makes it difficult to implement any technological and communication advancements.

However, despite differences in economy, politics, culture and society, second and third worlds have adopted educational ideals from western thought and are anxious to appear modern and therefore promote education as a symbol of modernity and development of their own population and the foreign countries. The spread of education internationally, as a result of globalization, has clearly had effects on cultures worldwide. The capitalist society is gradually becoming global with a strong emphasis on free trade emerging. Educational institutions have reacted accordingly, by becoming more market oriented, focusing their energy more on creating funds rather than providing sufficient education for students.

The Internationalization of higher education can be linked to various internal and external changes in the international system. Externally, there have been changes in the labour market, which have resulted in calls for more knowledge and skilled workers, and workers with deeper understandings of languages, cultures and business methods from all over the world. "Modern education… is almost exclusively focused on preparing children for an urban future,

The role of education has become more linked to globally competitive positions. Subsequent changes in university functions have lead universities toward "direct entrepreneurial activity to sustain themselves." This in turn produces a change in institutional approaches to the development of overseas education. University courses must now be cross-cultural in content, which is in association with the growing number of students, particularly in the 1990's, searching for higher education outside of their own country.

Education is becoming more invaluable to individuals. In today's environment, education provides individuals with a better chance of employment, which in turn leads to a better lifestyle, power and status. Under the prevailing global forces, higher education institutions everywhere are subject to global trends. Universities now facing more challenges than ever before, the rise of a globalised knowledge based economy has brought universities in many countries under closer scrutiny for the economic contributions they make. Governments have been particularly concerned that universities serve national interests in the global marketplace. There is an international tendency to emphasize the practical, technical value of higher education. The Co modification of knowledge as intellectual property has occurred particularly with regard to connecting the intellectual work of universities with community, business, and government interests and priorities. While such a tendency is often welcomed by so-called applied disciplines, it causes tensions between the more profitable applied subjects of science and technology, and those of basic theoretical inquiry, particularly arts and humanities subjects. It also creates institutional winners and losers.

Universities providing a high quality education in the globalised world, despite its focus on internationalism and cross-cultural communication, are still based on an individualistic model of teaching. Education should not become a means of westernizing the world. On the contrary, it should treat each unique culture and society with due respect, realizing that global education is not only learning about the West, but also studying different cultures of the world, using different approaches, Lack of regulation is a major issue with the globalization of higher education. The current globalization of higher education creates both challenges and opportunities. The relationship between universities education and globalization gives special attention. Education will be the answer to many problems raised by globalization. Educational goals are seen to be an area of great concern in the era of globalization. It is here that universities play a crucially important role, for creating a better society. It is impossible to ignore the global; universities need to reflect on the impact of globalization. They must engage with the issues of globalization, both theoretically as analysts and researchers, and practicing as academic workers involved in an increasingly globalised enterprise.

It is very surprising that today's global school system, supported by numerous international institutions (UNESCO being one of them), which has already achieved so much in the Internationalization of pre-University and University education, is suffering a global crisis in the area of primary education.

CONCLUSION

Globalization has had many obvious effects on educational technology and communication systems change the way education is delivered as well as the roles played by both teachers and students. The development of this technology is facilitating the transition from an industrial based society to an information-based one. At the same time, there is a dark side to globalization and to the very openness of the new information systems. While the richest countries grow richer, the poor are becoming poorer. Income, information and education gaps between the rich and the poor are widening not narrowing; economic crises, trade imbalances and structural adjustments have precipitated a moral crisis in many countries, tearing the basic social and cultural fabric of many families and communities apart, resulting in increasing youth unemployment, suicide, violence, racism and drug abuse and antisocial behaviour form schools. In the 21st century, education systems face the dual challenge of equipping students with the new knowledge, skills and values needed to be competitive in a global market while at the same time producing graduates who are responsible adults, good citizens both of their country and of the world. Thus globalization challenges us to rethink not only how much education is needed but also its ultimate purposes.

REFRENCES

Agrwal, R. (2002), Globalization of Higher Education and WTO, *Journal of Higher Education,* Vol. 40, No. 34. AIU House, New Delhi.

Banerjee, Brojendra Nath, (1998), *Globalization, Rough and Risky Road,* New age, International Publishers.

Beteille, A. (1995), Universities as institutions, *Economic and Political Weekly,* March 18.

Die, A. (2001), Creating learning Communities to meet the Challenge of Globalization – Can Open and Distance Learning help? *Indian Journal of Open Learning,* IGNOU, Vol. No. (10) No. 3, p. 269.

Harsolekar, D.D. (2000), Globalization of Indian Higher Education, *Journal of Higher Education,* Vol. 28, No. 28. AIU House, New Delhi.

Josephine, Y. (2008), *Globalization and Challenges for Education.* Shipra Publications, Delhi.

Khanna Kewal and Premila Khanna, (2001), *Indian Economy Towards Globalization,* Raj Publishing House, Jaipur.

Knight, J. and de Wit, H., (1997). Internationalization of Higher Education in Asia Pacific Countries, European Association of International Education, Amsterdam.

Patel, I.G., (1998), *Economic Reform and Global Change,* Macmillan India Ltd, New Delhi.

Singh, S.K, (1993), Building Institution of Higher Education, *Journal of Education Planning and Administration.*

Sharma. G.D. (2000), Internationalization of Higher Education – Status and Policy Suggestions, National Institute of Educational Planning and Administration, New Delhi, Monograph.

Spring, Joel, (1998), *Education and the Rise of the Global Economy;* Lawrence Erlbaum Associates, Publishers, Mahwah, New Jersey.

Trivedi, Pratima, (2000), *Economic Programme and Social Justice Towards Social Sector Development* (Ed.), Deep and Deep Publications, New Delhi.

Venkatasubramanian, K., (2002), Financing of Higher Education, *The Hindu,* February.

6

Internationalization of Higher Education: An Action on Call

Peeyush Kamal

The higher education sector has witnessed a tremendous increase in its institutional capacity in the years since Independence. The number of universities/university-level institutions has increased 18 times from 27 in 1950 to 504 in 2009. The sector boasts of 43 central universities, 297 State universities, 113 Private universities, 130 Deemed universities, 65 Institutions of national importance (established under Acts of Parliament) and five institutions (established under various State legislations). The number of colleges has also registered a manifold increase with just 578 in 1950 growing to be more than 33,000 in 2012. While we have made this impressive expansion in the field of higher education, we somehow seem to lag behind in 'Quality', there is also very great diversity in the educational institutions with respect to funding growth and the types of the systems in international standard with the exception of a few islands of excellence and institutions of national importance. In the recently announced Quality Standard World University rankings 2012 of top 200 educational institutions none from India found a place file in the Times Higher Education World rankings 2012-13 of the top 400 institutions only three IITs are listed. Time Higher Education World rankings 2012-13 judges' universities on parameters such as teaching, research, knowledge transfer and international outlook based on 13 calibrated performance indicators to provide the most comprehensive and balanced comparisons available, which are trusted by students, academics, university leaders, industry and governments. These 13 performance indicators are grouped into five areas: 1. Teaching: the learning environment (worth 30% of the overall ranking score) 2. Research: volume, income and reputation (worth 30%) 3. Citations: research influence (worth 30%) 4. Industries income: innovation (worth 2.5%) and 5. International outlook: staff, students and research (worth 7.5%). These indicators or parameters for Indian universities need to address in our educational institutions which were found very low in Times Higher Education World Rankings. There are various issues for the improvement of the quality of higher education in the country like Bureaucratic set up, obsolescence of infrastructure, shortage of faculty, outdated curricula and other related management issues.

In India, higher education is mostly looked after by the government, but due to shortage of resources to meet the increasing demand, private sector has been allowed to share the responsibility. Liberalization policies also open up the sector to foreign investment and permit the unregulated entry of private players will have only a marginal impact on the sector's basic problems such as access and quality. So far, these policies have induced foreign providers to focus only on certain technical and professional fields of study that can earn them good market returns. Private sector in Higher education also emphasize more on commercial aspect other than creation of knowledge which becomes the reason of deterioration in quality of education. In contrast to these modes, it is better to design a strategy that taps foreign universities and institutes of acceptable quality to work together with Indian universities/institutes to improve both access and quality. India has a broad educational set up in terms of a range of programmes and their acceptability in local industry or market, but it is inferior in comparison to international quality standards. The responsible bodies (councils and government) for quality assurance do not able to have international quality norms and an effective evaluation system to monitor and control violation of the existing norms by the institutions. Further, the government manipulates the issues of access and equity in higher education for their own interest rather than taking the right steps to improve the quality of higher education. As a result those who can afford the high cost of higher education look forward for the opportunities abroad while the others have to compromise with sub-standard education. If India becomes preferred location for higher education in the globalizing world it will have to develop an effective policy to take the challenges of substandard quality, Accessibility, Equality, increasing GER, ineffective systems of monitoring and control, red-tapism in growth and development and political interference. To overcome these problems India should have to take the shelter under the tree of Internationalization. Internationalization gives commercial advantage, knowledge and language acquisition, enhancing the curriculum with international content, and many others such as branch campuses, cross-border collaborative arrangements, programmes for international students, establishing English-medium programmes and degrees, and others have been put into place as part of Internationalization.

INTERNATIONALIZATION OF HIGHER EDUCATION

Hudzik's 'definition' of comprehensive Internationalization with the generally accepted definition by Jane Knight on Internationalization of higher education: "The process of integrating an international, intercultural or the global dimension into the purpose, functions or delivery of post-secondary education" Indian higher education needs comprehensive improvement in the education system of institutions at the national and international level to Internationalization of higher education. Like any new initiative, there will be some risks of misuses like there may be some institutions, which misrepresent, over-commercialize and perhaps make higher education affordable in the name of Internationalization. However, good policy framework has an ability to distinguish the wheat from the chaff. Internationalization of higher education is relevant when it is according to the needs of the country and its policy environment, which encourages innovation and experimentation but restricts misrepresentation, is much needed. It is high time for Indian higher education at policy and institutional level to reflect on how best to leverage the concept of Internationalization and engage it to achieve the goals of excellence, diversity and capacity building.

Internationalization entails connections between domestic and foreign parties interested in these activities. It also includes the policies and practices undertaken by academic systems and institutions – and even individuals – to cope with the global academic environment. The developed countries have an interest in exporting educational services in which they hold a lead. Developing countries, on the other hand, are recipients of the services from the former. This is not to say that they cannot export services in which other countries are interested. Some developing countries such as China and our country India are attracting overseas students to their institutions. It means that ultimately they may develop the capacity and incentive to engage in both the export and import of educational services.

WHY IT IS NEEDED?

- India is the second largest populated country in the world. India surely needs more universities because India has only 348 universities for its 1.2 billion people but, Japan has 4,000 universities for its 127 million people and US has 3,650 universities for its 301 million.
- To maximize the relevance of education
- Infusing Excellence
- Integrating an international, intercultural or global dimension
- Encouraging diversity and capacity building
- Bringing global best practices and more institutions with higher quality
- Global competition for talents,
- Higher Educational Institutions in India could be sensitized to adopt standards to facilitate "Global Benchmarking".
- Mobility and Exchanges for Students and Teachers
- Teaching and Research Collaboration
- Academic Standards and Quality
- Research Projects
- Co-operation and Development Assistance
- Curriculum Development
- International and Intercultural Understanding
- Promotion and Profile by Institution
- Diversify Source of Faculty and Students
- Regional Issues and Integration
- International Student Recruitment
- Diversify Income Generation

CHALLENGES TO THE INTERNATIONALIZATION OF HIGHER EDUCATION

- Democratic setting of the country.
- Affirming Academic and Professional Values in Internationalization of Higher Education.
- State governments and the central government have had their share of conflicting views.
- Managements of private sector institutions and public universities differ on several counts.
- Diversity of views held in different parts of the government, experts and other stakeholders.
- Ministry of human resource development and ministry of commerce have divergent views on the role of foreign providers and investment.
- Regulatory bodies such as the University Grants Commission (UGC) and the National Knowledge Commission do not see eye to eye on the role and nature of regulation.
- Country's direction in terms of Internationalization is neither clear nor coherent.
- Expand student intake (access).
- Upgrading quality and achieving excellence.
- Mobilizing the needed resources.
- Strengthening the regulatory function.
- Trained international staff storage.

MODE OF INTERNATIONALIZATION OF HIGHER EDUCATION

- Study abroad by students is still the most visible mode of Internationalization.
- Foreign education providers are setting up campuses or partnerships with local institutions in many developing countries.
- Distance learning involves foreign institutions.
- Twinning arrangements: students study in their home countries for the most part, but go overseas to complete the course and receive degrees from the foreign university.
- Education hubs to attract and serve foreign students. To make our top universities/institutes a destination for foreign students on a large scale.
- Virtual education: over 100 higher education institutions from different parts of the world launched the "open courseware consortium", each pledging to offer online course materials for at least 10 courses without any charge.
- Franchising.
- Award contracts to reputed foreign universities to collaborate in the creation of world-class universities in India.
- Encourage Indian institutions to set up campus/collaborations in other countries to meet the growing international demand for higher education.

SUGGESTIONS

- Increase governments interest.
- Identify the areas in which foreign imports are most useful.
- Adequate resources to pay for the providers' services.
- Equip the Indian institutions to absorb the needed inputs.
- Place an effective regulatory framework.
- Attract Foreign staff, students and institutes.
- Positive attitude of regulatory bodies.
- Access to Higher Education.
- Maintain Quality and Standards of higher education of international level.
- Invite Foreign institutions in domestic territory.
- Meet demand and supply of education.
- Strong institutional infrastructure.
- Achieve High gross enrolment ratio in higher education.

CONCLUSION

In the changing context of the emergence of the knowledge economy, higher education institutions need to embrace the concept of Internationalization. The functional character of higher education should imply and support the technological society by producing knowledge worker. This requires that the institutions should prepare themselves for addressing the issues of quality education. In improving the quality of higher education, many efforts have been put into the system with regulatory yardsticks identified and implemented, best practices incorporated and accreditation emphasized. The Indian institutions face tough competition for quality faculty, good students and global placements etc. Though the Indian economy has been opened up in the nineties, there has been resistance in India to allow foreign educational institutions due to several apprehensions. Understanding the realities, we should try to internationalize our university system and improve infrastructure to match the international standards.

REFERENCES

Altbach, P.G. and Knight, J. (2007), "The Internationalization of Higher Education: Motivations and Realities" Downloaded from jsi.sagepub.com at Narodna Univ Knjiznica on April 6, 2011.

Hangaragi, S.S. (2012), "Need to Improve the Quality of Higher Education Institutions in India for Sustaining long term growth" *University News*, Vol. 50, No. 39, Sep. 24-30, 2012.

Mathur, P.P. (2012), "Quality in Higher Education: Challenges of Internationalization of Higher education Institutions" *University News*, Vol. 50, No. 43, Oct. 22-28, 2012.

Thakur, J. (2012), "Quality in Higher Education System in India: Contemporary issues and challenges", *University News*, Vol. 50, No. 43, Oct. 22-28,2012

http://www.timeshighereducation.co.uk/world-university-rankings/2012-13/world-ranking/methodology dated 30.10.2012.

http://www.universityworldnews.com/article.php?story=0111021215849411 dated 30.10.2012.

7

Internationalization of Indian Higher Education: The Need of Time

Brajesh Kumar Shukla and *Tulika*

Education is a process by which a person's body, mind and character are formed and strengthened and enable him to develop his all round personality, exploring the best in him or her. It is a humanizing process of transformation to be able to think, relate to others meaningfully and understand the world and society clearly. A nation advances in the promotion of education and intelligence spread among the masses. Development of any country depends 20 per cent on natural resources, 16 per cent on infrastructure and 64 per cent on human resources. This call for high quality and well trained human resources from our education system. Without education one cannot differentiate between good or bad, right or wrong, true or false and lovely or ugly. The purpose of education is therefore to make human being capable competent and wise to meet the challenge of life. Jawaharlal Nehru declared that if all were well with our educational institutions, all would be well with the nation. Education institutions are intimately linked with society at large. They are the temples of knowledge, social change and transformation. Therefore our schools, colleges and universities are the makers of the destiny of a nation. The Kothari communication has rightly said that "The destiny of India is now being shaped in her classrooms. This we believe is no mere rhetoric. In a world based on science and technology it is education that determines the level of prosperity, welfare and security of people. On the quality, and number of persons coming out of our schools and college will depend our success in the great enterprise of national construction whose principal objective is to raise the standard of living of our people.

Higher education in India has an ancient tradition. The earliest known university was in Takshashila in the 7th century BC that had scholars not only from India but from all over the world. Everybody knows about Nalanda University and its most famous foreign student Huan Tsuang of China. Sanskrit used to be the language of higher education, a place presently occupied by the English. Not with handing this hoary past the present system of university education was actually introduced by the British in the 1857 when the universities of Calcutta, Bombay and Madras were established. Lord

Elplinstone, Lord Macaulay and Sir Charles wood were the early pioneers of the modern system of education in our country. They were good utilitarian's in the sense that the shrewdly recognized that. India was the jewel in subjugating and administering an empire on which the sun never sets. Hence they contrived to set up an educational system which will provide an army of trained manpower which would administer the country on behalf of their masters. This I was feeling on of the crucial reasons that the British were able to rule our country for the next 90 years with minimum man power and that too from a distant London. This was also the inflection point in higher education system as the medium of instruction became English throughout the country. With the dawn of Independence, the leaders of our national movement recognized that education is the tool of lift our massages from the missing of poverty and ignorance. In fact Pandit Jawahar Lal Nehru while delivering a speech at the special convocation of the Allahabad University on October 13, 1947 said that "A university stands for humanism for tolerance for reason, for progress, for the adventure of ideas and for the search for truth. It stands for the onward march of the human race towards, even higher objectives. If the universities discharge their duty adequately, then it is well with the nation and the people. But if the temple of learning itself became a home of narrow bigotry and petty objectives, how then will the nation prosper or people grow in stature?"

Thus the government of newly independent India recognized the importance of higher education and in spite of their pressing problems appointed several commissions and committees such as Radhakrishan Commission (1948-49), Kothari Commission (1964-65), Rammurti Committee (1990), Punnaya Committee (1992-93) etc. for suggesting an improvement and extension in higher education system desirable for the present and future requirement of the country. The University Grant Commission (UGC) the apex body of higher education was established in 1956 under an act of the Parliament of India.

At the time of independence we had only 20 universities. Today, we have 519 universities. Similarly our colleagues have grown from 592 to 25,951 and the student enrollment stand around 11.5 million. Even though these numbers are impressive in absolute terms. There is no way comparable to what other countries have achieved. Incredibly developed countries that are supposed to be an embodiment of capitalistic values have achieved 55 per cent enrollment of eligible age groups in higher education whereas our only 11 per cent even transition countries are ahead of us in this respect. Even more than the quantity mismatch what is worrying is the quality of our institutions.

DRAWBACK OF INDIAN EDUCATION SYSTEM

Some drawback of our educational system as like:

(1) The educational system has acquired a dualist character. It operates with a strong class bias with a wide disparity inequality. While 75 per cent of our Indian children go through an educational

programme of poor by government school and college 25 per cent benefit from a smaller number of quality institution run by private organizations

(2) Academic and administrative problems faced by our educational institutions are further compounded by government control and rigid regulation of the councils or universities
(3) One of the greatest difficulties is that teachers and students feel a tremendous academic pressure on them.
(4) Government policies and programmes in education are not effectively implemented.
(5) Our educational institutions in general and professional institutions in education in particular have become knowledge industries manufacturing graduates and postgraduates without consideration of quality
(6) Examination reforms have been miserably slow paced.
(7) Curricular reform and pedagogic reforms are not coping with the rate of advancement of knowledge.
(8) Lack of involvement of teachers, administrators in system.
(9) Evil practice of collecting capitation fee for admission.
(10) Caste, community or money base opportunities for teachers.
(11) Poor quality of teaching, Poor performance by college teachers Most of them have poor motivation.
(12) Negative a Heated towards research among college teachers.
(13) The evaluation system is qualitatively poor and corrupt.
(14) Examinations are not connected according to schedule and the results are not announced in a reasonable time after the examinations.
(15) Political interference in the autonomy of higher education.
(16) Poor leadership at higher levels of administration both in colleges and universities.

When we discuss about Internationalization of higher education then first of all we define it. Internationalization of higher education is the process of integrating an international, intercultural and/or global dimension into the goals, functions (Teaching, learning, research, services) and delivery of higher education. According to Organization for Economic Co-operation and Development (OECD) that "It is the complex of a process whose combined effect, where planned or not is to enhance the international dimension of experience of higher education in universities and similar educational institutions."

Therefore it can be finally stated that Internationalization of higher education means all types and models of delivery of higher education programmes, or set of courses of study, or educational services (including those of distance education) in which the learners are located in a country different from the one where the awarding institution is based. Such programmes may belong to the education system of a state different from the state in which it operates, or may operate independently of any national education system.

GOALS AND GENERAL PRINCIPLES OF INTERNATIONALIZATION OF HIGHER EDUCATION

The goals of internationalization of higher education are: creation of favourable condition for outwardly mobile students and faculty, who wish to do a part of their studies or teaching in another country, creation of conditions that enable foreign student to gain access to local study programmes and addition of an international dimension to the course contents and teaching programmes, cooperation with foreign partners in developing relevant curricula and educational methods, another study suggests that the aims of inter that the aims of internationalization of higher education may be grouped into four categories, in the future the quality and marketability of higher education programmes will be measured according to the international dimension they have and the international competence they are able to provide to their students.

PRINCIPLES OF INTERNATIONALIZATION OF HIGHER EDUCATION

Equal access for all even if students are financially weak, the system of international co-operation in higher education should be transparent and convincingly evident between the countries, long term sustainable collaboration and co-operation in the field of higher education needs to be emphasized with a focus on the social and cultural impact of Internationalization of higher education.

ADVANTAGES OF INTERNATIONALIZATION OF HIGHER EDUCATION

There are some most advantages of Internationalization higher education:

- Promotes value and culture
- Generates goodwill
- Includes the teaching-learning process
- Enhances the quality of education
- Encourages competitiveness
- Helps generate financial resources.

INTERNATIONALIZATION IN INDIA

India is the preferred destination for international students from developing countries due to the factors mentioned below:

- Low cost
- Education in English
- Global recognition to India professionals
- Strong university network
- Quality education (select institutions)
- Infrastructure – International standard (select institutions)

- Liberal visa policy for students.

Internationalization of higher education is today a fact of life and needs to be promoted for the academic, cultural, social, political and economic benefits that accrue from it. India has large potential to expand qualitative higher education but needs organized efforts and political will. Out of the top ten universities, is even our public funded universities who attracts maximum international students because of their long standing credibility, quality and relatively low cost, to grow further, they need more flexibility in handling and expanding the scope of international students. It is observed that the major chunk of students is about developing and neighboring countries. There is scope to increase their number at the same time we need to enroll more students in higher education system from our own country. We have to draw a balance between international students and national students. A changing scenario in all walks of life towards Internationalization is very dynamic, we have to reschedule our strategies to match the global speed with Indian identity, which is a Herculean task but not impossible. We would like to be higher educated country, the vision of Rabindranath Tagore regarding higher education is worth remembering. "The higher education is that which does not merely give us information but makes our life in harmony with all existence."

SUGGESTIONS

To promote Internationalization of Indian higher education, we will have to design a policy which promotes Internationalization bring transparency and credibility to the system. To reduce the problems of the foreign students we have to adopt single window policy for processing the admission. We need to provide adequate facilities (academic and residential) to attract them. We also need flexibility in changing subject combination for different courses and international dimension in course content. Universities will have to become proactive to attract international students. The ideal way of attracting the talented foreign students is introduction of merit scholarships for limited student which has long lasting impact quality credibility, competition and image of the country. Some other suggestions should also follow to improve the higher education as like – Enhancing the quality of teaching, learning and evaluation methods, focus on continuous development of faculty, removal of knowledge obsolescence to provide relevant and advanced information, Promotion of interdisciplinary teaching and research, to gear up to meet the increasing demand for quality higher education at low cost. The norms of higher education, input process, product, placement and promotion – all need to be validated and perfected, Higher education should integrate modern methods and media. It adequate facilities should be provided to teachers to undertake research. Admission to university course should be highly selective and based strictly on merit.

CONCLUSION

It can be finally say that the core mission of higher education is to educate, to train, to undertake research and to provide service to the community. In the context of globalization, the scope and demand for higher education is increasing the new paradigms in higher education involve creation of intellects of the world standards and also training of skill human power at mass level without compromising on quality. Higher education is no longer a luxury, it is essential for survival. In India, higher education has had a long history but its achievement has been mixed. While some institutions have been spectacularly successful at the international level, many institutions are now languishing due to a number of factors. Government of India is in the process of designing policies for foreign higher education providers in India. The authority which is entrusted with statutory powers should play an active role and bring clarity and credibility to the whole mechanism of foreign providers. There is a need for more transparency to attract foreign students, especially in professional courses. Similar is the need for foreign providers in the country. There are institutes and universities as mentioned in the category of foreign providers, illegally openly operating in India. This is the biggest challenge to their administrative and governing system. We as a country will have to deal with the irregularities with conviction, without further delay, otherwise we will damage our credibility. In the process of Internationalization we must not lose our national priority, national ethos and social structure.

REFERENCES

Bhalla, Veena (2001) International Students in Indian Universities (data for 1988-89 to 1999-2000), selected statistical data on India Higher Education, Association of Indian Universities, New Delhi.

Chauhan, C.P.S., (2002) Higher Education in India Challenge of Global Trends, Aligarh Muslim University, Aligarh, *University News*, April 29-5 May.

David, S.A. and Wildemersch, D. (2009). Globalization Growing Global Perspective in India, Higher Education Curriculum-General Tendencies in India (http://liars.kuleuven.be)

Pathak, R.P. (2007) *Education in the Emerging India*, Atlantic Publishing and Distributor (P) Ltd. New Delhi.

Powar, K.B. Ed. (2002) Internationalization of Higher Education, Association of Indian Universities, New Delhi.

Throat, Sukhadeo (2009) Higher Education: Approach Strategy and Action Plan in the 11th Plan, Convocation Address, *University News*, 47 (37) September, 14-20.

8

Internationalization of Higher Education: Preparation Policy, Implementation and Recognition

Rakesh Kumar Keshari

Internationalization is an ongoing and future-oriented process of integrating various international perspectives into our higher education. The perspectives may be related to the curriculum, programmes offered, top managers, faculty members, students, facilities and even the institutional visions, to suit the diverse and ever-changing environment and demands that are more global now. In realizing the transformation process, strategic changes involving all the aspects including financial commitments need to be planned realistically by each institution and their respective stakeholders. Then, the issue of recognition needs to be addressed as well. The reasons or rationales for Internationalization should be divided into two categories; the institutional level category and the national level category. The first category rationales will be mainly academic based, whereby among others it may facilitate exchanges and mobility of staff and students, carrying out collaborative research and projects, and enhancement in terms of quality and standard of the institutions. The national level rationales for Internationalization generally are more related to the economic, technology, political and social and cultural aspects. The concept of Internationalization of higher education is not new. In the more developed countries such as the USA, UK, Canada, Japan, France, the loose concept and definition of international higher education has long been practiced. Traditionally, students from former colonies were sent to universities in these countries to gain tertiary education and to come back and serve their native countries. This was seen as short-term training ground solution to fill the vacant administrative and technical posts in the native countries immediately after independence. Thus, this it looks like a "one-way traffic" of student movements from less developed countries. Although Internationalization of higher education can be defined in many ways, but in general the definition should include the key elements such as Academic Programme, Students, Academic Staff, Curricula, and Infrastructure and Facilities, that may also be considered as the bench-mark for Internationalization.

Programme or courses: The programme or courses of the programme offered should be global in nature, accepted and recognized internationally.

Student enrolment: The acceptance of students into the institution should be country, region, race, religion or cultural independent. In other words, students' acceptance and enrollment should be multinational in nature.

Multinational staff: The institution should be able to attract and gather expertise, especially teaching and research staff that is multinational in nature as well.

Curricular and co-curricular competencies: The co-curricular activities and informal non-academic training along with the formal academic activities should be able to prepare students to meet global challenges and needs related to the subsequent employability and marketability of the graduates.

Infrastructure and facilities: The institutions' physical and information must be at Par with those used by top-rank. Resource Centre (such as library and internet communication) classrooms, science and language laboratories are up-to-date with the latest appropriate facilities.

In the present Internationalization concept in line with globalization and democratization of education, however, economic and financial exchanges are not the only major consideration. By internalization we wish to strengthen research and innovation activities in local universities through international collaborations and network, and wider recognition. We wish to attract international students to enroll in Malaysian universities, even in highly competitive programmes. More international academic staff, either permanently or through exchange programmes will be employed. Where human capital and capacity development is concerned, graduates are expected to gain wider employment opportunities.

Internationalization of higher education is not a "phrase concept". It's a process with planning and analysis stages, glazed with human and financial commitments. The main initial objective is to gain international recognition on the local institutions and their respective academic curricula and programmes. Then, nation's policies and quality assurance are to be dealt with judiciously. To ensure its success, related individuals and organizations/bodies must execute their roles positively.

TRANSFORMATION AND IMPLEMENTATION

Physical transformation involves improvement in the internal infrastructure and environment of the institution, such that the physical beings and facilities are of "international nature". Other transformations are related to improvement in curriculum and programmes, research activities, services and networking. And, to ensure continuous recognition and improvement, the institutions need to have a short and long term strategic plan of Internationalization. Again, the realization of the transformation must be supported by an ample financial commitment and able players in the institutions. Having identified the needed transformations, the next step is to identify the key players that will ensure the success of the transformation to international status. A study by the International Association of Universities (IAU) in 2003 indicates that at the institutional level the major impulse for Internationalization is coming from the faculty members. Faculty member mainly will be involved in reevaluating and restructuring of programmes offered, and internationalizing the curriculum. Enhancement of research, development and innovation through international networks, cooperation and linkages also laid on the shoulders of academician, and of course with the support of institutional leaders. However, the main role of institutional leaders and administrators are inevitably important, especially where infrastructure transformations and the formulation of the Internationalization strategic plan are concerned. They are also expected to be involved in generating or finding financial sources to implement the transformations Internationalization of higher education will involves high mobility of students from one nation to another. In fact, the same study by IAU found that respondents considered students mobility as the most important aspects of Internationalization. Thus the role played by students and their presence in ensuring that higher education is really "international" must be appreciated by all quarters. However, the programmes offered, curriculum, services and facilities within the institutions will always be the pulling factor for international students.

Besides the institutional players above support from the government, private sectors and accreditation and recognizing bodies are also important in internalization of higher education. Although a study by IAU indicated that the idea of Internationalization was somewhat "bottom-up", initiated by faculty members and institutional leaders, the role played by government through the related ministries in facilitating the efficient implementation either in the form of policies (for public and private institutions) and financial support (mainly for public institutions) is crucial. The implementation of Internationalization policies in terms of student intake, visa requirements, programmes available to international students, international academic staff, setting-up private universities or colleges, etc. are to ensure the smooth Internationalization process without denying the tertiary education opportunities to local students.

For private sectors, their contribution will be more on the linkages, collaboration and cooperation in research enhancement, input for curriculum development, training for graduating students and staff, as well as recognition of the graduates. These roles are crucial since they are the one will be the main supply of employment market and job opportunities for the graduates.

KEY ROLES OF INSTITUTIONAL LEADERS

The policies laid down by government regarding Internationalization of higher education serve as guidelines and pointers to be followed by the individual institution. The roles of private sectors will only appear after the blue print of Internationalization has been sturdily laid down by the institution. Therefore, the onset or commencement of Internationalization of an institution depends very much on the institutional leaders. Many studies have shown that much is expected out of institutional leaders in leading their institutions to become globally recognized international higher education institutions. *Making a case for paradigm change* to stakeholders, academic and administrative staff, students and community towards successful

Internationalization, effectively will be the first and important role of institutional leaders. The leaders have the necessary institutional rank and leadership abilities to engage the symbiotic coalition between the parties to work together towards the goals of Internationalization. They should be able to develop the necessary organizational structure in the institutions that could facilitate Internationalization smoothly. Setting up some central and visible unit to become the standard bearer for international activities is very much recommended.

The ideas, plans and implementation of successful Internationalization need to be made known, especially to those who are not directly involved in the activities. The institutional leaders need to *stay focus and communicating effectively*, by shining the importance of Internationalization regularly and at any opportunity available to him. As the journey for Internationalization is long and winding, and the destination will keep on changing and improving to suit the local and global policies, demands and situations, staying focus are crucial. They must be focused on their goals, and able to steer the institutions to face all the unexpected challenges in the course of achieving the intended goals. Every information, directive, policies and rules related to Internationalization must be able to be communicated effectively through whatever means of communication within the institution.

Internationalization of higher education is attached with recognition for the institutions, both internal and external recognition. *Gaining recognition* is another key role of institutional leaders. Generally, recognition is related to the programmes, curricular and co-curricular activities offered and run by the institutions. In India, the UGC, University grant commission and AICTE, is the body that actively monitoring and regulating the higher education institutions especially for recognition purposes. However, the programmes, especially the professional programmes such as medical, engineering, architecture, law etc., must also be recognized by the regulating bodies in that professional field. The issue of non-recognition of qualification might affect the prospects of getting international students. To meet this ever-changing requirement, leaders, such as deans and heads of departments at faculty level must be given the encouragement and support to regularly and continually review and improve their programmes and curricula. Internationally recognized programmes would be able to attract international students as well as academic staff to enroll and serve the institutions. The graduates in that field would be able to compete in the job market both at home and abroad. Gaining recognition must be complimented by *recognizing transnational and foreign preparatory programmes and foreign university degree programmes*. Foreigners graduated from these programmes are the prospective feeders for undergraduate and post-graduate programmes in the institutions. However, except for developed countries such as UK, USA and Australia, provision for recognizing such transnational programmes from developing and undeveloped countries remains unregulated. The institutional leaders must be proactive in evaluating feeders from target countries such as China, West Asia and Africa, especially in terms of English language proficiency and the required level of basic knowledge in the respective fields. This will involve the evaluation and comparison of secondary education practice in the countries in what is presently practiced in India, in terms of both subject matter or contents and number of residential years in the level.

At the onset of Internationalization plan, the institutional leaders must realize that the plan will by no mean be a "single person war". Therefore they must *encourage wider involvement and participation* in the Internationalization movement, especially among his subjects at all levels. As mentioned earlier in the definition or benchmark of Internationalization, all levels of staffs have their respective roles to play to full-filled the requirement of the benchmarks. Their task and goals need to be clearly specified and monitored, and the appropriate recognizing awards are given for active and effective participation the Internationalization movement. Institutional leaders should also appreciate that the public, private sectors and NGO have roles to play as well. The government is encouraging the establishment of linkages between institutions of higher learning with these sectors of society, especially in terms of training, research, innovation and commercialization. Some public universities in India are encouraged to create a post of Vice Chancellor in charge of Industrial and Society Linkages.

Institutional leaders must *share the leadership aspiration* for Internationalization with his subjects, especially the young middle leaders and managers in their institutions, to continually identify and mobilized new leaders and followers. As Internationalization of higher education is a constantly changing and continually improving movement, the traveling time span involved to reach the perfect goals will be long. There will be a time when new leaders undertake the present institutional leaders' task and roles, smoothly without creating harmful vacuum to the Internationalization movement.

STRATEGIES FOR INTERNATIONALIZATION

Full-filling and sustaining the benchmarks of Internationalization need appropriate and workable strategies. The University of India spelled out five strategies in their internalization promotion plan These strategies can be considered as universal in nature, and may be applicable to any other institutions in trying to emulate their plan. Again, in implementing the strategies every individual from all levels in the institution must understand and effectively execute their roles and duties. Briefly, the five strategies is

A. Provide an Internationally High Standard of Education

- Strengthening constructive and creative learning in the interdisciplinary fields, and actively expanding cooperative learning.
- Publicizing overseas through the internet and providing the advice programme for prospective overseas students.
- Students exchange and credit transfer programmes with international alliance universities.

– Improving and providing external funds and scholarship for the best students from abroad.
– Having an international interim programme for the best students from the university, through alumni network.
– Exploring the potential of establishing overseas branch campuses.

B. Enhancement of Research Culture through International Network

– Establishment of advanced research institute for top level researchers to conduct research and academic activities.
– Inventory and mapping of international research network of individual faculty members.
– Foster joint research and exchange of faculty members with major foreign universities.
– Organizing international symposia and forums.
– Consolidate system for visiting researchers from foreign countries.

C. Promoting Cooperation With International Society

– Facilitate support and contribution system of international institutions and aid agencies for international development programme.
– Establishment of foreign liaison offices.
– The central role played by Corporate and International Division of the university to promote collaboration between industry and academia.
– Public relation activities to create an excellent international reputation.

D. Improve Infrastructure

– Training of staff to improve relevant skills to handle international support services within the university.
– Provide comfortable and conducive living, study and research environment for foreign students and researchers.
– Encourage local and state government to improve regional infrastructure such as schools and hospital.

E. Formation of Long Term Strategic Plan for Internationalization

– Obtain and exchange of information with foreign universities to draw strategic plan.
– Evaluate the current status of Internationalization.
– Based on examination results, evaluate the current progress of the Internationalization of the institution, and incorporate the changes needed with respect to goals and plans.

CHALLENGES FOR INTERNATIONALIZATION

As in any other processes of implementing a plan, implementation of Internationalization of higher education is also faced with multitudes of challenges that need to be overcome by the key players. Since the major tasks of the implementation rest on the shoulders of faculty members, with the support of institutional leaders, a study by Madeleine Green in the USA has found that the challenges can be individual or institutional in nature. Although the study was carried out in the USA, it is expected that these challenges are applicable in our present scenario in India. As movers of Internationalization plan in our institution, knowledge of these challenges would ensure us to be more prepared in our plans by finding ways to neutralize and minimize the retarding effects. Some of the individual challenges or barriers are:

(a) *Lack of competency* – especially the cognitive competence, whereby due to the lack of international experience and mindset, the faculty could not be able to connect knowledge to their teaching of international students.
(b) *Negative attitudes* – Individual perception of Internationalization is often correlated to their personal experience with people from other cultures. They may doubt the importance of global competencies through Internationalization of higher education as compared to competencies in their own field.
(c) *Absence of incentives* – Players for Internationalization plan in an institution mainly are academic staff with teaching and research loads. Without appropriate incentives either in financial, promotional or "equivalent time off" form, the individuals may feel unappreciated by the institution in performing their Internationalization tasks.
(d) *Lack of personal knowledge and expertise* – The willingness of an academician to engage with Internationalization activities depends on his personal capacities and experience with other cultures and languages. Lack of this will likely lead to opposition, unwillingness to participate or indifference towards Internationalization movement.

Some of institutional barriers or challenges that may hinder the Internationalization of higher education, and applicable to any institutions need to be appreciated as well. Briefly some of them are

(i) *Lack of financial resources* – Finding sufficient fund to bear the initial cost of Internationalization especially in providing the physical infrastructure, programme development and review, travel and accommodation for fact finding and promotional work is the main challenge of an institution. As for students, lack of financial support either from government or the private sector is the main significant barrier to study abroad.
(ii) *Scarcity of human resources* – This is related to the provision of international standard programmes and curricula, and promotion. Without competent human resources in the related academic fields, the intended programme could not be developed. Without competent promoter, the internationalized institution will not be promoted effectively.

(iii) *Educational structure* – Each country in this world has their own educational structure starting from pre-school, through primary, secondary, pre-university and terminating tertiary education. Mismatch between the educational structure of the host institution's country to that of prospective international students' countries would create problems even in the beginning of the study. The challenges will be even greater if the students were inferior in their pre-university preparation in their own country.

CONCLUSION

This presentation loosely discusses the aspects of Internationalization of higher education in terms of definition, policies, preparation, implementation and recognition. Roles of leaders in higher education, strategies for implementation, and possible challenges have been listed. These listings are by no means exhaustive. They were listed with the assumption that they are generally applicable to any institution. However it must be appreciated that each institution is an individual of their own right, they may have their own strategies, and facing challenges peculiar to that institution only. In this presentation no specific solutions to the challenges were given. It is hoped that by knowing the roles and the possible barriers that they may face, the main players would formulate their own solutions, acceptable within the constraints of their institution. As a concluding remark, let us look at the present scenario of higher education in India that may give some ideas to the Internationalization movement.

REFERENCES

Altbach, P.G. (1989). "Twisted Roots: The Western Impact on Asian Higher Education." *Higher Education* 18(1): 9–29.

Chakrabarti, R., A. Bartning, *et al.* (2010)."Developing Globally Compatible Institutional Infrastructures for Indian Higher Education." *Journal of Studies in International Education*, 14(2): 183–199.

Das, S. (2007). "The Higher Education in India and the Challenge of Globalization." *Social Scientist* 35 (3/4): 47–67.

Ellingboe, B. (1996). *Divisional Strategies on Internationalizing Curriculum*; MA Thesis, University of Minnesota, USA.

Gillan, M., B. Damachis, *et al.* (2003). "Australia in India: Commodification and Internationalization of Higher Education." *Economic and Political Weekly* 38 (14): 1395–1403.

Green, M.F. (2002). *The Challenge of Internalizing Undergraduates Education: Global Learning for All*; Paper of Global Challenges and US Higher Education Conference, Duke University, USA. Available at www.jhfc.duke.edu/ducis/globalchallenges/pdf/green.pdf. (Retrieved on 28 August 2007)

Hall, M. (2004). *The Importance of Internationalization of Higher Education*; International Education Association of South Africa, Cape Town, SA.

Hamrick, J. (1999). *Internationalizing Higher Education Institutions: Broadening the Approach to Institutional Change*; Occasional papers on Institutional Change and Transformation in Higher Education, University of Michigan, USA.

Knight, J. (2003). *Internationalization of Higher Education Practices and Priorities*: 2003 IAU Survey Report; International Association of Universities, Paris, France.

Pelan Strategik Pengajian Tinggi Negara Melangkau Tahun 2020, Sisipan Khas, Utusan Malaysia, 29 August 2007 (In Malay).

Prakash, V. (2005). *Internationalization of Higher Education: The Indian Context*; UNESCO, International Institute for Education Planning, Paris.

Roselle Tapsir, Ahmad Saat, Suzana Meor A. Aziz; (2007); *International Education: Diversity, Dilemmas, Differences and Direction*; Proceedings INCUE 2005, UPENA, UiTM Shah Alam.

Stella, A. and A. Gnanam (2005). "Cross-border Higher Education in India: False understandings and true overestimates." *Quality in Higher Education*, 11 (3): 227–237.

University of Tokyo; 2005; The University of Tokyo Internationalization Promotion Plan 2005–2008. Available at http/www/dir.u~tokyo.ac.jp/ en/ut/suoshinkeikaku-e.pdf. (Retrieved on 28 August 2007)

9

Internationalizing the Higher Education Curriculum

Shalini Rajput and *Dr. L. Mishra*

The universities today have re-imagined the purpose of Internationalization to address the changing social, civic and global trends. Therefore, apart from the economic aspect of Internationalization, universities in the 21st century have begun to pro-actively address the geopolitical and socio cultural issues that have sprung up as a result of and as a response to Internationalization of higher education. The process and the notion of Internationalization has become a strategic component of a broad range of university activity from the specification of mission statements, through the responsibilities of senior management, curriculum development, cross-border partnerships, classroom teaching and learning, even to the ways in which the university buildings are constructed, as is perhaps most neatly illustrated on the new campus for Shanghai International Studies University with its diverse architectural styles reflecting the countries that students study and the languages they learn.

The idea of Internationalization and the numerous processes and operations that it entails seems to add to the already super-complex nature of the university (Barnett, 2000). In particular, while the idea of Internationalization has become indispensable in higher education discourse world-wide, the meanings and actions which construct this particular nation remain largely vague (Turner and Robson, 2008). The connection between higher education and Internationalization can be analyzed in multiple ways. The meaning and purpose of Internationalization may be defined in contradictory ways, even across different departments within the same university. This issue of multiple meanings and complexity becomes of particular significance when considering the meaning of the Internationalization of the university curriculum.

What is Meant by Internationalization of the Higher Education Curriculum?

There is a lack of clarity around the concept of the Internationalization of the higher education curriculum and its boundaries and further research is needed with respect to meaning and process. In particular, there is a need to construct a broader perspective on the concept, which stretches beyond just curriculum content. Equally, thinking in the area must move away from a narrow focus on international students and provide international experiences to all universities staff and students so that they will perform successfully (professionally, economically and socially) within diverse contexts.

International curricula may be defined as (IDP, 1995, p. 1): "Curricula with an international orientation in content, aimed at preparing students for performing (professionally/socially) in an international and multicultural context, and designed for domestic students as well as foreign students." Support for those seeking to internationalise curricula is provided in the form of a useful nine category "Typology for Internationalizing Curriculum" proposed by Bremer and van der Wende (1995). Other writers exploring Internationalization have discussed the relevance and importance of student outcomes, teaching strategies and knowledge content and inclusive curricula and Nevertheless Mestenhauser's (1998, p. 28) conclusion still stands – the literature about international education "is generally silent about the nature of the international curriculum, and yet every field and discipline in international education makes assumptions about what to teach, how to teach it, when and to whom, in what sequence, and of what quality and quantity. None cite any research findings on which this form of the 'curriculum' is based". The means to "internationalize the curriculum" may still be unclear, partly because, as Cairo and McTaggart (2003) indicate, internationalizing the curriculum is a construct, not a clearly defined set of ideas or best practices. The concept "internationalizing the curriculum" needs to be further explored and strategies defined such that the academic community is more able to consider implementing such a curriculum within the various disciplines. It seems fundamental that the stakeholder group most concerned with designing and implementing curriculum in higher education be widely consulted as to the relevance of internationalization and what might be required of them within their teaching programmes. Bremer and van der Wende (1995) suggest a typology that illustrates the range of programmes that may be considered in planning for internationalized curricula. Appropriate initiatives include curricula where the content has been specifically designed for international students; curricula dealing with an international subject; curricula involving an internationally comparative approach and interdisciplinary programmes exploring regions or areas rather than single countries. In the vocational arena, curricula which prepare students in defining international professions or lead to internationally recognized professional qualifications represent internationalization, along with programmes where the study of foreign languages explicitly addresses cross-cultural communication issues and provides training in intercultural communication skills. Finally, in terms of academic mobility, Bremer and van der Wende regard joint or double degrees and programmes in which compulsory parts are offered at institutions abroad, with local faculty, as examples of internationalized curricula (Bremer and van der Wende, 1995). The typology is clearly useful in terms of deciding what specific features characters internationalized programmes, and may in turn, suggest a number of alternative approaches when HEIs consider the issue of 'concertizing' policy, that is, how to in practice, internationalize their curricula.

Why is Internationalization of the Higher Education Curriculum Important?

- The 21st century university faces numerous challenges at local, regional and global levels (mass migration, environmental and geographical issues, super-diversity of the student cohorts, as well as the knowledge paradigms, the information overload, and global interconnectedness);
- Problems and issues in the current socioeconomic and geopolitical aspects demand broader, multi-perspective understanding about the world, life and work;
- As the most visible and significant site of knowledge creation, the university has a social responsibility to equip the members of the society with necessary competencies, knowledge, understandings, and new skills so that they can constantly negotiate the changing nature of Work, the force, information technologies and cultural identities of people. Intercultural learning and Internationalization of the curriculum Intercultural learning is clearly an important part of Internationalization of the curriculum in any context. Knight (2003) describes the intercultural as 'relating to the diversity of cultures that exist within countries, communities, and institutions'. Intercultural engagement and learning is not, however, an easy thing to achieve. As Paige (Paige 1993, p. 1) points out, 'professional intercultural educators know that communicating and interacting with culturally different others is psychologically intense' and has several risk factors associated with it, including risk of embarrassment and risk of failure (p. 13). 'Intercultural education strives to develop critical engagement, self-reflection and sensitivity towards any aspect of interaction and communication between "self" and "others"' It involves the development of understandings of how the languages and cultures of others influence their thoughts, values, actions and feelings, and it is argued that this cannot occur unless we also understand the ways in which our own language and culture influences our actions, reactions, values and beliefs. This is complex and challenging and involves students and staff moving into a 'third place' (Lo Bianco, Liddicoat *et al.* 1999, p. 13), a meeting place between different cultures where there is recognition of the manifestation of cultural difference, and where equal and meaningful reconstructive cross-cultural dialogue can occur. This place may be simultaneously uncomfortable, challenging, enriching and exciting.

However, intercultural learning is often assumed to be an automatic outcome and benefit of intercultural contact whether that be contact resulting from having a range of cultures together on campus (AEI 1998, p. 2) and in class. The assumption is that proximity → intercultural Contact → intercultural learning/competence. Given that 'Australia now has one of the highest proportions of international students on campus of any country in the world', we would therefore expect there to be high levels of intercultural competence amongst the university community in Australia. However, research in Australia and overseas into the interaction and engagement between different cultural groups on does not support the crude proximity → intercultural contact → intercultural learning/competence equation. If intercultural learning does not occur automatically as a result of intercultural contact 'at home', it is probably therefore unlikely that it will be an outcome of offshore teaching for either staff or students without strategic intervention.

HOW CAN WE PUT THE INTERNATIONAL CURRICULUM INTO PRACTICE?

Problems and Issues

A key question is what Internationalization might mean at the disciplinary level, for example, what should an engineering, psychology or arts curriculum look like if it is to meet the needs of the 21st century student? We are shortly going to include some links to work in this area, however, when it comes to looking at each of the disciplines there is often not as much guidance at the level of curriculum content as might be expected although clearly much work is currently being done in this area. This type of work provides an exciting opportunity as by engaging with your communities of practice, such as professional bodies and Subject Centers, you can listen to, debate and contribute to the process of curriculum Internationalization within your subject area.

Some disciplines are already 'internationalized' (such as International Studies, Comparative Religions etc.) or lend themselves to Internationalization more easily. Internationalization could mean providing a broader knowledge base through including conceptual and theoretical work from non-Western sources; providing opportunities for practice in diverse cultural contexts; or examining practices in the discipline in different parts of the world. The ultimate aim is to better equip students with the knowledge and skills they will need in their future careers as well as to generate and pluralize knowledge. I shall here consider five contemporary competing epistemological pressures on the higher education curriculum, suggesting that the future of the higher education curriculum will hang significantly on the way in which this competition is resolved:

- the deconstruction of the subject, as reflected in, for example, the modularisation of the curriculum;
- the cross-curricular 'key' skills movement;
- the learning through experience movement and the shift of the seat of learning outside the academy; · the anarchic potential of web-based learning; and
- the reaformation of the subject as the academic and organizational identity.

Although it may be argued that to devote time to the development of skills is a diversion from a student's main studies, and that the potential list of skills becomes so long that it is self-defeating, we believe that four skills are key to the future success of graduates whatever they intend to do in later life. These four are:

(i) Communication skills;
(ii) Numeracy;
(iii) The use of information technology;
(iv) Learning how to learn. We believe that these key skills are relevant throughout life, not simply in employment. All institutions of higher education should Aim for student achievement in key skills to become an outcome of all programmes.

POSSIBLE SOLUTIONS: SUGGESTIONS FOR ACTION

Consider with students how knowledge/content might be alternatively constructed in different cultures; Ensure that learning outcomes include values and skills as well as knowledge; Discuss relevant ethical issues in international contexts; Give time between sessions to considering how professional practices might differ across the world.

- The term 'International' itself is problematic in the process of teaching and learning.
- Teaching–learning sites in the 21st century university are super-diverse and participants bring multiple perspectives, understandings and competencies to the classroom. Knowledge creation cannot be constrained within nationalities.
- Hence, this paper suggests that the term 'international curriculum' should be replaced by the term 'multi-perspective curriculum'.

Putting the Multi-Perspective Curriculum into Practice

- Continuously expose students and staff to multiple views of the world (create different socio-cultural/educational societies, promote interdisciplinary activities, harness experiences of all the students in teaching and learning, value alternative world views, use comparative approaches to teaching).
- Encourage reflexive learning and teaching (reflexive dialogue, keeping reflexive diaries, reflexive teaching/learning logs) so that students can constantly and critically reshape their approaches and views about learning and teaching.
- Seek to create a culture that makes students and staff feel that the university is a democratic meeting place where the encounter of diversity (in terms of gender, maturity, culture, nationality) creates opportunities to develop new competencies, knowledge and understandings.
- Increase opportunities for collaborative learning (communities of practice, group work, workshops, seminars) which exploit the diversity within the student body.

There are several different ingredients to this particular curriculum agenda, some of which are perhaps more readily acceptable to traditional academics than others. These include:

- an attempt to draw attention to and develop some of the more generic capacities which underlie traditional university education (e.g. critical thinking and problem solving) and which are prominent in what employers expect or are looking for in a graduate employee;
- a fresh emphasis on what might be called the interpersonal dimensions of working in an academic as well as an employment context (e.g. on team working and oral as well as written communication and presentational skills and the development of personal confidence in social situations);
- an understanding of the world of work', of the way businesses function and of how knowledge can be applied in these settings (which leads of course to pressure for the inclusion of work experience as part of undergraduate programmes; see below); and
- the establishment of basic skills which, it is claimed, many of today's entrants to higher education lack (numeracy and basic writing skills as well as competence in the use of information technology).

WEB BASED CURRICULUM

The combination of vast arenas of data on the web, increasingly sophisticated search engines and accelerated delivery systems all readily accessible to anyone with a PC will totally undermine the continuing dominance of a curriculum which provides for the transmission of knowledge and demands its replacement by a curriculum which supports its distillation, analysis, ordering and manipulation. Given the total lack of any quality control or scholarly screening of the stuff that is available on the net, it will place greater onus than ever on students' capacity to read this material critically and to assess its reliability for themselves. As still and moving images and sound become much more readily and speedily accessible on the web, the heavy emphasis in the traditional curriculum on words and figures will be extended to include the handling of multimedia resources and the presentation of work, not just in the Higher Education in the 21st Century written essay but in the multimedia formats that all sorts of contexts of working life will expect as standard. Conventional patterns of linearity in the reading and representation of knowledge-driven hitherto by the technology and sequence of the book and miniaturised in the form of the essay will be replaced or extended By representations which allow multiple connections and layering of content in both the forms in which it is accessed and in the forms in which it is represented. Individual learners will thus be located at the centre of a multi-layered, multimedia, multi-dimensional learning environment through which they have the power to construct their own learning; in other words an environment ideally designed to support the kind of constructivist approach to learning, and with it the individualised curriculum which is so strongly favoured in contemporary educational psychology. The technology will allow for all sorts of interaction between learners, scholars and researchers and between them and the professional and lay public which cross every institutional, social and national boundary. The community of learners is thus transformed, and the experience of learning will allow extended opportunities for collaborations in the construction of knowledge.

REFERENCES

Bridges, D. (1998), British Educational Research Association conference at York on an earlier version of this paper. http://itslifejimbutnotasweknowit.org.uk/files/CPLHE/CJEBridgesCurric.pdf download 13, April 2013

Caruana, V. and Spurling, N. (2007), *The Internationalization of UK Higher Education: A review of selected material*. Project Report. Higher Education Academy.

Haigh, M.J. (2002), Internationalization of the Curriculum: designing inclusive education for a small world. *Journal of Geography in Higher Education*, 26 (1), 49-66.

Huddart, T. and Jackson, E. (2010), *Understanding Internationalization of Home Students for Improvements to Curriculum Design.*

IDP Education Australia (1995), *Curriculum Development for Internationalization: Australian Case Studies and Stocktake*. Canberra: DEETYA.

Jones, E. and Killick, D. (2007), Internationalization of the curriculum. In E. Jones and S. Brown (Eds.). *Internationalizing Higher Education*. London: Routledge.

Leask, B. (2005), Internationalization of the curriculum: Teaching and learning. In J. Carroll and J. Ryan (Eds.), *Teaching International Students: Improving Learning for All* pp. 119-129. London: Routledge.

Webb, G. (2005), Internationalization of the curriculum: An institutional approach. In J. Carroll and J. Ryan (Eds.), *Teaching International Students: Improving Learning for All*, pp. 109-118. London: Routledge.

10

Internationalization of Higher Education: Banaras Hindu University, Varanasi

Savita Gupta, Vidhi Singh and *Kawendra Kumar*

GLOBALIZATION, INTERNATIONALIZATION AND ACADEMIC CAPITALISM

Globalization and internationalization are related but not the same thing. Globalization is the context of economic and academic trends that are part of the reality of the 21st century. Internationalization includes the policies and practices undertaken by academic systems and institutions – and even individuals – to cope with the global academic environment. The motivations for internationalization include commercial advantage, knowledge and language acquisition, enhancing the curriculum with international content, and many others. Specific initiatives such as branch campuses, cross-border collaborative arrangements, programmes for international students, establishing English-medium programmes and degrees, and others have been put into place as part of internationalization. Efforts to monitor international initiatives and ensure quality are integral to the international higher education environment.

GLOBALIZATION

The concept of globalization is complex and contested. It usually refers to the greater interconnectedness of the world. Two main approaches to the concept of globalization can be distinguished. The first, politically neutral, approach defines globalization as an empirical reality in terms of the compression of time and space or 'action at a distance,' particularly associated with instantaneous communications technology. The second approach identifies globalization as an economic discourse actively promulgating a market ideology. The concept of globalization spans separate yet overlapping domains. It is ultimately a process spearheaded by multinational financial and industrial conglomerates. The widely discussed globalization phenomenon fundamentally results from the globalization of economic life, which is largely the universalization of capitalism. With a market mechanism at the core of globalization, one strand in the debate on globalization and higher education suggests that market regulation should reign supreme. These values, reflected in the neo-conservative and neo-liberal agendas, promote less state intervention and greater reliance on the free market, and more appeal to individual self-interest than to collective rights. Parallel with globalization is the shift from social to corporate welfare and co modification of cultural goods. Cultural and scientific endeavours become profitable activities, cultural goods become commercial products, the public is redefined as customers, the university becomes a provider, and the learner a purchaser of services. Globalization is the most fundamental challenge facing universities in their history. Most of the new changes are expressions of a greater influence of the market and the government over university affairs. Arguably the most significant is the worldwide drastic restructuring of higher education systems. At the core of these is a redefinition of the relationships among the university, the state, and the market, with a net result of a reduction of institutional autonomy.

INTERNATIONALIZATION

The definition of internationalization has been the subject of much discussion. While globalization is radically reshaping the face of the university worldwide through market competition, internationalization is entailed. According to Knight, "internationalization at the national, sector, and institutional levels is defined as the process of integrating an international, intercultural, or global dimension into the purpose, functions or delivery of postsecondary education." With the advancement of human understanding and the universality of knowledge as its fundamental focus, internationalization is principally different from globalization in that it refers to the reciprocal exchange of people, ideas, good and services between two or more nations and cultural identities. In the Indian case, while internationalization signifies an integration of the international community with India's higher education community, the Indian government regards it instead as a strategy to strengthen national economic competitiveness. For institutions, internationalization means the awareness and operation of interactions within and between cultures through their teaching, research and services functions. In practice, however, individual institutions often care most about their research strength and international ranking. Internationalization is also perceived differently by scholars from different fields of academic enquiry. Most contemporary Indian academics in social sciences and humanities place their focus on international scholarly communications and emphasize the increasing participation of Indian scholars into the world academic community. In contrast, scholars from science and technology often respond more specifically, with concrete emphases on international similarities of science. Despite the disparities, these views collectively demonstrate that in addition to concrete contents of courses, internationalization encompasses commitments, attitudes, global awareness and orientation.

ACADEMIC CAPITALISM

The term academic capitalism was proposed by Slaughter and Leslie. According to them, To maintain or expand resources, faculty had to compete increasingly for external dollars that were tied to market-related research, which was referred to variously as applied, commercial, strategic, and targeted research, whether these moneys were in the form of research grants and contracts, service contracts, partnerships with industry and governments, technology transfer, or the recruitment of more and higher fee-paying students. We call institutional and professional market or market-like efforts to secure external moneys *academic capitalism*. The focus that has been placed by Slaughter and Leslie is on the political economy of the relationship between universities and external business firms. They are concerned with both the external environment and academic culture. Based on their empirical investigation, they argue that academic work has been fundamentally altered. The model of government-funded research has shifted from long-term programmes of 'pure' research under academic control to university-industry partnerships in which the direction of research is directly shaped by potential commercial applications. Universities are now more incorporated in industry, and their ethos shifts from the client welfare of their students to the economic bottom-line. The shift from full public funding to partial dependence on market sources of income undercuts the tacit social contract whereby universities have been treated as unique institutions.

A BRIEF HISTORY OF BHU AND ITS EARLY INTERNATIONALIZATION

The seeds of modern western education were laid in the country along with the development of business and power of the British East India Company during the early 19th century. The company needed educated locals to carry out its business properly in India, and the local masses started feeling the need for proper certification of qualification for the purpose of serving the administration and other government departments. The result was the foundation of the first three universities of the country by Earl Viscount Canning, the British Governor General, in 1857. In a time of nationwide political disturbances and turmoil in the form of the Indigo Revolutions, the Santhal Revolutions and the Sepoy Mutiny, the country slowly progresses towards what we now know as proper institutionalized and global education. Banaras Hindu University is an internationally reputed temple of learning, situated in the holy city of Varansi. This Creative and innovative university was founded by the great nationalistic leader, Pandit Madan Mohan Malviya, in 1916 with cooperation of great personalities like Dr. Annie Besant, who viewed it as the University of India. Banaras Hindu University was created under the Parliamentary legislation – BHU Act 1915. It played a stellar role in the independence movement and has developed into one of the greatest centers of learning in India. It has produced many great freedoms through a large number of renowned scholars, artists, scientists and technologists who have graced its portals. The University family consists of about 15000 students belonging to all streams of life, castes and religions and races, about, 17,000 teachers, and nearly 8,000 non-teaching staff. A large number of students from foreign countries like the U.S.A., the countries of Europe, Asia, Middle East, Africa etc., come to study here. The university has taken a leadership role in promoting new ideas, the spirit of integration of the world, and cultivation of intellect and culture.

Banaras Hindu University ranks among the first few in the country in the field of academic and research output. This university has two campuses, 3 institutes, 16 faculties, 140 departments, 4 advanced centers and 4 interdisciplinary schools. The University is making its mark at the national and international levels in a number of frontier areas of Science, Social Science, Technology, Medicine and Agriculture etc. A university can grow successfully only when research and teaching mesh together seamlessly – one without the other is incomplete. Therefore BHU has ensured the development of a collaborative environment conducive to learning, exposure to the best international practices and promotion of innovation and creativity. BHU today has nearly twenty thousand students including 2,500 research scholars and 650 foreign students from 34 nations, under one roof who are pursuing different academic programmes at this campus as well as the newly established Rajiv Gandhi South Campus. These are some of the brightest young minds in the country and abroad, who have joined this University after clearing a rigorous All India Entrance Test. The rapid pace of development in the country has raised the awareness as well as expectations of the people. Institutions of higher learning are instrumental in providing equality of opportunities, which is the essence of participatory democracy. This will not only remove a sense of alienation and neglect in the backward regions but also prevent out migration from these areas.

BHU has established the Rajiv Gandhi South Campus at Barkachha about 75 kms. southwest of Varanasi on 2760 acres of land. The first academic session commenced from 2006-07 with six programmes which has increased to more than 25 in the present session. This campus is emerging as a potential hub to impart education, training and entrepreneurship development skills, to the youth, women and marginalized sections of society in the backward region of Mirzapur and adjoining districts of Uttar Pradesh, Western Bihar and Northern Madhya Pradesh. The Campus is heading well for education to generate new breed of human resource who would be job creators and not job seekers. The University at Buffalo (UB) New York has signed an agreement with Banaras Hindu University (BHU) to establish a comprehensive exchange programme between the two. UB President John B. Simpson and Professor Panjab Singh, vice-chancellor, BHU signed the agreement at a formal ceremony held in the varsity premises. Prof. Singh is on a two-day visit to the varsity. "The UB community is delighted to celebrate the establishment of a formal exchange programme with Banaras Hindu University, a partnership that will enhance our university's ongoing internationalization and provide an outstanding partner in a critically important region of India," Simpson said at the signing ceremony." India's importance on the world stage – both as an economic and as a strategic power – is growing very rapidly, and its global influence will only continue to increase in the years ahead," he said. Simpson also pointed out that there are large numbers of Indian students currently enrolled at UB, who are contributing in many ways to the varsity. Similar to UB, BHU has large comprehensive research facility, with more than 20,000 students in 14 faculties and 124 departments. BHU, the largest residential university in Asia, has more than 12,000 students living on its campus.

"We are delighted to formalize our relationship with Banaras Hindu University, a truly world-class institution," noted Stephen C. Dunnett, UB vice provost for international education. "We look forward to working with Vice-Chancellor Singh and his colleagues to develop a range of collaborative activities of mutual benefit to our universities," Dunnet added. Banaras Hindu University ranks among the first few in the country in the field of academic and research output. This university has two campuses, 3 institutes, 16 faculties, 140 departments, 4 advanced centers and 4 interdisciplinary schools. The University is making its mark at the national and international levels in a number of frontier areas of Science, Social Science, Technology, medicine and Agriculture etc. A university can grow successfully only when research and teaching mesh together seamlessly – one without the other is incomplete. Therefore we have ensured the development of a collaborative environment conducive to learning, exposure to the best international practices and promotion of innovation and creativity. BHU today has nearly twenty thousand students including 2500 research scholars and 650 foreign students from 34 nations, under one roof who are pursuing different academic programmes at this campus as well as the newly established Rajiv Gandhi South Campus. These are some of the brightest young minds in the country and abroad, who have joined this University after clearing a rigorous All India Entrance Test. We realize that the rapid pace of development in the country has raised the awareness as well as expectations of the people. Institutions of higher learning are instrumental in providing equality of opportunities, which is the essence of participatory democracy. This will not only remove a sense of alienation and neglect in the backward regions but also prevent out migration from these areas. BHU has established the Rajiv Gandhi South Campus at Barkachha about 75 kms. southwest of Varanasi on 2760 acres of land. The first academic session commenced from 2006-07 with six programmes which has increased to more than 25 in the present session. This campus is emerging as a potential hub to impart education, training and entrepreneurship development skills, to the youth, women and marginalized sections of society in the backward region of Mirzapur and adjoining districts of Uttar Pradesh, Western Bihar and Northern Madhya Pradesh. The Campus is heading well as per your vision for education to generate new breed of human resource who would be job creators and not job seekers.

PERCEPTIONS OF INTERNATIONALIZATION

It should not be a surprise to see that while internationalization is becoming more accepted and more central to the provision of higher education in India, people are using the same term with very different definitions. This echoes the international situation: despite many attempts to formulate a 'tight' definition the core idea remains conceptually elusive. There is no simple, unique, or all-encompassing definition of Internationalization. Also echoing the international situation, most people at BHU understand internationalization in terms of categories or types of activities. These include academic and extra-curricular activities such as *Internationalizing Higher Education* development and innovation; scholar, student and faculty exchange; area studies; technological assistance; intercultural training; education of international students; and joint research initiatives. Indeed, as a result of the comprehensive changes in the contemporary world, internationalization could be interpreted from various perspectives.

Internationalization of higher education should encompass some administration, management and the training of student with skills, as well as knowledge and perspectives of other societies and cultures. In order to develop scholarship, a university needs to have frequent exchanges with its counterparts in foreign countries. Another point at issue is the relationship between internationalization and institutional identity. In the present era of increased globalization, there is a constant threat to the healthy survival of national identities and cultures of smaller and/or developing nations, the homogenization or 'McDonaldization' of cultures. How to preserve and promote national culture is a common question faced by non-Western countries, which often consider internationalization as a way either to respect cultural diversity and counter-balance the perceived homogenizing effect of globalization, or to expand the influence of their traditional cultures.

Internationalization Achieved

Internationalization is high on the agendas of national governments, international bodies, and institutions of higher education. Correspondingly, BHU has placed greater emphasis on international co-operation and exchange in all areas, and developed its own strategies to internationalize research and teaching. The International Centre of Banaras Hindu University was established in 2004, with an objective to deal with all matters related to Foreign Nationals viz. Collaboration with Foreign Universities/ Institutions, Foreign scholars visiting India as Visiting Lecturer/ Professor, Alumni Association of Foreign Students, Admission of Foreign Students etc. The International Centre is headed by the Chairman of International Centre, assisted with the Coordinator, International Students Affairs and International Collaboration and Dy. Coordinator, International Students Affairs and International Collaboration. The International Centre is housed in Tagore Bhavan, one of the oldest buildings of BHU, so named after the Noble Laureate Gurudev Rabindra Nath Tagore, who stayed in this building during his visit to BHU in the year 1923.

The International Centre, at the time of its inception was assigned the following role:

- Facilitate, assist and help international students in all their academic pursuits.

- Develop, coordinate and strengthen International linkages.
- Collaborate with foreign Universities/Institutions.
- Coordinate study abroad programme.
- Foreign Scholars visiting India as Visiting Lecturers/Professors, etc.
- Alumni Association of Foreign Students.

Organize International Cultural Festivals for Friendship by way of an Exhibition, Food Festival and Cultural Show, etc.:

A base for the ICCR (Indian Council for Cultural Relations) and to assist scholars and enhance bilateral relations.

International Centre has been established with a view to provide single window system for admission of International Students. Therefore, all the International candidates, seeking admission to Banaras Hindu University (except Medical and B. Tech.) have to fill up the application form obtained from the International Centre, BHU or by downloading from its site. The forms are also submitted at the International Centre which processes the forms for admission. Admission letters are also issued by the International Centre and the candidates report at the same place for admission. Thus the International Centre is working towards providing hassle free admission process for the International students.

The International Centre has been processing the proposals received from various International Universities/Institutions, seeking MoU in academic area, exchanges of study Programmes, students and faculties. A number of MoU(s) have been done and/or under consideration with various Universities/ Institutions abroad. The list of such University/Institutions is a follows:

The University has the provision to invite/accept the proposals for the appointment of Language teachers under the permission of the Government of India, under this scheme and presently some teachers are already on roll in foreign languages. Likewise, the International Scholars have the opportunity to be associated with the BHU as Visiting Professors/Fellow for which applications/ proposals are received by the International Centre.

The International Centre has organized various cultural shows/festivals, exhibition etc. within the very short span of its establishment (hardly two years). Amongst these, following may be noted: Horizon Series, 'Azadi Vatan Ki', a play by Cultural Centre of Mauritius organized in collaboration of ICCR, play and exhibition based on the story of B.P. Koriala (January 2007) in collaboration with the B.P. Koirala Foundation, Nepal, deputation of students for Soufest held at Jammu and ICC.camps organized at various places in the country.

The International Centre is actively sharing with the ICCR for the implementation of Councils policies for International Students, admission, distribution of scholarships, other programmes of ICCR held at BHU in particular and Varanasi and adjacent area in general.

APPRAISALS IN DIFFERENT CONTEXTS

Despite this impressive list of achievements in international communications,

BHU numbers reported a generally similar assessment: it is still far from adequate. Such consensus aside, however, people from various fields have different assessments of the achievement in their own specialties. These differences result from the different perspectives utilized to evaluate the achievement. No matter what the frame of reference is, however, an accurate overall assessment is, as one interviewee suggested, difficult. When compared to its development from the 1916 to the 2012, BHU has obviously made remarkable progress in international communications. However, overseas travel for faculty remains quite inadequate. Library collections of foreign language books and journals are far from sufficient, especially due to increasing prices and financially straitened circumstances. All these stifle the Internationalization process at the University. BHU respondents noted almost unanimously that the acknowledgement of an international dimension was clearly expressed in the BHU mission statement, and Internationalization at BHU is well ahead of the majority of Indian universities. This is largely due to the favourable conditions at BHU. It has a long history; and its former graduates have long occupied positions of influence both within and outside India, something that has helped BHU establish international links. The overall picture is that Internationalization is much better implemented in the natural sciences and engineering than in the arts, humanities, and some social sciences. In some science departments, international contacts have become extremely popular. This is mainly because these departments are much more likely to be successful in winning external funds, and thus have more resources to attract a higher proportion of young faculty who have recently returned from overseas with higher degrees. Their personal contacts, fresh knowledge, and international links, coupled with newly purchased teaching and research equipment and laboratory facilities, particularly with the assistance of a World Bank loan, have enabled rapid Internationalization in these departments. A very different scene is presented in the arts and humanities, and some social sciences.

BASIC RESEARCH IN DIFFICULTY

With the central focus of Internationalization on international understanding, a country's unique history, indigenous culture(s), resources, priorities, and so on shape its response to and relationships with other countries. National identity and culture is then key to Internationalization. It is in this sense that basic research plays a crucial role in promoting Internationalization. As a public good itself, basic research often needs substantial investment to deliver long term, but highly uncertain, benefits. The market, however, is not good at funding such research on its own.

BHU, however, has focused on basic theoretical studies since its early days. The separation of its engineering, agriculture and medicine departments in the 1916s further strengthened the central role of basic research as its focus and advantage. It has made every endeavour maintain strengths in basic research. One major task is to undertake key research projects. In recent years, BHU has undertaken some 100 national key projects including the

National 863 High-Tech Development Plan and other national basic research projects, as well as 60 selected projects as priority to tackle scientific and technological problems. From 1916-2012, science research at BHU won 434 prizes from the State Natural Science Foundation Committee, the then State Education Commission and Uttar Pradesh Government. BHU has also increased its scientific publications substantially. BHU ranked third among all Indian higher education institutions, winning five first prizes from the State Education Commission. From 1916 to 2012, 4,271 research articles from BHU were published in scientific journals, of which 783 were in internationally refereed journals published overseas, 132 research findings were selected for national prizes (one first prize, three second prizes, eight third prizes, and four fourth prizes), and ministerial/provincial prizes (one special prize, nine first prizes, forty-six second prizes, and sixty-one third prizes).

Despite this impressive list of achievements in international communications, BHU numbers reported a generally similar assessment: it is still far from adequate. Such consensus aside, however, people from various fields have different assessments of the achievement in their own specialties. These differences result from the different perspectives utilized to evaluate the achievement. No matter what the frame of reference is, however, an accurate overall assessment is, difficult. When compared to its development from the 1916 to the 2012, BHU has obviously made remarkable progress in international communications.

REFERENCES

Arora, Jagdish, Valuable Resources for a Progressive Policy for Higher Education in India

Ninnes, Peter and Merri Helsten 'Internationalizing Higher Education – Critical Explorations of Pedagogy and Policy'

www.abri.com

www.bhu.uni.ac.in

www.indianhighereducation.org/Book_Review.pdf

www.ncert.ac.in

11

Internationalization and Turkish Higher Education System

Osman Titrek

Internationalization became key theme in the 1990s, both in higher education policy debates and in research on higher education. Based on recent research over mobility and cooperation in the framework of European programmes, there are three areas of learning and research related to Internationalization: – knowledge transfer, – international education and research, and – border-crossing communication and discourse. The Turkish Higher Education system is becoming more international day-to-day. Especially student and academician nobilities with EU countries are increasing. However there are lots of problems about international publication number, international academician number and international university number. Developing Internationalization of Turkish Higher Education System, we have to increase the foreign academician number, international university type, scientific publication number, academician foreign language skills, knowledge transfer systems etc. The contemporary university was born in the nation state, not of medieval civilization, and it was only in the nineteenth and twentieth century, following the establishment of clear national economic interests, that universities acquired their identification with science and technology. Their regulatory and funding context was, and still is, national; their contribution to national cultures was, and still significant; students tended to be, and are still trained to become national functionaries; and universities played, and still play a considerable role in what some have called the military-industrial complex of nation states. In this perspective, they are very much national institutions. It is appropriate, therefore, to see current trends as part of a process by which national systems of higher education are being challenged by new forces of Internationalization. Universities are thus objects as well as subjects of "Internationalization" or "globalization". They are affected by and at the same time influence these processes (Enders, 2004).

"Internationalization" and "globalization" became key themes in the 1990s, both in higher education policy debates and in research on higher education. Higher education policy is still predominantly shaped at a national level; and as such, it still tends not only to reflect but to underscore the specific traditions and circumstances of individual countries. However, a number of different trends, many of which can be grouped together under the general heading of

"Internationalization", have begun to challenge the predominance of the nation state as the main determinant of the character of universities and colleges, and of the experiences of their students, their graduates and those who work in them. Internationalization is contributing to, if not leading, a process of rethinking the social, cultural and economic roles of higher education and their configuration in national systems of higher education (Enders, 2004). According to Ercan (2002), higher education includes all the educational institutions which provide at least 2-year higher education based on secondary education, and train the staffs whom the top-level manpower and the areas of scientific research want. The main body of higher education is university. According to Keohane (2006), higher education institutions and especially universities have been the institutions in which knowledge is produced, interpreted, enriched, criticized and transferred throughout the history. Therefore, the higher education institutions have become so active socially and politically in the modern times (Meriç, 2012).

According to Delors (1996), higher education is at the top of the educational pyramid and determines to a large extent the state of the education system of the country, especially its quality. As such it has a responsibility towards the whole education system as it has towards the whole of society (Sanyal, 2001). According to World Declaration on Higher Education for the Twenty-First Century: Vision and Action adopted by the World Conference on Higher Education (1998), the missions and functions of higher education are given in the Table 1 (Sanyal, 2001):

Table 1: Role of Higher Education Institution (HEI) to promote 'Education for All'

Role of HEI	*Task*
Education and training	To improve access and equity in basic education: 1. Introduce teaching of local languages and ICT literacy for potential teachers. 2. Reinforce teacher education and teacher management training, especially female teachers for basic education. 3. Introduce teaching of cultural factors promoting education. 4. Introduce teaching of educational planning, especially in formulating access policies and equity policies for basic education. 5. Introduce affirmative action for admitting female students and students of lower socioeconomic status in the teacher education programmes. 6. Introduce distance learning and learning through suitable ICT to reach the unreached.
Research	1. Investigate the effect of medium of instruction on motivating children of lower socioeconomic status to pursue basic education and literacy programmes. 2. Investigate the role of culture on demand for education for children of different socioeconomic status, especially girls. 3. Investigate the reasons for children remaining out of school, dropping out of school and failing examinations at the basic education level and formulate policies for achieving greater access and equity.

Role of HEI	*Task*
Services	1. Initiate adult literacy classes in campus. 2. Introduce a national service for students to teach in basic education schools as a condition for graduation. 3. Launch campaign through the media and other means in extra mural studies department for motivating and encouraging children of lower socioeconomic status and women to pursue basic education.
	To improve quality and relevance of basic education:
Education and training	1. Train teachers for teaching/training materials suitable for local contexts and environment. 2. Involve the community in designing content, method and structure of teacher training so that basic education can make school leavers employable either in the formal or in the informal sector. 3. Modernize teacher training taking into account the development of ICT and new pedagogy. 4. Introduce courses on methods of assessing quality and relevance of basic education and their improvement. 5. Introduce in-service courses on teacher management for heads and managers of basic education programmes. 6. Introduce training programmes on how to conceive, produce, distribute and evaluate textbooks cost effectively.
Research	1. Investigate the status of quality and relevance of basic education programmes (content, method and structure) through the perception and experience of the parents, the community and the employers. 2. Investigate the reasons for lack of quality and relevance and formulate policies for improvement. 3. Investigate the needs for skills of basic education completed in the labour market, formal and informal, and formulate policies for education, training and service departments of the Institution. 4. Investigate the difference in the quality and relevance of education offered by different methods. 5. Evaluate and monitor the progress made in 'basic education for all'.
Services	Organize evenings for the community within the 'extra mural studies department' to discuss the usefulness and the quality of the basic education programmes in so far as they concern the institution of higher education (e.g. An adult literacy programme of the department, the training of teachers, the standard of the content of the training materials prepared within the institution of higher education, etc.). Prepare programmes of neo-literates for the media for sustainability of education received.
	To improve efficiency/finance/management of basic education:
Education and training	1. Introduce courses for heads of schools/programmes in educational planning and management, focusing on ways of better utilization of resources, financing of programmes through community participation and other means and in school management and management of programmes at the national, provincial and local levels.

Role of HEI	Task
Research	1. To prepare state of the art papers on 'good practices' in efficiency, financing and management of basic education and literacy programmes from around the world. 2. Investigate the roles of the State, the community and the school in improving management of basic education and literacy 3. Identify reasons for inefficiency and wastage of resources (including student and staff time) and formulate corrective measures (e.g. Demotivation of teachers and corrective measures; internal and external inefficiency and methods of reducing them using new technology where applicable). 4. Investigate cost-effectiveness of alternative delivery systems for different target groups 5. Assist the government to prepare a 'viable and sustainable plan for achieving education for all' to mobilize funds from international agencies.
Services	1. Organize 'open door' evenings for meetings with the community to identify any inefficiency perceived and experienced by them and discuss possible means of correcting them. 2. Organize meetings with potential donors to finance programmes of improving basic education. 3. Organize evening in-service classes for school and programmed managers inviting extension lecturers on educational management.

Resource: (Sanyal, 2001).

INTERNATIONALIZATIONS IN HIGHER EDUCATION

Higher education has become increasingly international in the past decade as more and more students choose to study abroad, enroll in foreign educational programmes and institutions in their home country, or simply use the Internet to take courses at colleges or universities in other countries. This growth is the result of several different, but not mutually exclusive, driving forces: a desire to promote mutual understanding; the migration of skilled workers in a globalised economy; the desire of the institutions to generate additional revenues; or the need to build a more educated workforce in the home countries, generally as emerging economies (OECD, 2004).

Internationalization is undergoing constant change, influenced by external and internal social, economic, political and academic factors. Over the past 25 years, the international dimension of higher education has risen on the agendas of international organizations and national governments, institutions of higher education and their representative bodies, student organizations and accrediting agencies. This process is also described as the mainstreaming of Internationalization (Beelen and De Wit, 2012).

According to Knight (2004) and Stier (2004), the forces that drive Internationalization of higher education have been classified in the literature as academic or economic. *Academic motives for Internationalization* includes as follows:

- internationalizing to fulfill the institution's educational mission,
- internationalizing to remain academically relevant in an interconnected world that is becoming increasingly global,
- internationalizing to attract the best students and faculty worldwide.

Economic benefits of Internationalization include as follows:

- internationalizing to grow revenues,
- internationalizing to reduce operating risk via geographical diversification, and
- internationalizing to fund activities in the home campus (Hawawini, 2011).

According to Teichler (1999), a review of the complex and dynamic processes of Internationalization at different levels in higher education reveals that these processes are prompting increasingly rapid change in two rather different respects. First, there is now a wide range of border-crossing activities, many of them resulting from institutional rather than governmental initiatives, and these are certainly still on the rise. But we can also see more substantial changes towards systematic national or supra-national policies, combined with a growing awareness of issues of international co-operation and competition in a globalizing higher education market. Under the first heading there is a growth of specific, clearly visible international co-operation, including activities such as student and staff mobility schemes, cooperative research activities and foreign language teaching to support them; under the second, we can see trends towards Internationalization, regionalization or the globalization of the actual substance and structures of higher education – for example, proposals for convergence in institutional patterns, study programmes or curricula (Enders, 2004).

According to Knight (1996), Scott (1998), Teichler (1999) and van der Wende (2001), when higher education issues are discussed on a supranational basis, obviously three terms are most often employed in Europe: international, European and global. The uses of these three terms are similar in two respects: First, all three terms claim there is a trend or a policy direction away from a more or less closed national system of higher education and therefore, as will be pointed out below, towards a growing role of long-distance transport of knowledge in higher education and a more complex setting of multi-level actors and other forces. Second, all three terms might refer either to the changing context which poses a challenge for higher education or to changes which occur within higher education itself.

The uses of the three terms, however, differ in two respects as well. First, they vary in the prime meaning:

- Internationalization tends to address an increase of border-crossing activities amidst a more or less persistence of national systems of higher education.
- Globalization tends to assume that borders and national systems as such get blurred or even might disappear.

- Europeanization is the regionally defined version of either Internationalization or globalization. At present it is more often the regional version of Internationalization than of globalization.

Second, specific issues tend to be linked to the use of the individual terms:

- Internationalization is often discussed in relation to physical mobility, academic cooperation and academic knowledge transfer as well as international education.
- Europeanization is addressed frequently when referring to cooperation and mobility. Beyond that it also covers such issues as integration, convergence of contexts, structures and substance ("European dimension", "European culture", "European citizen", "European higher education space") or to segmentation between regions of the world (fortress Europe).
- Globalization is often associated with competition and market steering, trans-national education, and finally with commercial knowledge-transfer (Teichler, 2004).

THE RATIONALES FOR INTERNATIONALIZATION OF HIGHER EDUCATION

According to Knight and De Wit (1995), there are there are four categories of rationales. Rationales can be described as motivations for integrating an international dimension into higher education. They address the "why" of Internationalization. And different rationales imply different means and ends to Internationalization (http://www.ipv.pt/millenium/wit11.htm). These categories of the rationales are as follows (http://powershow.com/view1/):

a. Political Rationales
   - Foreign policy – National security – Technical assistance – Peace and mutual understanding – National identity – Regional identity
b. Social/ Cultural Rationales
   - Cultural rationales – Social rationales
c. Academic Rationales
   - Providing an international/intercultural dimension to research and teaching – Extension of the academic horizon – Institution – building – Profile/status – Enhancement of quality – International academic standards

According to Gümrükçü (2010), the rationales for Internationalization are as follows:

- The increase in the number of the academicians getting his socialization or education abroad.
- The necessity of taking into consideration of copyright.
- Scientist tourism.
- The transfer of knowledge at light speed.

- The transfer of native speaker instructors in language academies for foreign language teaching.
- The establishment of sections for different cultures and social structures.
- The implementation of exchange programmes such as ERASMUS Programme, etc.
- The dissemination of network.
- The universality of English.
- The common construction of joint projects.
- The appearance of offshore universities.
- The Bologna Process and EU credit transfer system.

THE KNOWLEDGE DIMENSIONS OF INTERNATIONALIZATION

According to Opper *et al.* (1990), there is not any generally agreed conceptual framework for structuring or classifying knowledge with respect to Internationalization. Various efforts have been made at systematization. For example, the first major comparative project on student mobility, which was undertaken in the 1980s, drew from preceding research and discussions over classifying learning areas and the possible impact of learning supported by study abroad as educational, linguistic, cultural and professional (Teichler, 2004). Based on recent research over mobility and cooperation in the framework of European programmes, Teichler (2004) observes three areas of learning and research related to Internationalization: – knowledge transfer, – international education and research, and – border-crossing communication and discourse.

Knowledge-transfer: Knowledge in normal disciplines (i.e. Not specialized on international issues) is more frequent, more intense and more rapidly transferred from one country to the other. This is undertaken, as will be discussed below, through various means, notably through media (books, electronic media and similar means), physical mobility (conferences, study abroad, academic staff exchange, etc.), joint curricula and research projects as well as trans-national education.

International education and research: Certain areas of knowledge focus on the international dimension, for example on border-crossing, foreign and distant phenomena and international comparison (e.g. foreign language philology, area studies, and international relations). At times characterized by a trend of Internationalization, the role of international education is clearly growing. On the one hand the number of students and the needed teaching and research capacity are likely to grow in the areas that genuinely address other cultures, societies, comparison or international relations because there will be more demand for these skills in the graduate labour market and research-based problem-solving. On the other hand, in areas not primarily addressing other cultures like comparison and international relations, demand is also expanding for foreign language proficiency and field knowledge from other countries.

Border-crossing communication and discourse: Learning and research in an international setting is one way of experiencing different views in a creative manner (e.g. being confronted with different theories, methodologies and field knowledge in order to reflect and relativism one's own past conceptual frameworks, to broaden one's horizon, to think comparatively and eventually to develop more complex perspectives). International communication and discourse is not necessarily the only possible means of promoting leaps forward in reflective thinking but it is a relatively safe and successful strategy for shaking the old established perspectives because of an all-embracing confrontation to a culture different from that at home. Results of analyses addressing student mobility suggest that this is the most salient impact of study abroad. Internationalization is one of the most important keywords of our university life. Concepts and definitions that have been attached to this word sometimes create confusion. Especially in the light of different structures, value systems and resources affiliated with different universities, it is critical to get the definition right to avoid conceptual vagueness. Internationalization appears to be an inevitable development that institutes of higher education have to confront. However, it offers both great opportunities and risks. Therefore, institutes of higher education need to be active adjusting themselves to the demands of Internationalization (Sağlamer, 2012).

TURKISH HIGHER EDUCATION SYSTEM AND INTERNATIONALIZATION

The most important system for Turkish Education and Higher Education System is European Education programmes. The European Union programme name is Life Long Learning programmes such as Erasmus, Grundtvig, Comenius, Leonardo DA Vinci, Youth etc. Especially, Erasmus programme is directly related to Higher Education System. There are four types of Erasmus programme: 1. Mobility, 2. Densily Language Education Programmes, 3. Densely Education Programmes and 4. Preparation Facilities. Mobility activity is the most important facility for Erasmus programme and the Internationalization of Turkish Higher education system nowadays for going students and academicians abroad (http://www.ua.gov.tr/index.cfm?action=detay&bid=9, 2012). Erasmus became part of the EU's Lifelong Learning Programme in 2007, covering new areas such as student placements in enterprises (transferred from the Leonardo DA Vinci Programme), university staff training and teaching for business staff. Erasmus is the perfect example of a European success story: close to 3 million students have participated since it started in 1987, as well as over 300 000 higher education teachers and other staff since 1997 (this type of exchange was also expanded further in 2007). The annual budget is in excess of 450 million Euro; more than 4 000 higher education institutions in 33 countries participate, and more are willing to join (http://ec.europa.eu/education/lifelong-learning-programme/erasmus_en.htm, 2012).

Table 2: European Union (EU) Erasmus Programme Digits of Turkey

	2004-2005	*2007-2008*	*2010-2011*	*2012-2013*
Learning Mobility	8.370	962.277	1,191,000	1,581.250
Giving lecture mobility	1.000	119.077	119.550	78.750
Having education mobility	0	21.265	28.100	34.300
Internship mobility	0	53.885	40.800	38.050
Organizations of Mobility	2.104	47.120	51.800	61.650
Total	**11.474**	**1,203.624**	**1,431.200**	**1,.794.000**

Resource: Kenar, 2012.

According to the Table, the number of learning mobility has recently risen to 1.581.250 while it was only 8.370 between 2004 and 2005. The number of giving lecture mobility has reached 78.750 in recent years while it was only 1.000 between 2004 and 2005. The number of the organizations of mobility is 61.650 while it was only 2.104 between 2004 and 2005. When the changes in the number of learning, giving lectures and organizations mobility are examined it is seen that these changes start with a certain number. However, this situation is different for having an education and internship. According to the table, the number of having education is 34.300 between 2012-2013 while this number was only 0 between 2004 and 2005. Having the same situation with having education, the number of internships is 38.050 in recent years while it was only 0 between the same years. When the Table is evaluated totally it is seen that the digits have reached 1.794.000 in 2013 while it was only 11.474 in 2004. In this respect, it can be expressed that EU Erasmus digits of Turkey have expanded nearly 156 times in nine years. Therefore, Turkey has gained a huge grow in terms of EU Erasmus digits between the years.

Table 3: EU Erasmus Programme Digits of Sakarya University

	2004-05	*2007-08*	*2010-11*	*2011-12*
Student Learning Mobility	3	355	347	345
Giving lecture mobility	1	99	56	108
Having education	0	19	22	18
Internship Mobility	0	21	13	25
Learning Mobility (Incoming student)	0	40	74	130
Internship Mobility (Incoming student)	0	0	2	2
Giving lecture/ Having education	0	43	15	35
Total	**4**	**577**	**529**	**663**

Resource: Kenar, 2012.

In the Fig. 1, the circumstances of Sakarya University are examined. This choice stems from the reason that Sakarya University is the biggest university having the huge EU Erasmus digits in Turkey. According to the Table, the number students learning mobility have risen from 3 to 345 between 2004 and 2012. The number of giving lecture mobility has risen up 1 to 108 between the same years. When the changes in the number of learning and giving lecture mobility are examined it is seen that these changes start with a certain number. However, this situation is different for the other criteria. The number of having education is 18 in 2012; the number of internship mobility is 25; the number of learning mobility for incoming student is 130; the number of internship mobility for incoming student is 2 and the number of giving lecture/having education is 35 while they all were only 0 in 2004. When the Table is evaluated totally it is seen that the digits have reached 661 while it was only 4 in 2004. In this respect, it can be expressed that EU Erasmus digits of Sakarya University have expanded nearly 165 times in eight years. Therefore, Sakarya University has gained a huge grow in terms of EU Erasmus digits between the years.

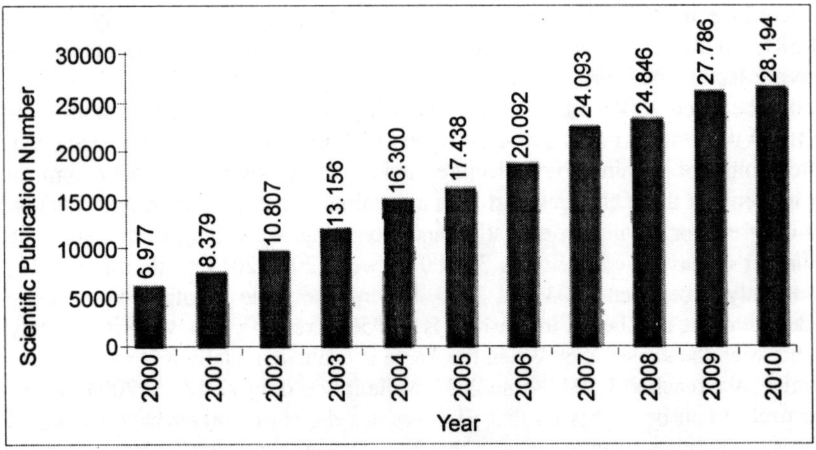

Fig. 1: The Number of Scientific Publications of Turkey

Resource: http://www.tubitak.gov.tr/tubitak_content_files/BTYPD/istatistikler/BTY60.pdf

According to the Fig. 1, the number of scientific publications in Turkey has risen to 28.194 from 6.977 between 2000 and 2010. However, this huge proceed is not seen in the evaluation of universities according to their academic performances. According to University Ranking by Academic Performance in 2011-2012 academic year, Turkey has only 2 universities – METU and Boğaziçi University – in the first 500 ranking. Besides, Turkey has 14 universities – 12 state and 2 private universities – in 1000 in this ranking. When we look at these rates in terms of internationalization it can be stated that this ranking is insufficient for Turkish higher education system. Therefore, Turkey should get its universities on the tops as much as possible in order to support and live internationalization of higher education.

CONCLUSION AND SUGGESTIONS

When we observed the higher education system according to the dimensions of Internationalization, it is seen that Turkey has developed its system in the fields of knowledge transfer, international education and border-crossing communication/discourse. However, the student and academicians mobility is limited to only through Europe. Turkey is an important country because of both its geopolitical location and history. Turkey's education system is similar to the American higher education system. Therefore, this mobility shouldn't be only one way through Europe, it should have multi-ways through also Turkey's cross roads Balkan, Middle East countries.

Moreover, the number of universities has changed continuously in recent years. Turkey has reached such a position in which its number of university was only one state university in 1933; 27 state universities and only one private university in 1984; 53 state and 23 private universities in 2001 and 122 state and 47 private universities and is 169 universities totally (OSYM, 2012). However, this enterprise of opening new universities is not enough for Turkey's Internationalization. Therefore, the foreign language capacities of academicians in Turkey should be developed especially in writing and speaking. When we look at the digit of foreign academician studying in Turkey it is seen that there are 126 professors, 105 associated professors, 261 assistant professors, 406 instructors, 326 lecturers, 10 specialists and 226 research assistants between 2011 and 2012; totally 1460 academicians. This number is insufficient and nearly only one thousandth of the Turkish total academician number 116.788 (OSYM, 2012). Most of these academicians study in the field of foreign language, and the rest is originally Turkish. Therefore, these academicians should study in different fields in order to get Internationalization. Besides, these academicians don't have any institution in which they can be managers. This situation is negative for Turkey and some institutions should be opened in order to make the Turkish educational system internationalized.

Although SCI and SSCI publications have increased in recent years, Turkish academic publication numbers are still insufficient. Some agreements and system supporting academicians' language skills, their international connections and cooperation, national and international joint projects should be formed. Besides, the government should help academicians and provide necessary supports to them for publication and projects. When the Turkish higher education system is observed it can be seen that the ECTS system still being used in Europe has been in-use. This system has been spreading all the Turkish universities through The Bologna Process. Therefore, Turkey has been trying to make great strides in the way of Internationalization in order to adapt and support it. However, this development is not enough for only EU countries or Turkey. Internationalization should be maximized globally. Therefore, a common credit system and a common transfer area should be created all over the world universities. At the same time, a Higher Education Council should be formed in order to create and supervise this system and area. Therefore, a common quality standard frame for higher education can be formed and can be practiced by this council in the world.

REFERENCES

Beelen, J., and De Wit, H. (2012). Internationalization revisited: New dimensions in the *Internationalization of Higher Education.*

Enders, J. (2004). Higher education, Internationalization, and the nation-state: Recent developments and challenges to governance theory. *Higher Education* (47), 361-382.

Hawawini, G. (2011). *The Internationalization of Higher Education Institutions: A Critical Review and a Radical Proposal.*

Kenar, N. (2012). The Erasmus Increasing Quality for personal mobility meeting. Retrieved from http://www.ua.gov.tr/index.cfm?action=detay&yayinid=22481C86A820A3FD5E6472FC0640763D87D4 at 25 Mayıs 2012 Turkish National National Agency *http://en.wikipedia.org/.* (2012). Downloaded at 28.11.2012 2012 from http://en.wikipedia.org/wiki/Higher_education

Meriç, N. (2012). *Higher education.* Unpublished Master Thesis, 18 Mart Üniversity, Çanakkale. Turkey.

OECD Report (2012). *Internationalization of higher education.* Downloaded on 05.11.2012 from http://www.oecd.org/education/educationeconomyandsociety/33734276.pdf

OSYM (2012). 2011-2012 years statistics. http://www.osym.gov.tr/belge/1-13575/2011-2012-ogretim-yili-yuksekogretim-istatistikleri.html

Sağlamer, G. (2012). *Internalization in higher education. Is it Global* Downloaded at 2012 from http://www.eaie.org/dms.

Sanyal, B.C. (2001, August). *New functions of higher education and ICT to achieve education for all.* Paris.

Teichler, U. (2004). The changing debate on Internationalization of Higher Education. *Higher Education,* 48, 5-26.

http://ec.europa.eu/education/lifelong-learning-programme/erasmus_en.htm,2012"*http://ec.europa.eu/education/lifelong-learning-programme/erasmus_en.htm,*2012. Downloaded on 05.11.2012 http:// powershow.com/view1/1a9bba-ZDRiO/Changing_Rationales_for_Internationalization_of_Higher_Education_in_a_new_Global_Area_powerpoint_ppt_presentation, 2012. Downloaded on 06.11.2012

http://www.abvizyonu.com/egitim/prof-dr-harun-gumrukcuuniversitelerin-ve-yuksekokullarin-uluslar-arasilasmasi.html, 2012. Downloaded on 06.11.2012

http://www.tubitak.gov.tr/tubitak_content_files/BTYPD/istatistikler/BTY60.pdf

http://www.urapcenter.org/2011/sci.php?q=NTAxLTc1MA==, 2012. Downloaded on 06.11.2012

http: //www.ua.gov.tr/index. cfm? action=detay&bid=9" *http://www. ua.gov.tr/index. cfm?action=detay&bid=9,* 2012. Downloaded on 05.11.2012

12

Problems and Issues in Higher Education

Ankur Gupta, Naushaba Parveen and *J.S. Verma*

The higher education system in India is the largest among the Third World nations and the second largest in the world with four million students, enrolled in about 7,000 colleges and about 200 universities. India is also the Third World's research super power spending about 8 per cent of the Third World funds for research and development and producing a large proportion of Third World's scientific output in terms of books, journals and articles. It is without doubt that India has one of the oldest higher education systems in the Third World with universities dating to 1857 and collegiate institutions older than that. There has been a phenomenal growth and expansion of higher education since independence. As a result of this unplanned expansion, the entire system has been enveloped by number of sub-standard colleges and universities. Though number of plans and proposals have been formulated to guide the system, yet at the macro level, very few have been successfully implemented, It has been noticed that though there has been some positive changes in higher education but much of the changes have acquired a negative quality. There comes a time, when new directions have to be given to age old processes. The need for change and drastic reforms has been felt since quite some in higher education scenario and attempts have to be made to tide over the acute crisis which exists today. The issues of performance appraisal of administrators and teachers, training of administrators and teachers, autonomy with regard to recruitment of teachers, admission of students, finance in the higher education scenario, These are some of the factors which are responsible for the acute crisis which we face in Higher Education today.

Expansion has taken place at all levels of the academic system and still continues, despite the recommendations of various commissions and committees against unplanned growth. Professional institutes, postgraduate, under-graduate arts and science colleges have mushroomed in rural and urban areas catering to the needs and demands of the society. The quality of these institutions is definitely in peril.

OBJECTIVES OF HIGHER EDUCATION

University Education Commission (1948-49)

Headed by Dr. Radhakrishnan University Education Commission was instituted to report on the conditions of Indian Universities and offer suggestions to revitalize it. The report has given the following objectives for higher education–

1. India is rich in natural resources and human potential. University should educate and train students to bring these two resources together and raise our living standards.
2. Universities should produce leaders with intellectual analysis and imaginative insight.
3. Intellectual adventure should be promoted.
4. Life has meaning. An integrated way of life leads to human betterment.
5. No amount of factual information would make ordinary men into 'educated' men, unless something awakened in them, an innate ability to lead a higher life.
6. Higher education should promote a new social order based on democracy, justice, liberty, equality and fraternity.

The Education Commission (1964-66)

The Kothari Commission made a few radical recommendations, including the New Pattern of Education (10 + 2 + 3).

Accordingly many States shed the Pre-University Course. The Commission redefined the ideals of higher education as follows–

1. Seeking knowledge within the framework of truth, using traditional knowledge in new circumstances.
2. Developing leadership in every sphere of life.
3. Giving educated and trained man-power to society.
4. Promoting social justice.
5. Inculcating right values.
6. Reduction of social and cultural disparities.
7. Developing national sentiments.
8. Introduction of adult education programmes.

National Policy on Higher Education (1979)

In 1979 the Parliament of India approved the National Policy on education giving new guidelines about higher education–

1. Higher education should play a vital role in national development.
2. Unchecked growth of institutions of higher education without adequate facilities will endanger quality.
3. Alternative strategies like correspondence courses, part time courses and own time studies should be explored.
4. Quality of post-graduate education should be improved.

5. Linkages with the society should be strengthened through extension programmes.
6. Autonomous colleges should strive to become centers of excellence.

PROBLEMS AND ISSUES OF HIGHER EDUCATION

1. ***Quality versus Quantity***: There are about four million students in our Universities and Colleges. The demand for higher education is due to the socio-economic transformation that is taking place in the country. The Indian economy has neither the resources to expand higher education at the present rate nor the capacity to absorb the large number of graduates in gainful employment. A kind of Iron Law of Educational Growth whose logic is very simple, "universalization of elementary education leading to generalization of secondary and the latter to a corresponding growth of higher education" is evident. There is a lot of criticism about the deplorable fall in intellectual standard of the Universities. So, the developmental strategy must cover man's hopes, aspirations and welfare.
2. ***Lack of Competency and Research***: The volume of knowledge doubles every ten years. New skills and knowledge are required to be an up to date. Unlike in the West, the contribution of our Universities to Science, Arts or Literature is very meager. Research facilities do not exist in many colleges. University teachers do very little research work; college teachers do even less; many teachers are content with their present qualifications and record. Only a few voice their views on academic or national problems.
3. ***Defective Curriculum***: The curricula of higher education are full of defects. The subjects of study are old and out of date. The curricula fail to fulfill the interests of different types of students.
4. ***Lack of Guidance and Counseling***: There is no provision for giving proper guidance and counseling to the students. Hence, the students select their courses either according to their own choice or with the advice of some inexperienced persons. Many students select subjects which are either against their interests and tendencies or which they are not capable of studying.
5. ***Low Standard of Teaching***: In his book *A New Deal for Our Universities*, K.R.S. Iyenger has remarked, "Our standards whether in scholarship or teaching, never very high or exacting, are now fast racing to the bottom.
6. ***Defective system of Examination***: The Indian University Commission in 1902 pointed out "The greater evil from which university education in India suffers is, that teaching is subordinate to examination, and not examination to teaching." The University Education Commission of 1949 also pointed out, "If we are to suggest one single reform in university education, it should be that of examinations."

7. ***Indiscipline***: Prof. N.K. Siddhant, former Vice-Chancellor of Calcutta University, has mentioned the following types of activities coming within the indiscipline: (1) Financial irregularity, (2) Minor misconduct, (3) Disorderly misconduct, (4) Theft and burglary, (5) Sex misconduct, (6) Misuse of privilege, and (7) Cheating in examination. In his book Indian University Administration Prof. N.K. Siddhant said, "The problem of maintaining discipline in the seats of higher education is assuming greater importance every day."
8. ***Student Unions***: The student unions in educational institutions of higher education pose serious problems before us. The harms-which these student unions-cause to the students are well-known. The leaders of these unions interfere in each and every work of the college. If the teacher, principal or manager of the college does any work which is against their wish they strongly oppose such works. They want that the appointment of the teachers, their teaching work and all the policies connected with the college should be done with their advice.
9. ***Lack of Appraisal***: One of the weakest link in our educational system has been the appraisal of college heads, college and university administrators and university and college teachers, even though we have long been aware of their importance for effective and efficient operation of our educational institutions. In many institutions administrators are being evaluated in a very unsystematic and unscientific manner and the most common mechanism used is the confidential report if any. The judgmental remarks are usually subjective and are about personality traits which are complex and difficult to evaluate. This does not keep the individual in any constructive way and has become a mere ritual. Any formal system of periodic appraisal for teachers in higher education is yet to be devised.

REMEDIAL SUGGESTIONS

- There should be diversification of courses in curriculum of the universities as determined by the Mudaliar Commission for the curriculum of the secondary schools. The curriculum of the universities should be flexible so that it may adapt with the changing conditions and needs of the society. The University Education Commission has rightly remarked, "Educational systems are built for the time and not for all time. There are no changeless ways of educating human nature. A curriculum which was prevalent in the Vedic period of the renaissance cannot continue unaltered in the twentieth century."
- There should be a provision of experienced and trained persons to provide guidance and counseling to the students from beginning to the end. The suggestions given by Mudaliar Commission and Kothari Commission hold good for the higher education also.

- Suggestions for raising the standard of teaching include increase in the salaries of teachers; more than 18 hours of teaching work in a week; improvement in the condition of their service; provision of tutorial classes; well-organized libraries and laboratories and encouragement to debates and discussions. The Kothari Commission has recommended professional training to junior lecturers' organizations or Re-orientation Courses for new lecturers, etc.
- Examination system can be reformed by including scientific methods in the examination of students by progressive test, preparation of objective progressive test and determination of 70, 55 and 40 per cent marks for awarding first, second and third division to the students. Abolition of internal examination, starting internal assessment or evaluation system and training of teachers in new system of assessment may remove many of the defects of the present examination system.
- According to Prof. Siddhant the best way of solving the problem of indiscipline is to divert the activities of the young students into healthy channels including sports, games, co-operative living in hostels, self-management of messes, debates and symposia. He has also made the following suggestions for solving the problem of indiscipline among the students:
  (1) In each centre of higher education the statistics of different types of indiscipline should be maintained.
  (2) The family and social life of the students and records where the student has studied earlier should be studied.
  (3) The cause of each crime committed by the students should be discovered.

  It has rightly been suggested by the Education Commission that not only the teachers but the students, their guardians and parents, society, Government and the political parties will have to work in order to solve the problem of indiscipline among the students.
- V.K.R.V. Rao has pointed out, "Unfortunately, we have in our Universities certain very undesirable elements, many of whom are in contact with embassies, planning trips abroad and obtaining money from outside sources. All these have a demoralizing effect on the student-community and should be stopped. I should like to suggest that legislation be introduced for the registration of university or college societies to ensure that they observe certain rules in elections, method of keeping accounts and similar and other things.

OTHER REMEDIAL INNOVATIONS

Appraisal as a Remedy

McGregor (1960) contends that performance appraisal is often perceived simply as a technique of personnel administration, but when it is used for administrative purposes, it becomes a part of managerial strategy, the implicit logic of which is that in order to get people to direct their efforts towards organizational objective, management must tell them what to do, judge how well they have done and record and punish them accordingly.

Beach (1971) adds another dimension to this definition by stating that performance appraisal is the systematic evaluation of the individual with response to his performance on the job and his potential for development. In other words performance appraisal reveals the development need of an individual.

Appraisal: Importance for Teachers and Administrators in Higher Education

There are innumerable reasons why appraisal is the key to effective principal ship, administrator ship and teaching, which in turn leads to institutional effectiveness.

Stoner and Freeman (1992) have expressed that the two major purposes of formal systematic appraisal are:

1. to let individual know formally how their current performance is being rated;
2. to locate individuals who need additional training.

According to Everard and Morris (1990) well developed appraisal systems are of considerable benefit to both the individual and the organization as they enable the employee to measure their achievement, recognize their achievement, prepare them for advancement, open up opportunities, for personal growth and 'clear the air' of problems and build relationships with their superior.

Bhagia and Juneja (1988) identified the roles of heads of college their frequency of performance, and the relationship of personality and organizational variables with the performance of roles. The study shows that the college head spends most of the time in dealing with routine administrative chores rather than with academic matters, it also shows that role-performance is positively and significantly related to the organizational health of a college. D'souza and Prabhakar (1987) identified key performance factors for the appraisal of college teachers. They were-planning and preparation, class-room management, updating knowledge, interpersonal relations and communications, participation and co-operation, initiative, sense of responsibility and emotional stability. They have further recommended self-appraisal or self-evaluation for the head of institution/ departments.

Kulshrestha (1977) concluded from his study on the formats of performance appraisal of college principals, that the following are needed to be incorporated in their appraisal Performa. They were management of growth of institutions in terms of population, faculty development and research, innovation in administration, administrative procedures, information systems and conduct of examination, management of crisis, college environment as reflected by academic, extra-curricular, extension activities and discipline, stability in organization as reflected by better human relationships in college, proper communication system, grievance procedures and organizing ability in the case of a new college.

SUGGESTIONS

The performance appraisal of administrators and teachers in Higher Education should include the following:

1. The appraisal Performa should include the key responsibility areas of the concerned appraise. A five points or seven point scales can be used for performance rating. Appraisal by the management, external agency teachers and students would give a true and unbiased picture of the appraiser's way of functioning in the institution.
2. ***Self-appraisal***: The appraise is required to make a frank and a critical assessment about himself/herself in the appraisal format. It is imperative that there should be an atmosphere of complete mutual trust and they should not feel that their limitations would be used against them.
3. ***Appraisal interviews***: The idea of an appraisal interview is to be free and frank and should precede the working of the report, the appraiser would make tentative assessment of the appraises assets and limitations and make him aware of it. The appraise can then provide corrective data and even point out the organizational constraint, which prevent superior performance.
4. ***Appraisal by students***: This acquires special significance when the 'appraise' is the teacher. There seems to be an unfounded fear among college and university teachers that students give a biased judgment which is primarily based on the acquisition of marks or grades allotted to them. The fear seems baseless, the marginal number of students whose evaluation is affected by such factors get eliminated by the data analysis which is carried out year after year.

TRAINING OF TEACHERS IN HIGHER EDUCATION

Higher Education has very important role to play in the entire education system. Unlike school education, it has a very different role to play when it comes to the transmission of knowledge from the educators to the learners. Apart from the level of content to be provided, the psychology of learners is very different and hence keeping in mind both these factors, it is very clear that these learners need to be tackled in a different way than the school learners. Apart from this, the college teachers are not just supposed to restrict their function to merely class-room teaching but they need to think of making themselves aware of various types of evaluation techniques/procedures and tools.

In pursuance of NPE, 1986, and POA 1986, Central Government and UGC have taken several steps to improve the status and motivation of teachers which includes provision of training opportunities through Academic Staff Colleges.

These colleges organize orientation programmes for newly appointed lecturers and conduct refresher courses for in-service teachers. In 1991, the scheme of ASC was reviewed by an expert committee set up by UGC and they made some suggestions which were accepted by UGC and it decided to continue the scheme of ASCs during the Eighth Plan. Benal (1989) concluded from his study that training and orientation of teachers of higher education is required.

The effective and efficient utilization and mobilization of all the available resources depends on the administrators. Their role is very complex in nature. They need to perform a wide range of functions which are varied in nature. But in India, neither at the school or higher education level, the training programmes for administrators have been thought of conceived on a formal basis although the importance for such programmes is emphasized by various educators from time to time. For school level administrators, Secondary Education Commission (1952-53) emphasized on the role of Principals and mentioned that on him the proper working of the school ultimately depends. Glueck (1974) stated that the training for administrators at school level could reduce waste and increase output. Training can make contribution to the achievement of goals in efficient and effective way.

Similarly, Husen arid Postlewaite (1985) also emphasized training for school principals. In his study Hoyle (1975) stated that whatever the kind of organization, involvement of professional staff is proposed, it can be effective if there is an adequate programme for professional development of administrators. What is being stated for administrators at school level is also applicable for administrators in higher education and if the training programme has to be an effective one, there is a need of identification of the training needs of administrators. One such study for women administrators was conducted by Jaya Indiresan, Lena D'Souza and *et al.* from NIEPA (Now NUEPA) in collaboration with SNDT University in 1990. The areas identified for orientation were

1. application of computer in various areas of planning and administration,
2. role and identity of women administrators,
3. data base for planning,
4. cost effective analysis, and
5. Portfolio analysis etc.

There is a need of some more such studies to be undertaken. In future institutional management is going to become more complex.

AUTONOMY OF THE INSTITUTIONS

Concept of Autonomy

The word "Autonomy" in a layman's language sounds, something similar to "freedom". Every individual desires autonomy in his life/ work. Similarly, every institution which works for the primary task of attainment of its set goals, needs autonomy in its functioning. Every educational institution has its own academic goals and it engages it's human power for the attainment of the same and institutions of higher education are no exception to it.

Autonomy assumes greater significance for administrators of colleges/ university as they are ultimately responsible to run the entire show.

With regard to the recruitment of teachers, in case of some states, the recruitment of Government college teachers is done by the State Public Service Commission in a centralized way and thus it becomes more of a bureaucratic function where the colleges have hardly any option but to accept the teachers appointed by SPSC in the respected colleges. The university too, has no voice in it. In case of private colleges too, university has no autonomy to choose the teachers as it is done by the managing committees of that college where usually the local candidates get preference. In case of university departments too, the selection of the regular staff is done in a centralized manner where heads of the institution are just there in the selection committee as one of the panel member. The final composition of the committee too is done by higher authorities. Thus, the institutional head doesn't have much autonomy in this regard except in case of some powerful heads.

Autonomy and Admission of Students

With regard to admission of students: too, in a real sense, the heads of the institutions do not have much autonomy. The reasons are they have to follow certain Government norms with regard to reservation of seats. Further, in (case of private colleges and especially in case of non-aided colleges) the admission has to be given to them who can pay for it and hence it is not ability to learn but ability to pay gets the priority which, too, can lead to a situation of compromising with the quality.

The autonomous colleges were the brain child of NPE 1986 and POA 1986. Some studies have been undertaken in this area of autonomy. At NIEPA, research team of Sharma, Ahmed and *et al.* submitted a report of study visits to autonomous colleges with regard to autonomy and accountability in 1987 on the basis of the analysis of the data, some of the suggestions given were

1. Concept of autonomy and accountability needs to be dearly desired,
2. Universities must given full autonomy to colleges to frame their curriculum,
3. Autonomy should be extended to all the sections in the system, and
4. It is necessary, to introduce structure/changes with regard to planning, administration and financial practice.

REFERENCES

Altekar, A.S.; *Education in India*, Nawal Kishore Bros. Varanasi.

Bhagia, Juneja and *et al.*, "Role Performance of Heads of Colleges, NIEPA, 1988.

Chandra, S.S., Rawat, V.S. and Singh, R.P.; *Indian Education Development Problems, Issues and Trends*, Surya Publication, Meerut.

D'Souza, L. and Prabhakar, A., *Managing Performance Appraisal in Educational Organizations*, Education Management Series, Bombay, 1987.

Everard, B. and Morris, G., *Effective School Management*, Paul Chapman Publishing Ltd., London, 1990.

Kaul, J.N., Autonomy of the University Community 1985 in NIEPA *Research Studies, Annotated Bibliography* (1962–1993) by Nirmal Malhotra, Pub. NIEPA, New Delhi.

McGreger, D., *The Human Side of Enterprise*, McGreaw Hill, New York, 1960.

Ministry of Human Resource Development, *Challenges of Education–A Policy Perspective*, Government of India, New Delhi, 1985.

Ministry of Human Resource Development, *National Policy on Education*, Government of India, New Delhi, 1986.

Ministry of Human Resource Development, *Programme of Action 1992*, Government of India, New Delhi, 1992.

13

Higher Education: Issues and Challenges

Fauzia Khan

Since independence, higher education in India has expanded many folds. While there were only 20 universities in 1947, the number has increased to 540 in 2011. The number of colleges has increased to 25,951 from 500 at the time of independence. Significant increase is also visible in the number of teaching staff from 15,000 to 5 lakhs during the same period. The number of students enrolled in higher education has also gone up from 1 lakh in 1950 to 169.75 lakhs provisional students enrolled in various courses at all levels in universities and colleges in 2010-11. The enrolment ratio has also increased from less than 1 per cent in 1950 to 14 per cent in 2010. Thus, it is obvious that the institutional capacity of higher education in India has increased many times. These developments notwithstanding the Gross National Ratio (GNR) in relative terms with 60 per cent in USA and Canada over 40 per cent in several European countries and more than 20 per cent in many developed and developing countries. The main aim of the present Five-Year Plan is to increase the involvement of higher education system so as to increase the Gross Involvement Ratio by 15 per cent to 20 per cent. The most important component for sustaining higher economic growth is higher education, but it is very less in comparison to other developed and developing countries.

During the past two decades, there is a tremendous expansion of higher education, but education has become a money making business. Private institutions have entered in the system. Both the private and government institutions are drawing their interest from higher education. A large number of colleges, university level institutions and deemed universities have been established by state legislatures. But still there is a need for further expansion of higher education to meet the growing demands and increasing aspirations of the new generation learners.

ACADEMIC STRUCTURE

Higher education in India covers all the post senior-secondary education i.e. after class 12th, in different subject areas. There are different professional courses like engineering and technology, medicine, agriculture, teaching and so on. There are four levels of courses, viz., Undergraduate programmes, Masters/Postgraduate programmes, Pre-doctoral (M. Phil.) programmes and

Doctoral programmes (Ph.D.). Bachelor's degree (Undergraduate programme) requires three years of education after completing 12 years of schooling. A Master's degree is of two years duration and it could be based on course work with or without research work. M. Phil. degree is a pre-doctoral programme with main focus on the research methodology and research work. A Ph.D. degree is awarded two years after M. Phil. Degree and three years after Master's degree. With a Ph.D., the research scholars undergo a research project and then write a substantial thesis based on their research.

Higher education has a fixed curriculum. The choices are limited in the respective departments of studies. Efforts are being made to introduce the choice based credit system in higher education, but it is adopted by only few institutions. To gain maximum rewards from education in the present scenario, it is very important that there is greater flexibility with regards to subject choices of students in higher education system. It will ensure a greater horizontal and vertical mobility.

The most recent initiatives in higher education include the integrated graduation programmes and lateral entry of three-year bachelor's degree holders in science in the third year of the four-year engineering degree programmes. Similarly, restructuring of master's and graduate degree by introducing a four-year, flexible and modular Bachelor of Science (B.Sc.) programme and other integrated programmes are positive steps that will enhance student choice. The significance of such academic restructuring is a very important step in higher education reforms.

REGULATORY BODIES

The higher education system in India has many statutory agencies such as Indian Nursing Council (INC), Bar Council of India (BCI), Pharmacy Council of India (PCI), National Council of Teacher Education (NCTE), Council of Architecture (COA), the Medical Council of India (MCI), University Grants Commission (UGC), All India Council of Technical Education (AICTE), etc. Besides these agencies, the institutions are regulated by the Central and State Universities as well as by the Directorates of College and Technical Education. Each of the regulatory agencies is governed by its own individual acts (Table 1).

Table 1: Statutory Regulatory Bodies

Year	*Statutory Body*
1933	Medical Council of India (MCI) Act
1947	Indian Nursing Council (INC) Act
1948	Dentists Council of India (DCI) Act
1948	Pharmacy Council of India (PCI) Act
1956	University grants Commission (UGC) Act
1961	Bar Council of India (BCI) Act
1970	Indian Medicine Central Council (IMCC) Act
1972	Council of Architecture (COA) Act
1987	All India Council of Technical Education (AICTE) Act
1993	National Council of Teacher Education (NCTE) Act

Since these Acts were created at different periods by different ministries, the regulatory provisions of these Acts were substantially different from each other. The UGC was assigned the overall responsibility for the whole of the higher education system, but it is observed that there exists very little coordination among the statutory bodies with respect to approval mechanisms, nomenclatures, degree durations, accreditation process etc. Regulation comprise of various stages such as approval, affiliation, accreditation and recognition; as a consequence of which a highly over-regulated system results in interference of multiple and multi-level agencies that hampers innovations and creativity. Thus, the Knowledge Commission proposed to establish the Independent Regulatory Authority for Higher Education (IRAHE) to overcome this limitation. A good regulatory system can facilitate and promote innovation and quality, or a bad one can discourage initiative and destroy the quality. Therefore, a well-designed regulatory system can help to reduce turbulence that exists due to rapid expansion of Higher Education. It could also ensure credibility of the academic programmes and protect the interest of the students and the society.

NATIONAL KNOWLEDGE COMMISSION RECOMMENDATIONS

The National Knowledge Commission (NKC) proposed establishment of IRAHE so as to facilitate setting up of new universities especially by private investors and also through public-private partnership, in consideration of the fact that the present system is over-regulated, but under-governed. One of the key objectives of IRAHE was to minimize conflicts of interest by creating an arms length relationship from stakeholders, and to decrease the confusing and overlapping mandates due to multiplicity of regulatory agencies. This was conceptualized as a single-window licensing authority for according degree-granting power to higher education institutions and would also be responsible for settling disputes and monitoring standards. The body would apply exactly the same norms to public and private institutions, as well. IRAHE will consist of a Chairperson, a distinguished academic personality who is appointed by the Prime Minister based on the recommendations of a Search Committee. IRAHE will also include six other members who are distinguished academics in different disciplines, along with some part-time members of outstanding distinction.

The functions of IRAHE, as given by NKC, are:

1. To determine eligibility for setting up new institutions based on transparent criteria.
2. To apply the same norms to private, public and international institutions.
3. Granting powers to higher education institutions to award degrees.
4. To monitor standards and settle disputes.
5. To determine the authority for licensing accrediting agencies.

NKC also proposed that the role of UGC should be limited to disburse public funds and maintenance of public institutions in higher education. NKC has also suggested curtailing the functions of other regulatory agencies like AICTE and MCI. IRAHE was to have a highly centralized role with unwieldy responsibility. Large size of higher education system has led to many diverse disciplines and varying level of imbalances are seen in different parts of the country. NKC recommendations have created a high level of controversy among educational experts, the academics, and the policy makers. Considering the past experiences and present political environment in the country, many observers seriously question the possibility of independent status of this body. Because of the fact that IRAHE would be free from political and functional constraints, it is highly likely that there may be increased scope for politicization and high-level corruption. Moreover, abolishing the present statutory bodies like AICTE is not an easy task. Some others consider this recommendation as an indication of neo-liberal and market oriented philosophy.

Earlier the NPE (1986) had also recommended a coordinating body at the state level for decentralization of power and for better coordination at the state level. According to it, "State level planning and coordination of higher education will be done through councils of higher education. The UGC and these councils will develop coordinated methods to keep a watch on standards".

If the bodies like IRAHE are established, we will have an elegant structure of regulated intermediaries consisting of:

I. National Board of Higher Education
II. National level Autonomous Bodies
III. State Councils of Higher Education
IV. Accrediting Bodies
V. Universities
VI. Colleges

It will form an academic hierarchy with proper decentralization and well defined functions. The working of the existing institutions may be examined for possible streamlining and improving as the case may be.

In order to reach at the desired goal for 15 per cent of the eligible group by 2015, India needs to have a large number of educational institutions. The most important challenge is to expand education system and to maintain and improve the quality of education to meet the need of globalized society. If higher education does not produce high quality graduates, we cannot stand with global markets. So higher education is a very important investment in human capital to produce specialized and globally competent human resources which is immensely important for economic growth of the country.

ENROLLMENT

The UGC Annual Report 2005-06 provides a level-wise and subject-wise enrollment data for the year 2005-06. It is seen that the majority of student enrollment is at the undergraduate level. There are 88.91 per cent (9,804,977) of total students enrolled in undergraduate programmes, only 9.42 per cent (1,038,810) in the post-graduate programmes and a mere 0.64 per cent (70,716) in doctoral programmes. The remaining 1.03 per cent (113,517) students were enrolled in various types of diploma and certificate programmes in the formal system of higher education. Overall 87 per cent student enrollment is in affiliated colleges.

If the level-wise enrollment was studied, it was found that while a bulk (90.3%) of the undergraduate students and two-thirds (66.6%) of the post-graduate students attend colleges, a majority (90.7%) of doctoral students are enrolled in the universities.

The post-graduate enrollment is fairly low and has significantly decreased from 13 per cent in 1980 to about 9 per cent in 2003. The proportion of doctoral students has also decreased from 0.88 per cent in 1980-81 to a mere 0.58 per cent in 2003-04.

EXPANDING ACCESS

The expansion of higher education was done without considering the quality of education until recently. There was an unplanned proliferation of Institutions of Higher Education (MHRD, 1992) with the main objective of expanding the existing facilities. There are several types of private institutions, while most of them are colleges and some are deemed to be universities and very few of them are established by religious and linguistic minorities. In the last decade, higher education has become international; it is one of the ways to increase the access to higher education. In spite of having high targets in 11-Five Year Plan, our nation is facing problem of unmet demand for higher education. Students have no choices but to enroll in foreign universities and pay high fees.

EXCELLENCE

In the present scenario, higher education is conceived as the production of highly qualified workforce. The earnings and status of people in their respective workplaces will determine the standard of education they have received. There are many stakeholders in higher education i.e., the students, the parents, the teachers, the non-teaching staff, government funding agencies, regulatory bodies and educational agencies. All of these have their own views about the quality of education, and these views are influenced by their interest and objectives. These views are very often different from their expectations from the system.

Different institutions have different views about what constitutes 'quality of education'. The deterioration of quality is very much visible in the output of universities. Still there are a few universities, colleges and deemed universities who have managed to maintain their standard of quality since their inception; IITs and IIMs are some such institutions. With the advent of globalization, there was an increasing concern regarding the quality of Indian Universities and Colleges. Consequently, National Assessment and Accreditation Council (NAAC) were established in 1994 to address the issues of quality in Indian Higher Education. NAAC had assessed 162 universities and 4096 colleges till March 2010. It was found that 37.65 per cent universities were A grade, 58.65 per cent were B grade and 3.70 per cent were low grade. This was the report of a National Body, however, if we consider International Level Assessment then the scenario is even worst. As compared to universities of other countries, only IIT Mumbai figured in the top 200 universities in the world in the prestigious QS World University Ranking in 2010. It was ranked in 187th place in 2010 and now in 2012, it is altogether missing from the list of top 200 universities of the world. It's really disheartening to mention that the Indian Higher Education is nowhere near the global standards.

The National Policy of Education (NPE, 1986) had raised serious concerns about the deterioration of the standard of higher education. It had observed at that time, that the then available machinery was unable to maintain the standard of higher education in the country. Various options were examined and the NPE reached at the conclusion that an external agency was required to assess the practices of higher education systems.

At present, there are many agencies that are responsible to assess the quality of education in the country, e.g., NAAC (National Academic Accreditation Committee) set up by the UGC in 1994 to accredit institutions of higher education, NBA (National Board of Accreditation) established by the AICTE in 1994 to accredit programmes of engineering and related areas, AB (Accreditation Board) established by agriculture department, and ICAR in 1996 to accredit agriculture institutions. The function of these agencies is to assess the higher education institutions on some predetermined criteria and they try to maintain quality assurance. The accreditation in India was earlier voluntary, but now many state governments have made it mandatory for the institutes of higher education. The impact of accreditation on quality of education is quite visible in the output of the institutions which have gone from this voluntary accreditation process, but still there are some institutes that are not interested in accreditation. This is the main reason that the number of accredited institutions is very less. Many reputed universities and colleges have, so far, not volunteered themselves for accreditation.

TEACHERS AND TEACHING IN HIGHER EDUCATION

Of the total enrolled population, 85 per cent are in affiliated colleges. These colleges have little or no autonomy to change their practices and curriculum. Out of 18,500 colleges, 14,000 have undergraduate courses like B.A., B.Com. and B.Sc. They teach a fixed and often outdated syllabus provided by their respective universities. A large number of these colleges have a small number of enrolled students (just a few hundreds) and have less than a dozen teachers each. Fixed courses are available to students and the students do not have much choice. The teaching-learning process followed in Indian Higher Education remains essentially teacher-centric where, till recently, a teacher in higher education was called a 'lecturer' whose main work was to give lectures to the students. Although the term is no longer in use, the dependence of faculty on lecture method still remains predominant. Therefore, there is a need to do away with the 'teacher knows all' model and the student must be actively involved in their own learning which results in learning for the teachers, as well.

NPE (1986) advocated a systematic and a well planned programme of vocational education. Vocational education was a distant stream of education intended to prepare students for identifying occupations. This scheme for the vocationalisation of education at the university and college level was started in 1994-95 of the UGC. This was redesigned in the year 2003-04 to bring in greater flexibility. Now, very few courses are there which are not attached to vocational training. Here, it is worth mentioning that we are in the age of demographic transition where population growth is slowing down but the population of young, ready as skilled workforce, is and would continue to increase. A majority of Indian population is in the age group of 15-65 years. According to Economic Survey, it is estimated that the average age of India would be 29 years by 2020 as compared to 37 years for the US and China, 45 years in Western Europe and 48 years in Japan. This could result in a low dependency ratio and substantial earning population, relatively high from other countries. This could be an opportunity to propel India ahead of other nations but only if quality higher education is accessible to the people, and if not, the same situation could turn into a disaster.

If the quality of teachers is improved, it will automatically improve the quality of teaching and learners' outcome. In the present scenario, this task is not easy. Employment procedures followed for selecting teachers is often marred by controversies, with allegations of nepotism and political influences remaining rife. Besides, the reservation policy followed by the state as a measure of social justice is considered by many as being contradictory to excellence. This conflict between social justice and excellence, and between equity and merit still remains debatable. Teaching ability is directly related to training and experience. Unfortunately, there is another drawback in the education system. It is the prevailing salary structure, which does not target high quality teachers (Manushek, 2005). The respect and esteem which the teachers used to have earlier in the society, is not available to the present day teachers. Now-a-days only those persons become teachers who could not release their first or second choice of career. Thus, the present day teachers are those who are having teaching profession as their 3rd choice as a career option. Also, the teachers do not have any well defined performance appraisal system, which is very strongly recommended by NAAC. Still the higher education system has not evolved or adopted any reliable procedure for assessment of the performance of teachers. Due to the career advancement and promotion schemes that currently exist, all the teachers get promotion, whether they perform up to the mark or not. As a result of which all the teachers, whether they are academically competent or not, rise to the top positions. This has obsessed the majority of individuals who are seeking promotion across the universities. This has also removed incentives for teachers to perform (Kapur & Mehta, 2004). However, the UGC has now laid down well defined procedure and credit system for various tasks in the system, as a means to assess the performance of the teachers in higher education. This, too, is not perfect and has some inherent deficiencies. Low salaries, lack of adequate respect in the society, and lack of any reliable performance appraisal system to discriminate the performing teachers with the non-performing ones, has resulted in decreasing levels of job satisfaction and motivation of the teachers due to which they are not able to teach whole-heartedly.

According to Jayaram (2002), teachers in higher education do not have any professional preparation, as well. The present day teachers enter this profession with no prior professional preparation other than a postgraduate degree. They undertake this challenging work without any training and accountability, with performance being no more than its own reward. Furthermore, there is very limited exposure of faculty of the institutes of higher education to any quality professional development programmes. The programmes that already exist are dull and ineffective to a large extent. In-house mentoring is usually non-existent and intra-institutional politics, which plague the institutions of higher education, is a major hindrance for creating an academic ambience that is suitable for bringing out implicit talent of the faculty. The exposure of faculty to international seminars and conferences is also quite limited as a result of which they remain oblivious of any new development in their respective fields. Due to this, the present day teachers at colleges and universities have been largely been reduced to the lowest common denominator. However, recently the government has taken measures to improve the academic contribution of the teachers by means of their upgradation and adaptation through various courses. Several measures, like enhancement of retirement age, increase in pay scales, etc., have also been taken to attract the interest of quality teachers.

RESEARCH AND INNOVATIONS

Despite India's poor performance in basic research (as measured by publications and education counts) and applied research (measured by Patent Control); there is a general optimism about India's political co-operative research (Agarwal, 2009).

Despite having knowledge and the potential, Indian Higher Education institutes fail miserably in the area of research, largely due to lack or inadequacy of funding by the government, due to which the talented faculty and scholars migrate to foreign countries. As a result of which there are hardly any instances of path-breaking research by Indian faculty. However, recently several measures have been taken by the UGC, to improve the quality of research. One such step is that of granting stipend for research scholars, which would help the scholars in many ways and would also foster quality in research. Several regulations have also been developed by the UGC to define systematic creation, collection and compilation of categorized information.

The need to improve teaching and research has also been emphasized by the National Knowledge Commission (2006). The National Knowledge Commission (NKC) also considered faculty members of institutions of higher education as an important element for improving quality of universities through knowledge creations and enhanced teaching performance. Synergies exist between research and teaching and they mutually enrich each other; thus, as universities are the natural home for teaching, so are they for research, as well. NKC, therefore, emphasizes that research is essential for the pursuit of academic excellence for institutions of higher education. It further adds that the research outputs of these institutions shall be vital contributors to India's socioeconomic development and progress in science and technology.

The major problem with research is the access to material available in the area (Agarwal, 2007). The quality of research outcomes depends significantly on the easy and ready access of the researchers to scholarly communication. Most of the scholarly journals are very expensive for most of the higher education institutions in India. Scholarly communication through electronics and the internet provides an innovative solution to the affordability problem as it incurs low or almost no cost in distribution.

Theses and dissertations are important sources of information but they do not find their way into various publication channels. These research works are of great help to the researchers for their work. New aspects are available for accessing the work but still it is not open to large groups as a result of which the quality of their research is adversely affected. Indian higher education institutions must improve access of the researchers to the information resources. Sometimes in certain institutes, research collections are kept closely guarded and closed to access for the outsiders, making it difficult for others to access them. So the candidates who want to pursue research are not able to consult them and are, thus, selecting the research problems without knowing that what type of work already exists in the area of their interest. Thus, restricting information for outside students and scholars results in duplication of work.

Major handicap face by doctoral researchers in India is poor visibility. Multiple linkages forming interconnecting institution or groupings, which are regional, national, international or subject specific, are extremely rare. Thus, people work in isolation, often disconnected from the latest ideas, trends and developments in research in their areas of interest, in the other parts of the world; and the same it true other way as well. This usually leads to what is called 'reinvention of the wheel' resulting in wastage of money, time and energy. However, now there is an International trend to preserve and centrally maintain an electronic thesis and dissertations and make them generally accessible, and this helps to not only prevent duplication of work but also helps to improve quality of doctoral research. Establishing DELNET and INFLIBNET in our country is an effort in this direction.

INTERNATIONALIZATION OF HIGHER EDUCATION

Higher education has become international in the past decade. It has now become a market-driven activity. Internationalization of Higher Education means the migration of students from one nation to another nation to get a desired qualification at higher education level. But now, due to advancements in the field of technology and education, cross-border education is possible without migration from one nation to another nation. Cross-border higher education is one way to increase the access to higher education for countries that face a problem in meeting the demand for higher education. There are many reasons or factors contributing to the growing number of enrollments in foreign universities. Many developing countries have under supply of seats in various courses, which create a great demand. Students from these countries have no choice but to leave the country and pay more for their education. Another main reason is the expectation of consumer group (parents and students). After graduating from a developed country, the students get better opportunities in their careers. These are the factors which make higher education a global export commodity in developing countries.

UNESCO (2009) presented a report on the 'World Conference on Higher Education'. According to the report:

- There were more than 2.5 million students in the world studying outside their own country.
- It was also predicted that the number of international students might rise approximately to 7 million.
- The main preferred destinations of international students are The United States, The United Kingdom, Germany, France and Australia.
- In recent years, some Asian and Middle East countries have started attracting more international students.

HIGHER EDUCATION AND CHALLENGES OF THE PRESENT ERA

Indian higher education has changed a lot over the past ten years. There is increasing competition in the field of higher education. Commercialization of higher education has increased. Cross-border delivery of higher education has challenged the values which were traditionally attached to exchange and partnership programmes. Measurement of success of a person is done on the basis of his/her occupation or career. Thus, there is an urgent need of the people to increase the levels of their vocation. Measurement of success of an institute of higher education is now being done on the basis of the number of student placement. The international ranking of higher education institutions is a controversial and a widely debated aspect. Quality assurance is an important issue that can not be overlooked by the institutes of higher education. The accountability of the management, deans and faculty members have greatly increased.

EFFORTS OF THE GOVERNMENT IN THE FIELD OF HIGHER EDUCATION

The outlay of government policies for higher education has seen a many-fold increase in the recent past.

- 11th Five Year Plan had focused on the establishment of new universities and colleges.
- The Technical and Medical Education Bill was passed in 2010 with an aim to discourage the malpractices prevalent in the technical and medical education. The engineering, medical and management institutions are being directly funded by the MHRD. All-India common admission tests like, IIT-JEE, CPMT, CAT etc. are used for selection of candidates for all professional courses.
- Privatization of Higher Education is also being done. There are several types of private institutions for higher education. While most of these are colleges, some are deemed to be universities. These institutions include:
  1. Institutions established by State Legislatures.
  2. Institutions established by religious and linguistic minorities.
  3. Old private institutions substantially funded by the government.
- The General Agreement on Trade and Services (GATS) of World Trade Organization (WTO), education has been identified as a service. This gives particular importance to the higher education and its Internationalization.
- Different modes of delivery by foreign providers have been identified. These modes include – Branch Campuses; Double/Joint Degree; Twinning; Franchised Programmes; Validated Programmes; and Distance and Open Learning, e-Learning, etc.
- The Foreign Educational Institutions Bill (2010) has finally got the green signal by the government. The MHRD has termed this Bill as a milestone in education, which will help benchmark quality education in a new way altogether, by enhancing the choices for students and increasing competition. If this Bill becomes a law, then it will gain following advantages:
  1. Different universities of the world are eager to open their campuses in India because India is a growing economy.
  2. These foreign universities will be granted the status of deemed universities under the Section 3 of the UGC Act.
  3. This will increase healthy competition, improve the standard of education and open up more seats in higher education.

But there is another side of the coin too:

1. These institutions can attract faculty from Indian Universities with better pay scales and perks.

2. There will be no reservation policy for SC, ST and OBC students and teachers.
3. The main aim of these foreign institutes will be to increase their profits in the field of higher education. They will launch the courses which the market needs, and will charge extraordinarily high fees.
4. There are no criteria prescribed for the assessment and accreditation of the foreign universities in India. They will be only assessed on the basis of their present reputation. This will lead to unhealthy competition among their equals.

Thus, the Indian higher education system needs a comprehensive Internationalization strategy at both national and institutional levels. A systematic approach is required to internationalize higher education in India. Best practices should be introduced into the system for its better functioning. There should be checks and control on the increased competition to attract students. Close monitoring is required to check over commercialization; otherwise the higher education will become unavoidable in the future.

CONCLUSION

Education liberates and it also democratizes by demolishing the barriers of caste and class, and is capable of obliterating inequalities that are imposed by birth and other circumstances. This is true not only for the local environment but also for the larger global environment. People are now realizing the importance of education in transforming an underdeveloped nation to a developing nation and a developing nation into a developed nation. Higher education has pervasive and substantial impact on development, since it arms an individual with necessary knowledge, attitudes, skills and competence for realizing important personal and social goals and thereby contributing to both personal and social development. In India, Higher Education has had an exponential quantitative growth since independence and same is true of the challenges that the Indian higher education faces.

One of the most important need of higher education is to reformulate the curriculum in accordance with the demands of the present era. The political, social, scientific and technological landscape of the world is changing very fast and the curriculum has to be sensitive to this change for it to stay relevant. With the changes in curriculum and with the introduction of new courses, there is the need for teachers also to constantly reinvent themselves through the updating of their knowledge, attitudes and skills for which best professional development programmes are required. These programmes should not only be limited to acquaint the teachers with new developments in their respective fields but they must also cater to the problems faced by the teachers in their day-to-day academic life. These programmes must help the teachers overcome the obstacles that they face in their in-hand practices, like the problems faced during the teaching and learning process, or the problems faced while dealing with the students and the staff. Therefore, there is a need to shift the professional development programmes from the usual lecture mode to workshop mode. The teachers and the administrative staff should be exposed to the good and innovative practices in higher education within and outside India; for which the staff should be encouraged to participate in national and international seminars where they can share their experiences of such practices and the results of their researches.

The research scenario in India too has been an area of concern. There are hardly any instances of path-breaking research by Indian faculty, in the past few decades. The M. Phil. and Ph.D. programmes must be combined so that a research scholar has a firm foundation in research before he/she could select a topic and its related methodology. The selection of the topic should be based on a thorough analysis of the national and international researches available in that area. It is, therefore, imperative that both the national and international bodies must make the researches freely available to all so that duplication and waste of funds and time may be avoided. The faculty must also be provided funds to carry out action research to find solutions to problems of in-hand practices which might lead to innovations in practices in higher education.

The politicisation of higher education is another area of concern. The effect of internal and external politics of higher education is counterproductive to the quality of higher education. The appointments of Vice-Chancellors to teachers to students are often influenced by the politics and politicians, as a result of which incapable people are appointed to lead to deterioration of the quality. The appointments should be fair and should only be based on merit. As pointed by UNESCO, the candidate's qualifications, aptitude and passion for the subject, course and the job must be given due consideration before appointments are made.

There is also an immediate need to craft progressive policies for higher education in India. The government should have a clear vision of its policies. We should have the wisdom to understand and appreciate new realities and to have the courage to take bold decisions regarding the educational system. We should seize this opportunity to shape our bright future. It is, therefore, what Kirpal said seems to be so apt,

> 'The single most important thing needed now is to get out of the rigidity of the system. In the rapidly changing world of today, one thing is certain; yesterday's education system will not meet today's need and even less so the need of tomorrow'. (Kirpal, 1994).

REFERENCES

Aggarwal, P. (2009). *Indian Higher Education-Envisioning Future*, New Delhi: Sage Publication Pvt. Ltd.

Ministry of Human Resource Development (1986). *National Policy on Education-1986*, New Delhi: Government of India.

University Grants Commission (2009-10). *UGC Annual Report 2008-09.*

University Grants Commission (2009-10). *UGC Annual Report 2009-10.*

University Grants Commission (2009-10). *UGC Annual Report 2010-11.*

14

The Feasibility and Fallacies of Internationalization of Higher Education in India

Bipasha Sinha

Internationalization of higher education in India is not a new phenomenon. The Universities of Takshsila, Vikramshila, Vallabhi and Nalanda bear witness to our magnificent educational legacy. These ancient Universities attracted great scholars from all over the world particularly during the Gupta and Maurya rule. Fa-Hein and Hein-Tsang of China came to Nalanda University for education during these periods. Medieval India boasts of famous scholars like Nuniz and Peaz from Portugal, Ibn Batuta from Africa and Nicolo Conti from Italy during the Tuglaq reign. During the British period, eminent scholars like Max Muller and William Jones did extensive study on India literature and culture. Foreign faculties to name a few like William Ward, Joshua Marshman, William Carrey, David Hare and Alexander Duff came to India for teaching and managing educational institutions. From the time of independence several Indian scholars have gone abroad especially to England to train in subjects like engineering, medicine and law. Foreign books and journals have always been a vital source of knowledge for our university students and teachers. Thus, teaching, learning, research and institution-building have all been of part of Internationalization of higher education in India.

In this millennium however, the Internationalization of higher education has taken a new dimension with new modes of delivery in higher education. It is widely documented that the international mobility of students and academicians permits developing countries to acquire current knowledge and research methodologies. The Eleventh Five-Year Plan (2007-2012) has accepted the urgency to develop India's higher education system to face the global challenge. The plan acknowledges the need for an international dimension, including linkages with other countries and international research programmes (Government of India 2007). Education is treated as a tradable service under the General Agreement on Trades in Services (1995) and the 'Foreign Education Providers Bill' of 2010 is a lead in permitting foreign investment in higher education in India. Higher education in four different modes are recognized for trade in services. The first mode is 'cross-border delivery' which refers to delivery of education services and obtaining degrees via the internet that is through distance education; virtual universities, tele-education, educational testing services etc. The second mode is 'consumed abroad' which refers to inflow and outflow of students for higher education. The third mode is 'commercial presence' which refers to joint degree providers, branch campuses, franchise-twinning arrangements, franchise establishment of local branch campus for foreign universities etc. The fourth mode is 'movement of natural persons' which refers to temporary movement of teachers and scholars to provide education services overseas.

THE FOREIGN EDUCATIONAL INSTITUTIONS BILL (2010)

The Foreign Educational Institutions Bill particularly aims at regulating mode three of trade in educational services which is commercial presence of existing foreign providers and aims at regulating the entry of new foreign providers. The Bill does not aid Indian institutions to go abroad, nor does it try to manage the matter of foreign students coming to India. So the bill doesn't deal with all four modes of Internationalization of higher education in India. Moreover, even if foreign education providers were not allowed to set up campuses in India, they could employ other means of delivery like the distance mode or informal twinning arrangements on which the Indian government may not have much control. In today's world, all sorts of services and online transactions are available on the net with the use of credit cards and it would be impossible to track them. Regarding twinning arrangements there are no legal barring if an Indian institution confers a student with degrees after completion of saying a semester in an institution abroad because it would amount to just a matter of credit transfer. Furthermore, with all the conditions stated in the Bill like ₹ 500 millions as caution deposit, strict compliance to government policies and with a clause forbidding the repatriation of profits, it is doubtful if there are going to be many takers (Gnanam, 2010).

FOREIGN EDUCATIONAL INSTITUTIONS BILL AND GROSS ENROLLMENT RATIO IN HIGHER EDUCATION

It is debatable on how the Foreign Educational Institutions Bill will be helpful in achieving India's goal of 30 per cent GER by 2020 (Shah, 2010). It may further raise the inequality between rural and urban, rich and poor; higher caste and deprived categories of students. The Foreign Educational Institutions Bill predominantly aspires to secure help from the foreign universities to improve the quality of education from mediocre to excellent rather than a quantitative increase in the Gross Enrolment Ratio in higher education. The champions of the Bill feel that permitting foreign universities would be beneficial as they would serve as models to the indigenous ones and help in enhancing the quality of education, increase the output of academic work and culture, increase student-faculty exchanges and the professional development of the faculty in terms of superior teaching and research. However these can only be ensured when Indian campuses have adequately equipped infrastructure.

Yet again, developed countries may not find it viable to transfer the entire faculty needed from their country. As of now there are about six hundred thousand teachers in our higher education system to cater to 10-12 million students (Gnanman, 2010). If the Gross Enrolment Ratio doubles or triples in a reasonable period of time, it is unrealistic to consider that the vast majority would gain from a few hundred visiting foreign nationals to serve in the Indian campuses. The education made available by foreign providers will be more expensive and indeed beyond the reach of common students. It may only be accessed by a privileged few students who are able to pay high fees. The reach of programmes offered through the electronic media is also limited to those dwelling in big cities and who have access to internet technology. Again most of the foreign providers offer programmes relating to business management and technology which are required by the specialized few and do not cater much to liberal disciplines that are relevant to the socio-cultural needs of the local people.

THE FOREIGN EDUCATIONAL INSTITUTIONS BILL AND OUTWARD MOBILITY OF STUDENTS

In our country 'Bilayati Shiksha' has always seen to add prestige value in spite of numerous incidents of discrimination faced by Indian students in Australia, violence in the U.S. and stringent visa norms in the U.K. The number of students who leave the country to study has risen over the years. Studying abroad is no longer meant for the elite few. Many students from the large and growing middle-class prefer to get educated abroad, knowing that this can open up better job opportunities back in India on their return (Khadria, 2007). Over 40,000 Indian students are studying in US courses and several thousands in Europe and approximately 3-14 billion dollars is drained out of India for students who go abroad (Powar, 2010). Currently, Indians constitute about 7.5 per cent of the world's mobile students, the second-largest group of students after China (Agarwal, 2010). However an approximation of the percentage of students going abroad for education revealed from the student visas issued by the various consulates show that the numbers are not significant for a big country like ours (Gnanman, 2010).

The Foreign Educational Institutions Bill assumes that the outflow of Indian students can be checked by endorsing foreign universities to come and offer their educational programmes in India itself. It is believed that the cost of living and travel could be diminished if foreign providers operate in our country. However, it is debatable as to how far the foreign education providers can re-create the same ambience and work culture of their country in India. The presence of a few foreign universities or their branch campuses from a country may not reverse this traditional mobility of our students to foreign countries for higher learning. Those Indian students who aspire for education abroad do so not only for good quality education but also to be an immigrant to these advanced countries where a better quality of life and earnings exists.

THE FOREIGN EDUCATIONAL INSTITUTIONS BILL AND INWARD MOBILITY OF STUDENTS

India has not been proactive in drawing international students and its coordination, communication and recruitment strategies are weak. The prevalence of international students in India is markedly low compared to that in China. China, which hosted only a few hundred students in the early 1990s, now hosts about 200,000 students, while in India this number increased from about 13,000 students in 1990-91 to the current 18,594 (Agarwal, 2010). Most of the international students traditionally come from neighboring countries in South Asia like Bhutan, Nepal, Sri Lanka, Bangladesh and Malaysia.

The Association of Indian Universities (AIU) faces many difficulties in collecting data, particularly for students from neighbouring countries like Nepal, Bhutan and Bangladesh as their borders with India are porous. Most institutions recruit foreign students themselves, though some universities coordinate recruitment four affiliated colleges. The coordination mechanism for promotion of Indian higher education abroad by the University Grants Commission in 2004-05 has not been very effective. Educational Consultants India Limited is the liaison agency for the admission of foreign nationals and overseas Indians, but it recruits less than a thousand students each year. Another thousand comes through the Indian Council for Cultural Relations, as a part of the public diplomacy of the government (Agarwal, 2008).

There are numerous causes for insufficient foreign student enrollment in India. Most of the international students in India are either self-financed or receive some funding from their home governments. The Indian embassies abroad do have handbooks that contain information about academic courses and universities but these are not updated on a regular basis. There is a lack of integrated sites on the internet providing comprehensive information to the students which is why Indian universities remain largely inaccessible to foreign students. Foreign students also have a difficult time in securing visas. The process starts in the months of February and March and by the time it materializes, the academic course may have already begun, leaving students with little or no time to plan their trip. Further, Indian universities lack good infrastructure like proper hostel facilities or cafeteria, lack of any international student's cell in the universities etc. Moreover, International students also face difficulties in opening bank accounts and in obtaining adequate information about transportation as roadmaps of towns are rarely available.

THE FOREIGN EDUCATIONAL INSTITUTIONS BILL AND FACULTY

Migration and exodus of teachers may be a major concern for India due to the effect of the Foreign Educational Institutions Bill on our already declining staff strength in higher education. India may face a real challenge of retaining their finest faculties. Indian faculties might leave their home country by being allured by the Foreign Educational Providers for better facilities for undertaking research in emerging areas.

According to a recent report of HRD Ministry, premier educational institutes like the Indian Institute of Technology (IITs) and the Indian Institute of Management (IIMs) is facing a faculty crunch with nearly one-third of the vacant posts. According to a report published in IANS (2010) around 35 per cent posts are vacant in the central universities, 25 per cent in the IIMs, 33.33 per cent in the National Institute of Technology (NITs). It is really a matter of concern as these massive vacant positions lead to more workload on teaching, affecting quality of teaching and research.

THE TASK AHEAD

It is explicit that only Internationalization cannot provide all the solutions in the field of higher education in India. India's higher education segment is presently encountering grave challenges like the need to expand student access, upgrading quality to accomplish excellence, mobilizing the required resources and strengthening the regulatory role. All these are complex issues and there are no simple solutions to it. The Indian government is making an effort by suggesting various reforms but it still has a long way to go.

In recent years, the government has taken steps to attract international students, including the streamlining of the visa process and the granting of multi-entry visas for long-term courses. Universities have been advised to set up international student centers, special websites, familiarization sessions and periodic monitoring of foreign students. Under the Promotion of Indian Education Abroad, during the 10th Five Year Plan (2002-07), the UGC has attempted to attract international students to India. The government has created an exclusive scheme called Direct Admission of Students Abroad wherein 15 per cent seats have been reserved in premier technical institutions such as the National Institutes of Technology and centrally funded institutions for foreign nationals and non-resident Indians. The Manipal Academy of Higher Education has offshore branches in Nepal and Malaysia. Manipal Academy in India also hosts a large number of Malaysian students in medical courses because of its twinning arrangement with the medical school in Malacca. Birla Institute of Technology has campuses in Oman and Dubai. IGNOU has thousands of students registered abroad. APTECH and NIIT also have branches abroad and as many as 16 Indian institutions have offshore centers (Power, 2010).

To restrain outward mobility of students it is important that we create world class Universities in India which would be recognized internationally. Singapore, Dubai and Qatar have a Knowledge City which provides high quality education. The government of India plans to set up five universities to cater to the needs of overseas Indian students, with half of the seats reserved for them. The first such university in Bangalore is to be set up in partnership with the Manipal Group. Several private institutions having world-class infrastructure like the Vellore Institute of Technology which already hosts several hundred students from China. On the same lines of the Knowledge City, Education Hubs at Chandigarh, Sonepat, and Lavasa are ongoing initiatives to allure international students. Developed as a center of excellence for education and research in hospitality and management education, Lavasa has already commenced academic programmes (Agarwal, 2010).

Very few Indian institutions find a place in the global rankings of universities. The Shanghai world rankings of the top 500 universities/institutes include only three Indian Institutes of Technologies and one Indian Institute of Management at the lower end. The Times global rankings of the top 100 also find a mention of just a couple of Indian institutions. In terms of published papers, India has slipped from the 8th place in 1985 to the 14th in 2006 (Paul, 2009). The report of the National Accreditation and Assessment Council (NAAC) shows that only 30 per cent of the universities and only 10 per cent of the colleges are "A" grade or "Five Star" institutions and the rest are tolerable or poor. NAAC proposes to introduce the India Education Index (IEI) for ranking institutes based on academic, research performance and other parameters. The outcome will help in the international comparison of institutes. NAAC has entered into an MoU with higher learning institutes in the United States, Taiwan, Norway, Kuwait and with the Commonwealth of Learning (COL) to facilitate collaborative work on quality assurance in higher education institutions (Muzammil, 2010).

In the 11th Plan, the public expenditure on education is only about three per cent of the Gross National Product; more particularly, only 0.37 per cent of Gross Domestic Product is spent on higher education in India compared to 0.50 per cent in China and 1.40 per cent in the US (Agarwal, 2006). Although government funding has gone up over the past couple of years, public funds continue to be scarce and unevenly distributed. As a result, most institutions face economic hurdles and have raised fees, particularly for professional programmes, to substitute or supplement public funds. This has made higher education expenditures and only a few students qualify for loans, thereby restricting access to higher education. Thus, since the funds received by Indian universities are small, they are not in a position to cope with the Foreign Education Providers who have a much better infrastructure, technology, pedagogical skills, faculties and well developed market driven courses.

The Indian government should offer tax concessions/fiscal incentives to private companies to set up campuses of higher education. The private sector should run universities not for a profit-basis but as a part of corporate social responsibility. Open Universities need to be encouraged to offer quality programmes at the least cost. There is great need for providing broadband connectivity to all students along with low priced computer accessibility. If online learning can be made available through rural and small town institutions, then the access to and quality of higher education can be improved. A majority of the country's students (88.9%) are enrolled in undergraduate programmes, with merely 9.4 per cent enrolled in postgraduate and just 0.7 per cent in doctoral programmes. Enrollment by major field of study is skewed in favour of the arts and humanities (45%), followed by science (20.5%) and commerce (18%). Only 17 per cent of students pursue professional studies, which are dominated by engineering and medicine (Agarwal, 2009). Most of our public Universities lack vocational focus and churns out graduates who have difficulty securing employment. These Universities need to start innovative courses like apparel design, jewellery design, animation technology, etc., which some private Universities like Amity University and Lovely Professional University offer. Also flexibility in switching streams should be introduced. A student should be allowed to study any subject-combination provided he has the acumen for it. The logic is that a student good in history or language can also be proficient in Mathematics or physics. Moreover, Indian Universities can encourage 'brain gain' by appointing Indians who are teaching abroad to teach in Universities in India through higher remuneration and adequate resources for advancement. With the increase in the standard of living in most of the metropolis in India, many non-resident Indians have come back to India and many more are seeking ways to come back to their homeland. The Presidency University of Kolkata has introduced such a flexible curriculum and has also absorbed a number of such Indian teachers from abroad.

So higher education in India needs to adopt a holistic approach by changing and aligning with global norms to ensure an internationally comparable academic structure, academic calendar, grading procedure, methods of instruction and granting of degrees which will be recognized internationally.

REFERENCES

Agarwal, P. (2006). "Higher Education in India: The Need for Change", ICRIER Working Paper (New Delhi) June.

Agarwal, P. (2008). India in the context of International Student Circulation. In H. De Wit (Eds.), *The Dynamics of International Student Circulation in a Global Context,* pp. 83-112. Rotterdam and Taipei: Sense Publishers.

Agarwal, P. (2009). *Indian Higher Education: Envisioning the Future*. New Delhi, Sage.

Agarwal, P. (2010). Internationalization of Indian Higher Education. *University News*, Vol. 48 No. 37, pp. 46-53.

Government of India (2002). Tenth Five Year Plan-Sectoral Policies and Programmes, Vol. 2, Planning Commission, New Delhi.

Government of India, (2007). Draft Report of Working Group on Higher Education-11th Five Year Plan, Planning Commission, New Delhi.

Gnanam, A. (2010). Can Foreign Providers Supplement the Indigenous Efforts to Improve Access and Quality of Higher Education In India? *University News*, Vol. 48 No. 37, pp. 42-45.

Khadria, B. (2007). "Tracing the Genesis of Brain Drain in India through its State Policy and Civil Society", In Nancy Green and Francois Weil, Eds., *Citizenship and Those Who Leave: The Politics of Emigration and Expatriation,* University of Illinois Press, Urbana and Chicago, pp. 265-282.

Muzammil, Mohd. (2010). Foreign Education Providers in Indian higher education: Motivation and Implication. *University News*, Vol. 48 No. 37, pp. 90-96.

NKC (National Knowledge Commission). 2007, 2008. *Report to the nation 2006* and *Report to the nation 2007*. New Delhi: Government of India.

Paul, Samuel. (2009). Internationalization of Higher Education: Strategic Implications *Economic and Political Weekly*, Vol. 64 No. 9, pp. 36-41.

Powar, S.K., (2010). Marketing of higher education through offshore campuses, *University News*, Vol. 48 No. 6, pp. 16-13.

Shah, Beena. (2010). Foreign Education Providers in India: Genesis, Actions and Reactions. *University News*, Vol. 48 No. 37, pp. 21-29.

http://www.edcil.co.in IANS (Indo-Asia News service) report of 18 August 2010.

15

Contemporary Issues and Trends in Higher Education

Jasim Ahmad

The world is progressing very fast in almost all aspects of development including higher education. There are some important points of views regarding key trends for higher education in the 21st century. The author addresses 15 key trends – some new, some ongoing, some evolving; as perceived by the author and published in different journals and media. Each trend is constantly evolving and new ones are emerging. By understanding these trends and technologies, higher-education institutions may be able to prepare students to become the next generation of productive employees and innovative leaders the world needs.

SOCIAL NET-WORKING

The biggest trend under this category includes the emergence of Web 2.0 and social net-working phenomena such as blogs and wikis, as well as new online video repository and delivery websites such as YouTube, iTunes U, Big Think, etc. The invention of smart phones and other intelligent devices has also enhanced mobile learning commonly referred to as m-learning, creating new channels for content delivery, video expansion online, and broadcasting. The adoption of virtual reality websites such as Second Life has provided higher-education institutions with new venues for classes and learning.

The Universities continue to examine ways in which they can integrate these tools to further enhance the campus and learning experience and improve productivity through flexible learning environments. Many universities view technology as a key asset that helps them create an intellectually vibrant and relevant campus to attract the best students and faculty.

RAPID EXPANSION AND INTERNATIONALIZATION

Higher education globally is the thing in demand the most, and its demand tends to continue to grow in future. There are more than 100 million college students worldwide, new campuses are being built, and existing campuses are expanding. For last few years, Indian higher education has grown at a break-neck speed. For example, Indian higher education has grown by 20 per cent in one year and added more than 5,000 colleges to the system. Likewise, Gross

Enrollment Ratio (GER) grew from 12.5 per cent in 2007-08 to 17.3 per cent in 2009-10. Clearly, access to higher education is very important for a developing country like India and it is encouraging to see the growth. Universities are competing internationally for resources, faculty, the best students, and educational funding.

The international expansion creates opportunities for students and faculty in terms of exchange programmes and expanded campus environments. Countries like China, India, and the Middle East have quickly become key areas for widespread campus growth. The learning model varies by country and institution, starting from replicating the home campus, to building local capacity, to participating in faculty exchanges. These global learning environments give students an opportunity to expand their portfolios to include experience that is valued in today's workforce. Universities in turn use their foreign campuses to attract top research talent and build international relationships, establishing a global presence and helping develop local capacity. This can be used in future to create a powerful manpower hub.

TECHNICAL AND INFORMATION LITERACY

Now-a-days the higher education institutions are taking steps to enhance technical literacy and create a campus culture that encourages faculty to use tablets, computers, power point, the internet, smart devices, and other innovative tools in their curriculum transaction.

Information literacy is another area of concern, while many students may be device-savvy, they may not necessarily be information-savvy. Students today, having for the most part grown up with technology, possess more technical abilities with computers and software, yet many have not learned how to use technology for academic purposes. Universities are addressing this through a variety of methods, such as library programmes that include workshops, training programmes and instructional services. At the same time, universities are creating a technology culture through a variety of venues – common areas, support desks, alumni meet, campus selection programmes and student employment programmes. Technical and information literacy continues to gain importance on campuses, ensuring that students are viable candidates in the global workplace.

BRAND CONSCIOUSNESS, ENROLMENT, AND RETENTION

Institutions realize that the Internet is a viable way to market academic programmes to prospective students while enhancing its brand. Universities are also establishing online parties and networking websites for newly admitted freshmen, allowing them to interact virtually with campus services and the campus community before they get into the institution.

YouTube's education channels and iTunes U are effective not only for teaching and learning, but also for marketing the university's products. Videos of sports rallies, seminars, concerts, and other events are posted to these sites, effectively giving prospective students a glimpse of the university's offerings.

Colleges are also using technology to help build an attractive brand – one that assures prospective students and parents that upon graduation, students will be prepared to participate in a technologically advanced, global economy. To attract and retain prospective students, some universities have developed student blogger programmes, where an assigned roster of current students blogs about their daily routines. Some universities also have respective "pages" on Facebook and Twitter to enable communications with incoming fresher.

MOBILE TELECOMMUNICATION AND E-LEARNING

The college students today depend too much on their mobile phones and PDAs. One-third of the 97 per cent of college students who own a cell phone no longer use land lines to make voice calls. The freedom, convenience, and cost savings that mobile phones provide are invaluable to students, whether they are living away from home or commuting daily to and from institution, home, and work place. With the spreading of mobile phones on campus, colleges everywhere are compelled to capitalize on feature-rich phones that are capable of much more than just voice calls. Adoption of the iPhone and other smart devices that have Internet access allows students and faculty to perform a wide range of tasks virtually anywhere they have cell phone services. These tasks range from administrative process of registration, to academic process of downloading class materials, to social process of instant messaging, to the functional process of checking transportation schedules. Mobile learning is also on the rise on college campuses that are exploring using e-book readers, PDAs and smart phones to deliver courseware, field data, short tutorials, and classroom polls.

INNOVATIVE CAMPUS AND PEDAGOGICAL CENTERS

In addition to new and renovated buildings, several higher-education institutions have created areas called "campus commons." These areas redefine how traditional buildings, rooms, and spaces are designed, built, and used. High-traffic areas such as the campus library or computer lab typically are the starting point for developing campus commons. For example, many universities are transforming their libraries into campus commons by building food courts, creating social gathering and computer gaming areas. and adding collaborative seating arrangements.

In these attempts libraries have been at the forefront as books are increasingly digitized and space is re-evaluated. Campus commons are evolving to become key locations where technologies can be showcased and explored. Some institutions are reinventing these spaces as pedagogical or innovation centers where faculty can learn how to integrate technology into the curriculum, or where students can go to watch and make video projects.

CAMPUS SAFETY AND SECURITY

The physical safety of college campuses has always been a top priority for institutions. In the aftermath of the Virginia Tech shootings (USA) in April

2007, almost 100 per cent of the institutions has revised their emergency plans, and 80 per cent have increased funding for campus safety. The United States House of Representatives passed a Bill in February 2008 that would require colleges and universities to issue public warnings within 30 minutes of an emergency or threat, as well as notify the public regarding campus safety information. In April 2008, the bill was revised to require public warnings within 30 minutes of confirmation of an emergency or threat. Universities must have the equipment to be able to issue these warnings quickly and directly to the campus population and surrounding community.

In India, the honourable supreme court has also made a remarkable judgment regarding ban on ragging in educational institutions to check malpractices and various incidents of death on account of ragging in college campuses.

EVOLVING PROCESS OF TEACHING AND LEARNING

The education process continues to evolve from one-to-one, i.e. teacher to student to collaborative learning. Web 2.0 and social networking tools such as blogs and wikis, and online social gathering websites such as Flicker, Twitter, etc. are enhancing and facilitating collaborative learning and are being used widely on many campuses. The delivery of content has evolved dramatically, as many professors opt to post all class material, including complete audio and/or video recordings of lectures, on sites like iTunes U and YouTube. Because students spend much of their time online, university professors see the value of posting academic materials on these popular sites where students can download and interact with the course materials in a location where they also seek entertainment. Open source course-management systems such as Module and similar systems on Facebook are just some applications being reconfigured to support more content and student collaboration.

COLLABORATION AND PARTNERSHIP OF PRIVATE SECTOR

Collaboration is a distinguishing attribute of higher education. Universities are seeking ways to facilitate collaboration to enhance research, classes, foreign exchanges, alumni relationships, and private sector partnerships. A variety of venues have emerged to make collaboration easier and more accessible.

Virtual meeting-place and application-sharing tools such as Cisco WebEx is efficient web-based collaboration solutions that help improve productivity and decrease communication and travel. WebEx simulates the visual communications that occur between students and teachers in the traditional classroom setting. For example, professors use the WebEx "attention indicator" feature to monitor whether students are giving the class their full attention. Professors can also require students participating in the WebEx session to turn on "desktop sharing" to ensure that the students are actively engaged in the class.

GREEN CAMPUS/ENERGY CONSERVATION AND SUSTAINABLE DEVELOPMENT

Green or eco friendly has become a key topic in many industry sectors globally, including higher education. Universities are continually seeking and identifying ways to conserve energy efficiently, provide energy using alternative methods and resources, and recycle discarded electronics, hardware components known as "e-waste." Carbon foot printing, green dorms, green institutes, and green blueprints are just a few examples of green programmes on college campuses. Common conservation practices include implementing cloud computing through server virtualization; installation of devices to generate alternative energy, providing resource sharing; collocating equipment to reduce energy consumption, costs, power, and space; buying energy-efficient equipment; donating IT equipment; deploying recycling programmes; and supporting teleporting.

DISTANCE AND OPEN LEARNING

For providing higher education to anybody who desires at any stages of life, distance and open universities are coming up at national as well as international level. These universities and schools of open learning provide opportunities to those who are somewhere employed or engaged in some activities or vocation and cannot get education through regular mode. It also provides chance to those who for any reason could not get education and at later stage of life want to pursue education. Through distance learning employees can also learn new and upcoming technologies and skills in the area of his or her work to make them up to date and effective. All the distance universities and schools are getting enrolment of large number of students in different courses due to mass awareness and desire of getting more and quality improvement in their lives.

STRATEGIC PLANS AND TECHNOLOGY

Budget and efficiency are ongoing concerns in higher education. In response, institutions are starting to adopt certain practices from private enterprises, such as strategic planning that integrates technology as a key component.

"Cloud computing" – a process that allows files and data to be stored on a remote network using the Internet – is another approach that may potentially lower IT costs and is also a current topic of interest among universities.

In addition, universities are developing long-term financial strategies to ensure that technology is incorporated into the budget. Leasing IT equipment is becoming a more common way to manage IT costs and budgets. Leasing has become more popular and is being used effectively by a number of higher-education institutions to ensure that the allocation of funds for new technology and upgrades is consistent.

ENTERTAINMENT IN EDUCATION (EDUTAINMENT)

Higher education along with entertainment is becoming more intertwined. This can be experienced on iTunes and YouTube, sites commonly used for entertainment only. Teachers are now combining the two, using various videos that contain both educational and entertainment value in broadcasts and posting course content on education channels to create a more engaging learning environment. Computer gaming is emerging in teaching and learning as well, and thousands of schools have a presence in Second Life, using these virtual spaces for socializing, teaching, learning, and branding.

Television broadcasting companies such as the BBC, MTV, NBC, DD, and ABC are quickly developing methods to integrate broadcast media with higher education. This trend supports the marked increase in the use of multimedia devices on college campuses where content is accessible not only through computers, but also through TVs and Smartphone. Campuses are evaluating the benefit of broadcasting campus TV programmes over IP networks.

VOCATIONAL, PROFESSIONAL AND TECHNICAL EDUCATION

In the age of economy, everyone wants to earn more and more. Now the very purpose of education has got transformed from a means of producing good human beings having high morals of human life to the creation of a person of high productive value in terms of money, goods and services. To achieve this objective of life, everyone needs to get vocational, professional or technical education, which provides employment and develop skills to open and run his own business and to become entrepreneur. Because of this fact a trend is observed that more and more institutions of this kind are showing mushrooming growth. It is being found that very few aspirants are seen to take admission in classical subjects or courses and seats in these courses remain unfilled whereas in technical, vocational and professional courses there are high levels of competition to get in.

QUALITY CONCERN AND CONSOLIDATION

Indian higher education has shown the growth of 20 per cent in one year and added more than 5,000 colleges to the system. The gross enrollment ratio (GER) grew from 12.5 per cent in 2007-08 to 17.3 per cent in 2009-10. These growths reflect the access of masses to higher education which is a very important signal for a developing country like India. It is satisfactory and encouraging to see this growth. This trend invites our higher education policy makers and regulators towards consolidation.

On the policy front, it is already recognized that systemic quality needs improvement. Improvement in quality and providing more funds to state universities should be the focus of India's higher education policy in the coming years. It will be interesting to see whether policy reforms in higher education move beyond politics and see the reality of implementation.

CONCLUSION

In the 21st century, technology is going to play an increasing role in higher education. Institutions will adopt innovative solutions that will change the way students learn, communicate, produce, collaborate, and study both on and off campus. Ways and means are needed to be found out that can improve interactions among faculty, staff, and students. Creating innovative services from current and future technologies requires a powerful, reliable, expandable, and secure IT infrastructure that has adequate bandwidth, quality of service, and storage. Many colleges and universities have already developed short- and long-term plans to ensure success in meeting their current and future needs. Growth, improvement in quality and internationalization are the great challenges for Indian higher education. A very good balance is needed in quality vs. quantity; private vs. public and for-profit vs. not-for-profit.

REFERENCES

Agarwal, Pawan (2006). Higher Education in India: The Need for Change, Working Paper 180, ICRIER, New Delhi

Agarwal, Pawan (2009), *Indian Higher Education: Envisioning the Future*, Sage India, New Delhi.

Bok, Derek (2003), *Universities in the Market Place: The Commercialization of Higher Education*, Princeton University Press, Princeton, New Jersey, USA.

David Lim, *Quality Assurance in Higher Education – A Study of Developing Countries* Hants, England: Ashgate Pub. Ltd., 2001.

Philip, G. Altbach, Robert O. Berdahl and Particia J. Gumport (1998), *American Higher Education in the Twenty-First Century: Social, Political and Economic Challenges*, The Johns Hopkins University Press, Baltimore and London.

Tracey Wilen-Daugenti and R, Alva Grace McKee (Aug, 2008), *21st Century Trends for Higher Education,* Top Trends, 2008–2009, Higher Education Practice, Cisco Internet Business Solutions Group (IBSG).

www.dreducation.com, Rahul Chaudaha, Policy India Higher Education Data, Posted 8th January 2012

www.ibbc.lt/economicreformshighereducation.pdf, dated 30.10.2012

www.indiastudychannel.com, dated 28.10.2012

www.wikipedia.org/wiki/Education_in_India, dated 25.10.2012

16

Tertiary Education in India: Challenges for Privatization

Gyanendra Kumar Rout

Universities are breeding ground of innovation. It is the place where the young and fresh mind gets the necessary conducive environment to develop. No wonder, all of the developed countries has put the biggest thrust on developing centers of excellences such as Oxford, Harvard, MIT and Stanford. Their strategy has borne fruit as would have seen one after another breath taking innovation churned out by these universities. Can anybody forget Google? The duo of Sergey Brin and Larry page, two novice university students, did something unthinkable. They created world's most powerful search engine 'Google' that has changed the world forever. The question is why similar success stories are not replicated in our country. The reason is not very difficult to fathom. The government has neglected demands of higher education for longer. The result is very obvious. We have failed to produce a single innovation that could take the world by storm.

Our economy is growing at the rate of 8 per cent and to sustain that rate we do not have skilled talents for the industries. We lack good teachers, good managers, good quality engineers and out-of-the-box-thinkers in every sphere of life. But how to ameliorate the situation is the immediate question which arises in mind. One will be surprised to know that India has around 250 universities and around 11,000 colleges and yet the world has not seen anything substantial from them. The point to pay attention is that the proportion of students going colleges and university is as dismal as 6 per cent. There are questions being raised about the mushrooming of colleges and universities but the irony is that we are not able to cater to the needy age group. In the scheme of providing higher education to the masses, finance has a very important role. One can understand that government alone will not be able to bear the huge financial implication thus we will have to seek private participation. The government has allocated an amount of 52,000 crore in the education sector. While presenting the budget, Finance Minister Shri Pranab Mukherjee had said "Over 70 per cent of Indians will be of working age in 2025. In this context, universalizing access to secondary education, increasing the percentage of our scholars in higher education and providing skill training is necessary."

One of the emerging challenges of privatization of higher education, certainly, will be the question of how higher learning being a scarce resource to be judiciously distributed to set the tune of democratic practice in a traditional hierarchical society like India. True, educational domain in general, higher learning in particular will be meaningless unless educational processes have filtered through desirable levels of democratic values. No doubt, democratic ethos is central to the way the education system is organized and pedagogy is practiced and knowledge system is evolving. However, given the peculiarities of material dimensions of the caste system in Indian society in terms of appropriating developmental opportunities, as empirical studies show (Bhatt, 1975 and Sarkar, 1978), socio-cultural backwardness falls back on to determine higher education as well (Raju, 2008 and Thorat, 2009). Nonetheless to mention, globally too, socially unequal have not been benefited, despite the fact that many policies envisaged to include them.

(Altbach, 2010). Increasing democratization, in other words, would gradually change elite domination in higher education (Yashpal, 2009) and the system of pedagogy and knowledge can be more inclusive and egalitarian so that it can accommodate diversities. True, for the marginalized, higher learning will open up certainly desirable, but multiple mobility patterns. To begin with it would transcend their deprived socio-cultural conditions that have historically been constructed and reconstructed with a set of exclusive practices. Secondly, it allows them to change their traditional occupations to secular occupation and gives opportunities in the decision making positions of the state institutions. Finally, above all, a new culture of modernity can be visualized (Weisskopf, 2004 and Ciotti, 2010). However, the issues social justice will be a challenging question and worry some in the institutions of higher learning, once its governing orderings shift over to the private agencies and to the global competitive players (Babu, 2010). At a time when the structural adjustments of the political economy of the state restructure its neo-liberal agenda, the state of education was thrown on to privatization. As expected, its logic is to minimize the state intervention and maximize market to grow. It has further extended in the form of cross-bordering of higher education services in the post-reform period in the backdrop of globalization. It is in this context, this paper would detour into the unintended consequences of privatization of higher education in general and the emerging challenges on the questions of equality in particular. Indian society, being held back on its diversity in a variety of forms, how the higher education sector, in the backdrop of the structural changes of society, grapples with the question of equality, has been a central theme to the policy makers, analysts and academics. Thus, the paper would narrow down to examine the socio-political and economic dimensions of higher education in India, so as to shed light on the larger question of development and equality.

In a new order of things in the backdrop of political economy nationally and globally, the regimes and its apparatuses of the state subject to structural changes. This can easily be observed the way neo-liberal policies were doctorate in higher education with consensus from the business establishments. Structural adjustments organized internally in the system tend to make the public institutions, their services and deliveries to be competent globally. However, these external factors as a set of policies and practices did reflect on the structural conditions of Indian society too. Although private education (mainly aided system) has already made their presence in the state of education, they were not exceptional from the issues of exclusion. External interventions to the educational system, for instance, high courts and the Supreme Court on the regulation and management of private educational institutions are a point of departure in this regard. Mushroom growth fake universities in different part of India also challenge the moral questions of the system.

On the other side of the spectrum, as the empirical studies show disparities and sure, it has been widening not only in terms of the economy, but also accessing higher education as well. In other words, having fed each other, the new forms of disparities, both vertical and horizontal, is leading to exclusion. For instance, high dropout rate in the schools, due to multiple factors, certainly will lead to legitimately exclude children for higher education, that too often not because of their own fault. Students drawn from the lower sections of society, including females, find difficult to cope with the situation as they underwent extreme humiliation within these enlightened institutions itself. Given the socio-structural conditions and the governing principles of domination with a variety of conditions of class/caste, perhaps, shed the light on the challenging issues of social justice in the education system. Scholarship on the questions about higher education shows that there has been a continuous elite dominating on the one hand and perpetual marginalization of the other, over the accessibility of this scarce resource. The gradual departure of policies on education from the fundamental principle of social justice to privatization requires new theoretical explanations and their ideological positions as higher learning being treated as a private meritorious good, than a public good. To foreground the intricacies in the changing domain, we focus on the following critical questions. To begin with, the structure of the political economy of education today has been undergoing tremendous change.

Admitting this fact, whether policy judgments towards massive privatization along with opening up of foreign direct investment in higher education, sustains the democratic practices in the pedagogy? Secondly, are essentially these mushrooming private educational institutions to be private in totality? In a corollary to that, what are the politics behind naming them as private for the entire cost of education is born from the public by imposing different kind of fees including governmental concessions? In such a condition, finally, can we imagine inclusive, participatory, and diverse critical thought in the emerging private education system as the inclusive strategies are being central to the on the going growth model of the political economy?

PROCESSES OF PRIVATIZATION OF TERTIARY EDUCATION

Privatization precisely means a form of free market capitalism that signifies the centrality of merits, efficiency and competition regulated by the state apparatus. Its process, as usual, underlines several dimensions and reflections on society at large. To begin with, new terminologies, such as, cost effective, market force, meeting demands, and delivering quality goods etc., help us to make sense of the process of privatization. However, at the policy level, its process is much complicated, for instance, it asks for selling the whole or part, charging for services, contracting out, buying out existing interest groups and repealing monopolies for diluting the public sector, encouraging alternative institutions, withdrawing state institutions, and divestment (Walford, 1990). The public on the other spectrum tends to interact differently or divert their imagination and perceives education as a commodity. Students in the context of Privatization, as is the inputs and examinations as a measured value for successful. By locating these new objective formations, in education, for Grace (1989: 207), is a robust way of thinking and encouraging academics who engaged in research activities of this kind. Hence, it is very clear by the fact that the social implications of the conceptual divide between private and public, and drawing the boundaries between these two critical domains. For analytical purposes, private education explains how public education is carried out through private means. In this scheme, public subsidies including tax rebates and land acquisition are being extended to the private education institutions. This would, indeed, attract the entrepreneurial groups to operate education in the private sector. However, for enterprising individuals, the policy of privatization would enable them to impose different kinds of fees upon students. Such practices would correspond to open market and result in Co modification of knowledge. While treating intellectual activities as commodities, social values of education would eventually be replaced by market values. Among other things, who would benefit from it is also a fundamental question. Obviously, it is alleged that the process of privatization has inbuilt class interest as well. Pooling resources into the privileged top stream of educational institutions for the elite sections will fundamentally be determined by one's capacity to pay. This would allow the private sector to grow and legitimize class its interest.

Many countries across the globe, introduced market-driven mechanism to coordinate their national higher education sector (William, 1995; Altbach, 2010). This paradigm shift in the domain of public investment can be seen as how the state reinvents new power structure in the education sector. New changes that are taking place in the domain of higher education, particularly ever growing private investments, have complicated the entire governing process in the academic environs. True market priorities would prevail in the new order of things. Instead of the single market in higher education, there are a number of market players who involved in the private investments. There are markets, for instance, for students and research staff, for lectures, for research grants and scholarship, for donations, for graduates, and for company training and so on. Through a market driven policy of the state, students and colleges are being encouraged to make their own cost benefit analyses, that too in economic terms (Jongbloed, 2003: 110-135). Fixing up of cost and profit calculation in education policy, no doubt, will erode the substantial aspects of education being a critical pedagogical activity (Dennison, 2003: 7-8). In other words, profit motives of the private higher education sector would also lead to the structural shift in the terrain of pedagogy to. This shift can largely be seen from social sciences to proliferation of job oriented courses, such as, professional and technical courses. Knowledge here becomes skill; whereas the process (teaching/learning) turns to be as products (students). In addition access/equity is negotiated by quality/excellence. Above all, the market will prevail over sociologies of education. Privileging professional/ technical knowledge over all other forms of knowing leads to hierarchies of knowledge, and disciplinary syncretism will be redundant. It is in this shift, standard of living determines the pursuance of education (Kunhaman, 2002: 105-106). Among other things, there is a cultural production of class and their interest in education. In such a situation, a fundamental question is that whether education would create and sharpen criticality and analytical power of the learner or, it would equip learners with marketable skills for the furtherance of capitalist to grow.

COUNTRY CONTEXT

The private initiative in education, especially higher education is not altogether new to India. Some of the leading universities namely, the Banaras Hindu University and the Aligarh Muslim University came up with the efforts of certain dedicated individuals and financial support of the community at large. Again, a large number of educational institutions in the country especially those concerned with general and professional higher education have been established on private and voluntary initiative with or without financial subsidy from the Government. Some of the prestigious modern universities in India even established by the efforts of certain dedicated individuals with private financial aid. This, indeed, was a unique in India as a form of public private partnership (Levi, 1994: 313). The concept of private institution, however, in the initial stage was meant to be sheer arbitrary, and was a relative category to express miscellaneous classes of educational institutions. Levi here argues that philanthropy lacks strong historical root in less developed countries in general with rare exception and Indian experience for him a rare exception. Arbitrary term, without much complexity gained public image from its inception and became a normative language in the domain of philanthropy (Cotton, 1999: 566-67). Hence, philanthropy was understood by the fact that private institutions were being supported by the public. During British rule, through the directives of the East India Company, the policy of grand-in-aid system was executed to encourage private institutions. There were three types of private institutions, for instance, nationalist, sectarians and caste communities, were operated with the support of individual philanthropist and local notables, before independence (Rudolph, 1972: 19). Even, in the post-independent India, the private sector was continuing to thrive and become a major domain in shaping the system of higher learning in the backdrop of the constitutional provision. Such historical patronage, led to the outgrowth of private higher education institutions over the years, and they constitute three-fourth of the total. There were two types of private institutions; aided and unaided. If the former was privately managed and publicly funded, the latter was both privately managed and funded colleges. In this respect, no doubt, the role of private initiative in higher education has been very crucial in the initial stages of independence.

It has been reported that many of the private educational institutions were to be nonviable and mediocre. It was largely due to the poor quality of delivery in their services and inadequate enrollment rates of students (Garg, 1977 and Kulandaiswamy, 2005). True, private aided educational institutions were to be abided the norms laid down by the statue of the concerned universities. They also used to receive financial aid from the state regularly, therefore, for financial matters; private aided institutions did not have any significant role in sharing the cost of education (Tilak, 1992: 131). In spite of the fact that the state has authority over affiliation, pattern of aiding, and regulation of education, it failed to comply with constitutional promises of social justice. In other words, the dominant culture has silently been reproduced in the educational institutions as the managements simultaneously enjoyed their local/estate power with knowledge governing power.

Indian Constitution provided the language and religion based minorities to establish higher education institutions of their choice under Article 30(1). Similarly Article 30(2) ensured financial aid to these institutions. In the Article 26 to the contrary, ensures freedom both to the majority and minority communities to establish and maintain institutions for charitable purpose.

As a result, these managements were continued to remain as sectarian and partisan organization of their own locality, community and organs of political parties. Moreover, these very institutions played key role in the local politics to circulate among the party cadres and supporters. Because of their affiliation with local political power structures, these managements used to receive under patronage and partisan prestige. The political elites simultaneously make governing rules of the system flexible. Conjoining local politics with governing power of education institutions, in a way, were benefited reciprocally both parties via nepotism, benefaction and influence. Much relaxed UGC Rule, in fact, fuelled the process from bad to worse. (Rudolph, 1972 and Krishna Kumar, 2004). Since most of the private agencies drawn from the elite sections of society, education was yet another domain through which they continued to govern on the state of education. In other words, a system of education thrived into half-backed capitalism, from half backed socialism, in the backdrop of the mixed economy of India. In addition to that, there were 20 fake universities illegally operating throughout India and highest number was found Uttar Pradesh followed by Delhi (UGC,

2006). Its logic is clear as the demands voucher for the creation of new institutions, no matter even for expanding private players in the education sector. This trend, perhaps, makes indispensability of the middle class in the private education sector as they are the only probable group can buy education by paying huge fees (Kapur and Mehta, 2007: 35). The outgrowth of self financial institutions, in the post-reform period, with one set of cross-border education system, has shown a paradigmatic shift in the higher education sector in India. This trend, in fact, draws our attention to the complexities of pedagogic practices on the one hand and its wide range of social consequence on the other. The emerging discourses on the privatization of higher education world over, especially among developing societies, indicates the fact that they have commercial intent to reduce education to be a sheer commodity. It is in this context, the state of education in India needs to be critically examined in the light of the political economy in general and education policy adjustments in particular. In the context of the current changing social and economic fabric of the country, it appears almost certain to go in for private funding of education. The recent paradigm shift in Indian economic and political philosophy has led to the demand of private universities so as to meet the challenge of the contemplated open economy and the demand for qualitative human resources and high level of R&D.

THE PARADIGM SHIFT

Recent shifts in the Indian economy opened up yet another entry for private universities, both domestically and globally, to enhance qualitative human resources and to contemplate with a new set of requirements in society. The state too has made a couple of attempts to rationalize privatization of education. To begin with, while presenting country paper in the UNESCO World Conference on Higher Education in 1998, HRD minister of India proclaimed that 'efforts have been mounted for mobilization of resources and recommended for a firm commitment to higher education, institutions of higher education should make efforts to raise their own resources by raising the fee levels, encouraging private donations and by generating revenues through consultancy and other activities'. Followed by it, the debates on private members Bill for Private Universities in the Parliament in 1995 and the new Act on the Establishment and Maintenance of Standards in Private Universities Regulations, 2003 can be seen in this context. Moreover, a series of Supreme Court verdicts in favour private players in education showed the attitude.

TOWARDS PRIVATE INVESTMENTS IN HIGHER EDUCATION

The basic objective of privatization of higher education in India was to reduce the number of publicly funded colleges and universities, authorize decentralization of academic administration and promote creativity, innovation and higher standard. In addition to that, in the post-reform period, the state, as it was stated earlier, brought about new avenues on how to mobilize alternative resources in the form of raising fee levels up to 20 per cent of the annual recurring cost per student, mobilization of internal and external sources such as sale of output, voluntary donations from industry, students loan and consultancy (Tilak, 1999: 63). In other words, the establishment of self-financing colleges which had the twin advantages in effects. Obviously, it would reduce the burden of the state, but at the same time these colleges get permission to charge high fees and mobilize their own resources as they wish (Shasrabuddhe and Srivastava, 1998: 422-423). But the concept of autonomous college and programme for their establishment brought severe criticism mainly because of the failure of delivering better education. Moreover, though the proclamation of the government was to encourage private funding without commercialization, in reality the intention of private agencies was to commercialize the education system. On the other side of the spectrum, industrial entrepreneurs like Mukesh Ambani and Kumarmangalam Birla were invited to prepare Policy Framework for Reforms in Education" for the Prime Minister's Council on Trade and Industry in 2000. On this trend, who would decide the fate of the education policy of the nation, led to a new shift in the history of higher education in India. Its logic, in fact, was as simple as to make education as a profitable market venture in favour of industrialists. True, at a time when economy, world over, has increasingly been knowledge based, education as it was assumed, opens new avenues for market expansion and competition to hit the market driven economy. This, perhaps the reason behind the entrepreneurial units like APTECH Company began with Aptech University, a peripheral unit of Aptech Education. (Babu, 2011). Society order to meet the artificially created market demand of growing IT professionals in India In this context, it is to be noted that albeit we tried to develop self-financing colleges in rural and urban areas to nurture competitive skilled, it will not sustain simply because of the rural poor cannot afford. Moreover, it is sure that these initiatives neither inclusive and nor socially oriented, as against what the policy makers imagined.

Among other things, to attract investment for educational institutions from individuals or corporate bodies, the state for instance, announced tax-free and gave free hands to mobilize resources. In case, institutions were unable to attract donations, then they were allowed to charge high tuition fee from the students. Liberal attitude towards fee structure and compulsory cost recovery from students at the policy level were justified so as to indiscriminately reduce the burden of public financing. In doing so, it was believed that the capitation fee colleges can tap untapped resources for the development of higher education by charging a higher fee. Understandably, UGC devised a fee structure for various professional courses, for instance, medicine and BDS for the private unaided colleges and deemed to be universities. Fee structure for various professional courses in private unaided deemed universities in which for medicine the fee rate was ₹ 1,30,000 while for BDS one lakh. For management courses, fee rate was ₹ 50,000 (see http://www.ugc.ac.in).

No concrete evidence is available to us to prove that these capitation fee colleges are delivering qualitative education (Kaul, 1993). From the supply side, profit motives and political influences of the private education providers led to the outgrowth of these capitation fee colleges (Tilak, 1990). As the recent reports suggest there were 82 private and deemed universities 7,964 private colleges and 150 foreign private institutions operational in India (Agarwal, 2007). However, from the demand side, there was a historically conditioned class of rich and well-to-do people consisting of politicians, top bureaucrats, business executives, small and big industrialists, traders, businessmen, technocrats, professionals and large land holders who are able and are willing to pay higher fee rate (Kothari, 1986: 594). According to Kothari, it was the pressure from the same group, which pursued for privatization policies. Though private education providers are adherent to the legal framework, the state of higher education under the private dispensation, have intrinsic problems of commercialization and therefore, education service can easily become an illicit business too. These institutions began to charge huge donations and capitation fees, almost 10 to 20 times greater than the actual fee of any publicly funded college. To fuel up the process of commercialization, the capitation fee institutions introduced job oriented courses. It has twin advantage, at one level it would attract the students as these courses guarantee quick job opportunities on the other hand the private providers would get freedom to fix the price tag of the course as they wish (Mukhopadhayay, 1996). In other words, the logic of mobilizing untapped resources for education, in the form of privatization, consequently produce the culture of making profit out of higher education.

CONCLUSION

No wonder, policies for enhancing accessibility and expanding more educational opportunities in India, are implicitly guided by principles of inclusiveness and social justice and at the same time, reducing the elite domination in the existing social system. The introduction of social justice is being debated, in this regard, becomes central to make sense of the conditions of equity and address cumulative inequalities that are structurally imprinted in the social system itself. However, the new challenges in the domain of the political economy of higher education in developing countries are in twofold; narrowing unequal accessibility between several social and cultural groups, and satisfying the requirements of the global market. The vision, principle and goal of higher education policy of India today delineate these broader themes. Of late, the policies on higher education extended to help a new perspective for the policy makers, governing institutions, practitioners and academics. The main objectives of the plan were expansion of enrollment in higher education with inclusiveness, quality, and relevant education, with necessary academic reforms at the university and college systems. It is true that, through time, public financing for higher education has been shrinking. This resulted to a huge expenditure and investment gap between the resources required and resources held by the state. The investment gap has been attributed to the consequential effect of market forces that guided the developments in higher education. Sharing cost of education by students was logically placed as the very education has been treated as a long term investment for personal economic growth. Hence, privatization and worse forms of commercial practices have guided the present phase in the development of higher education.

REFERENCES

Albach, G. Philip. (2010). 'The Global Academic Revolution: Implications for India', Foundation Day lecture and National Seminar. Thiruvananthapuram: The Kerala State Higher Education Council.

Agarwal, Pawan. (2007). 'Private Higher Education in India: Status and Prospects', *The Observatory on borderless Higher Education*, UK.

Babu, Suresh G.S. (2011). Privatization of Higher Education In India: Challenges of social Equality, *Global Conclave of Young Scholars of Indian Education,* New Delhi, NUEPA.

Babu, Suresh G.S. (2010). Emerging Challenges of Equality: Private Education Sector in Kerala in Yagati Chinna Rao and Sudhakara Karakoti (Eds.) *Exclusion and Discrimination: Concepts, Perspectives and Challenges*, New Delhi: Kanishka Publishers.

Bhatt, A. (1975). *Caste, Class and Politics: An Empirical Project of Social Stratification in Modern India*, Delhi: Manohar Publications.

Ciotti, Manuela. (2010). *Retro-Modern India: Forging the Low-caste Self,* New Delhi: Routledge.

Dennison, M. George. (2003). Privatization: An Unheralded Trend in Public Higher Education, *Innovative Higher Education*, 28(1).

Grace, Gerald. (1989). Education: Commodity or Public Good, *British Journal of Educational Studies*, 37(3).

Jongbloed, Ben. (2003). 'Marketisation in Higher Education, Clark's Triangle and the Essential Ingredients of Markets', *Higher Education Quarterly*, 57(2).

Kapur, Devesh and Mehta, Pratap Bhanu. (2007). '*Mortgaging the Future: Indian Higher Education,*' Brookings NCAER India Policy Forum.

Kaul, Rekha. (1993). *Caste and Class and Education: Politics of the Capitation Fee Phenomenon in Karnataka*, New Delhi: Sage.

Kothari, V.N. (1986). Private Unaided Engineering and Medical Colleges: Consequences of Misguided Policy, *Economic and Political Weekly*, 21 (14), 593-96.

Kulandaiswamy, V.C. (2005. 18th May). Reconstruction of Higher Education in India: *The Hindu*.

Kumar, Krishna. (2004. 12th March). Aiming Higher: Case for Private Capital in Education*: The Times of India*.

Kunhaman, M. (2002). *Globalization: A Subaltern Perspective*, Thiruvananthapuram: Centre for Subaltern Studies.

Levi, C. Daniel. (1994). Problems of privatization, in Jamil Salmi and Adriaan M. Vespers (Eds.) *Revitalizing Higher Education*, Pergamon: Publishers of the IAU Press.

Mukhopadhyay, Asok. (1996). Liberalization and Higher Education in India: *The Indian Journal of Public Administration*, Vol. XLII (3), July-Sept.

Raju, Saraswati. (2008). Gender Differentials in Access to Higher Education in *Higher Education in India: Issues Related to Expansion, Inclusiveness, Quality and Finance*, New Delhi: UGC.

Rudolph, Susanne Hoiber and Rudolph, I Lloyd. (1972). *Education and Politics in India, Studies in Organization, Society and Polity*, Madras: Oxford University Press.

Shasrabuddhe, Milind and Srivastava. (1998). Development in Higher Education: Caravan of 50 years, in Marmar Mukhopadhyay (*et al.*), *Education: The Next Millenium, Report of the World Conference Paper-III*, Howrah: Institute of Education, Rural Studies and Development.

Sarkar, N.K. (1978). *Social Structure and Development Strategy in Asia*, New Delhi: People's Publishing House.

Throat, Sukhadeo. (2009). *Dalits in India: Search for a Common Destiny*, New Delhi: Sage Publications.

Tilak, BG. Jandhyala, (1992). Capitation Fee Colleges: Some Issues for Discussion, *Journal of Higher Education*, 16(1).

Tilak, BG. Jandhyala, (1990), *Political Economy of Education in India*, Buffalo: State University Press.

University Grants Commission. (2006). Annual Report 2005-2006, New Delhi: *UGC* Verma, Vishiesh.1998. Privatization of Higher Education, in Marmar Mukhopadhyay (*et al.*), *Education: The Next Millennium, Report of the World Conference Paper-III*, Howrah: Institute of Education, Rural Studies and Development.

Walford, Geoffrey. (1990). *Privatization and Privilege in Education*, London: Routledge. William, G.L. 1995. 'The Marketisation' of Higher Education: Reforms and Potentials Reforms in Higher Education Finance', in D.D. Dill and B. Sporn (Eds.), *Patterns of Social Demand and University Reform: Through a Glass Darkly*, Oxford: Pergamon Press.

Weisskopf, E. Thomas. (2004). 'Impact of Reservation on Admissions to Higher Education in India', *Economic and Political Weekly*, 39 (39), 4339-4349.

Yashpal. (2009). Report of The Committee to Advise on Renovation and Rejuvenation of Higher Education. New Delhi: Government of India.

17

TQM for Quality Enhancement in Higher Education

Fauzia Khan and *Gaurav Singh Bafila*

Education is a deliberate enterprise and aim of all the nations is to provide good quality education to its citizens so that they may become capable of significantly contributing towards the development of the nation. Education, in general and Higher Education, in particular, all over the world is looked upon as a harbinger of all other changes – social, cultural, economic, scientific and technological. Higher Education, as a deliberate enterprise of mankind, always aims at providing quality programmes to the citizens of the nation so as to take them on an onward march towards progress and prosperity.

The Indian higher education system is the third largest in the World, after China and United States, and in a system that had been expanding so rapidly, quality has been a casualty. Higher Education in India is at crossroads and is passing through exciting times. Increasing competition, changing global character and enhancement of technology are some of the significant factors creating a great impact on higher education. It is high time, that calls for serious attention to be given to quality in Higher Education.

CONCEPT OF QUALITY

'Quality' is a much-debated term. To some it is like 'beauty' that lies in the eye of the beholder. Those who believe in this are 'relativists', whereas those who believe quality can be specific attributes that can be identified, they are 'objectivists' (NAAC, 2007). The word quality comes from the Latin word qualis meaning 'what kind of'. Quality, according to American Society for Quality (1990), is the totality of features and characteristics of a product or services that bear on its ability to satisfy the stated or the implied needs.

Modern definition emphasises that quality is meeting or exceeding customer expectations. Customer can either be external customers or internal customers. External customers are the recipients of an output but are not part of the organization supplying it, whereas Internal customers are the recipients of another person's or department's output within an organization. Students, faculty members, administrative staff, management and the donors are the internal customers, and the community, government and employers are the external customers. Stakeholders include both internal customers and external customers.

Quality can be of two kinds, intrinsic and extrinsic. The intrinsic quality of higher education refers to the basic value and ideals, which form the very heart of higher education. It focuses on the knowledge creating processes and student learning. It represents the core of academic quality. The academic community can be seen as the guardian of intrinsic quality. The extrinsic quality refers to the capacities of an educational institution to respond to the needs of the society with whom they interact. It concerns the demands that society directs towards education. It should be determined by economic demands and the state demands both of which form pillars of society (Mukhopadhyay, 2005).

Quality in education is a matter of global quest; for India this quest is all the more important for it to become a global player. In order to succeed in this and to attend global standards in local settings, it is necessary for Indian educational institutions to both improve and sustain quality. Quality, in today's era, has proved to be a decisive factor in determining the success or failure of any service and Higher Education is no different. In this context, Quality Management helps in designing and implementing quality in higher educational institutions. Therefore, there is a need to give due importance to Quality Management in Higher Education.

QUALITY MANAGEMENT

Quality, long considered an ineffable abstraction in academe, is now discussed as something that can be managed and improved (Seymour, 1992). The term quality management refers to the policies, systems and processes designed to ensure the maintenance and enhancement of quality within an institution. Quality management is usually thought of, however, as a means to an end, not an end in itself. According to Trow (1994), higher education institution needs quality management (principles) to make it more efficient and to improve quality.

Need For Quality Management In Higher Education

Higher Education is an important area of concern in our educational system. Some of the reasons for the need of Quality Management in Higher Education are:

- *Competition*: With the advent of globalisation and the GATS (Global Agreement on Trade in Services), the educational environment, too, is characterised by increased competition. In this new era, the educational institutions would have to compete with each other for funds and students. Therefore, to survive such a competition, educational institutions would have to lay more emphasis on quality and its management.
- *Customer Satisfaction*: The customers of educational institutions are the students, parents and the sponsoring agencies and they are now becoming increasingly conscious of their rights. They want to get value for their money and also for the time spent. The customers are

now insisting on good quality teaching and receiving employable skills, and therefore, it is essential that the courses and programmes offered by the educational institutions are relevant to the needs of the current era with due emphasis placed on the transaction of these courses and programmes.

- *Maintaining Standards*: Educational institutions must not only set their own standards and maintain it, but must continuously improve it year after year; for which the institutions must make sincere efforts to improve quality of the educational transactions and also of the educational provisions and facilities.
- *Accountability*: Every institution must be accountable to its stakeholders in terms of its effectiveness and its efficiency, and must also maintain transparency so that the stakeholders can take appropriate decisions. Quality Management will ensure appropriate, optimum and judicious use of resources to deliver best possible results.
- *Improve Employee Morale and Motivation*: With a Quality Management System in place, the internal processes would become more systematic as a result of which every department would complement each other. This would help in developing internal-customer satisfaction leading to high morale and motivation among the staff (both academic and non-academic) which would help them in carrying out their duties and responsibilities more effectively.
- *Credibility, Prestige and Status*: Quality Management would result in persistent high levels of quality which would result in bringing credibility to the institution which would further lead to prestige, status and brand value; as a consequence of which such institutions would have greater capacity to attract better students, increased donations and grants and higher employer interest for easy and good placement of graduates.

Out of all approaches to Quality Management, the most eminent and popular is Total Quality Management (TQM). Although Total Quality Management developed within the manufacturing environment, the benefits are equally applicable to service entities such as higher education institutions. (De Jager and Nieuwenhuis, 2005). Total Quality Management offers a unique and reliable method to design and implement quality in educational institutions (Mukhopadhyay, 2005). Total Quality Management in education has been tried in many educational institutions with impressive results (Sallis, 1993). Many Educational Institutions in India, such as Shri Ram School Delhi, Model School Lucknow, BITS Pilani etc., have also benefited by adopting Total Quality Management.

Total Quality Management

The term 'Total Quality Management (TQM)' was developed by Feigenbaum, in 1961. Total Quality Management can be defined as the process of integration of all activities, functions and processes within an organization in order to achieve continuous improvement in cost, quality, function and delivery of goods and services for customer satisfaction. It refers to the application of quality principles to overall process and all the management functions in order to ensure total customer satisfaction (Ali and Shastri, 2010). According to Witcher (1990), TQM is composed of three terms:

Total: meaning that every person is involved including customer and suppliers.

Quality: implying that customer requirements are met exactly.

Management: indicating that senior executives are committed.

TQM involves a number of essential elements such as customer focus, teamwork, leadership, employee involvement, their training, continuous improvement, tools etc.

The implication of Total Quality Management in education is ensuring quality management in all aspects of educational management in the higher education institutions. According to Indian scriptures, each person lives in multiple planes: the physical, the intellectual, the emotional and the spiritual. Mukhopadhyay (2005) argues that in the same way each educational institution exists in the physical, the intellectual, the emotional and the spiritual planes of living. Quality management of all these, forms an integral part of TQM and only when quality management comprehensively takes charge of the development of an institution in all its planes, will it make TQM meaningful and functional. He feels that for an educational institution, the infrastructure, personnel, finances, rules and regulations, protocols. etc., provide the physical basis or plane of living. The intellectual plane of an educational institution is indicated by the curriculum, curriculum transaction or the teaching-learning processes, evaluation and intellectual discourses among the faculty and among the students and the faculty. The mental or the emotional dimension of an educational institution is indicated by the interpersonal relationships, affiliations to the institution, concern for the employees, organisational climate and other such non-intellectual attributes. The fourth dimension is the spiritual dimension. Deriving implication from the word 'spirit', the spiritual aspect of institutional life is indicated by attributes like higher goals, innovation, experimentation, exploration of new areas and modes of working, social and community concern and service. Whenever we witness creativity, the inner health of the organisation – non-partisan decisions, non-exploitation of the weak and the low, inspiration, institution above self-we experience its spiritual qualities. All that strives to reach higher levels, transcending the mundane, is spiritual. It is this component that renders quality an endless journey in search of new heights all the time.

Thus, TQM as applied to higher educational institutions means management of quality of infrastructure, intellectual, emotional and spiritual dimensions of institutional life. Only such comprehensive TQM of an educational institution can lead to Total Quality Education.

Implementation Strategies

Actual implementation of a quality improvement approach to operations requires movement from the philosophical concept of TQM to a strategic framework for implementation. According to McCormack (1992), when TQM efforts do not meet expectations, it is often because of poor tactics and lack of a strategic framework. There is no single best approach to implementing the TQM philosophy. An approach unique to the needs and culture of the organisation must be developed. (Sohal and Terziovski, 2000)

Crumrine and Runnels (1991) offer a model for implementing TQM in a vocational-technical school or similar institution that identifies five phases or categories for implementation and the tasks associated with each category:

1. *Commitment*: Investigate, evaluate, adopt and obtain commitment to TQM.
2. *Organizational Development*: Integrate TQM into key management processes; educate, train and offer support to employees.
3. *Customer Focus*: Determine work teams; analyse customers, products/services.
4. *Process Orientation*: Identify, standardize, and improve process control.
5. *Continuous Improvement*: Develop method for identifying opportunities and integrating the improvement process into daily operations.

Sallis (1996) raised some guiding questions while proposing a six-stage strategic planning model (Table 1). Such questions are linked to each stage. The response to such questions can be building block of a strategic plan for effective implementation.

Table 1: Strategic Planning Process (Sallis, 1996)

Stages	*Questions*
Mission and vision	➢ What is our purpose? ➢ What are our vision, mission and values?
Customer or learner requirements	➢ Who are our customers? ➢ What do our customers expect of us? ➢ What do we need to be good at to meet customer expectations? ➢ What do our learners require from our institution? ➢ What method do we use to identify learner/customer needs?
Routes to success	➢ What are our strengths, weaknesses, opportunities and threats? ➢ What factors are critical to our success? ➢ How are we going to achieve success?
Quality performance	➢ What are the standards we are going to set? ➢ How are we going to deliver quality? ➢ What will quality cost us?

Stages	Questions
Investing in people	➢ How should we make the best use of our staff? ➢ Are we investing sufficiently in staff and staff development?
Evaluating process	➢ Do we have process in place to deal with things that go wrong? ➢ How will we know if we have been successful?

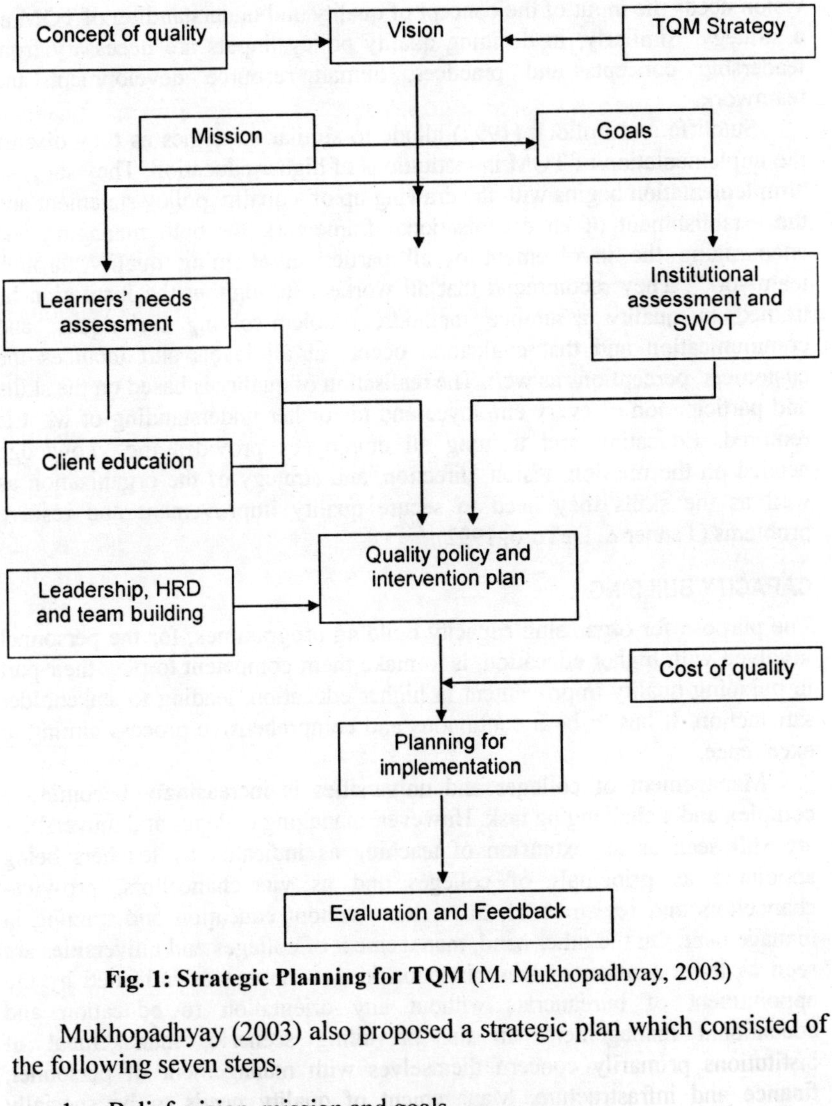

Fig. 1: Strategic Planning for TQM (M. Mukhopadhyay, 2003)

Mukhopadhyay (2003) also proposed a strategic plan which consisted of the following seven steps,

1. Belief, vision, mission and goals
2. Learners' needs assessment and client education
3. Institutional assessment and SWOT analysis

4. Quality policy and intervention plan
5. Cost of Quality
6. Planning for implementation
7. Evaluation and feedback

The interrelationship among the various stages and components can be seen in the Fig. 1. The model incorporates all seven stages. It indicates that vision needs the input of the concept of quality and understanding of TQM as a strategy. Similarly, in deciding quality policy, inputs are necessary from leadership concepts and practices, human resource development and teamwork.

Sutcliffe and Pollock (1992) allude to similar strategies as they discuss the implementation of TQM in institutions of higher education. They suggest, "Implementation begins with the drawing up of a quality policy statement and the establishment of an organisational framework for both managing and encouraging the involvement of all parties in attaining quality through teamwork". They recommend that all workers throughout the institution be trained in quality assurance methods, problem-solving techniques, and communication and that evaluation occurs at all levels and includes the customers' perceptions as well. The realisation of quality is based on the skills and participation of every employee and his or her understanding of what is required. Educating and training all employees provides the knowledge needed on the mission, vision, direction, and strategy of the organization as well as the skills they need to secure quality improvement and resolve problems (Tenner & DeToro, 1992).

CAPACITY BUILDING

The purpose for organising capacity building programmes, for the personnel involved with higher education, is to make them competent to play their part in pursuing quality improvement in higher education, leading to stakeholder satisfaction.•It has to be a continuous and comprehensive process aiming at excellence.

Management of colleges and universities is increasingly becoming a complex and a challenging task. However, managing colleges and universities are still seen as an extension of teaching as indicated by teachers being appointed as principals of colleges and as vice-chancellors, pro-vice-chancellors and registrars of universities without education and training in management. On the other hand, management of colleges and universities are seen as the extension of administration in government as indicated by the appointment of bureaucrats without any orientation to education and educational management. In the prevailing scenario, management of institutions primarily concern themselves with management of personnel, finance and infrastructure. Management of quality needs to be specially attended to. It is, therefore, necessary to train people, especially, in leadership position in higher education institutions in the methods and techniques of management of quality. Keeping this in mind, UGC should consider setting up Institutes of Quality Management to not only cater to personnel from Higher Education Institutions but also to provide training to personnel involved with school education (Mukhopadhyay, 2005). Certain private schools like Delhi Public School Society, Bharatiya Vidya Bhavan and others have already realised the importance of Quality Management and have been organizing specialised training programme on quality management.

Businesses all over the world have keenly adopted and adapted Total Quality Management to suit their particular requirements. Higher Educational Institutions must take help from such business establishments in capacity building of their staff. Hogg and Hogg (1995) cited the 1991 issue of the Harvard Business Review in which the CEO's of six major companies (American Express, Ford, IBM, Motorola, Procter and Gamble, and Xerox) wrote "An Open Letter: TQM on the Campus", in which they proposed partnerships between business and the academia. These partnerships would foster a shared responsibility to learn, to teach, and to practice TQM. They proposed that presidents, deans, and faculty leaders attend week-long sessions at each of the six companies to study ways to: 1) identify the core knowledge specific to TQM; 2) develop a research agenda in TQM; and 3) develop faculty understanding of and commitment to TQM. These six companies did this for the first time in 1992, each taking about 100 university people in their sessions. In 1993, another six companies also participated in this 'University Challenge' programme. Similarly, in India, experts, institutions and businesses having experience in successful implementation of TQM practices must playing a key role in the initiation of TQM at colleges and universities by organising capacity building programmes for the personnel of higher education.

CONCLUSION

The quality of the nation depends on the quality of its citizens. The quality of its citizens depends not exclusively but in significant measure upon the quality of their education. Today, there is an imperative need to prepare the citizens for the local as well as for the global demands. This fact is now being realised and thus, we need to bring in changes for the improvement of quality in higher education. Real change in an organisation is usually preceded by necessity. Necessity is not only the mother of invention, it is the mother of change as well. The "do more with less" era requires the higher education institutions to change structures and processes that promote inefficiencies.

With the advent of Globalisation and increased global competitiveness, quality management has become an absolute necessity, especially when there is a need to change the focus from adaptation of technology to invention of new technology and from literate society to knowledge based society. Total Quality Management (TQM) can usher in quality in higher education by providing continuous institution based quality improvement resulting in an effective and efficient organisation. TQM can be a powerful tool in the educational setting even though it was developed with manufacturing processes in mind.

Many experts have pointed the difference between educational setup and the industrial setup; this difference, according to them, would hamper the use of the principles of TQM in Education. There is an iota of truth in the above statement, no doubt. It would be unwise to think that one shoe fits all but experts at the same time also point out that each organisation has a personality of its own which implies that even when applying the TQM to different organisation in the industrial setup, care is to be taken to mould the TQM according to the personality of that very organisation. Similarly, while applying TQM to the organisations in the educational setup, the TQM needs to be moulded according to the characteristics of the organisations in the educational setup.

TQM is being used intensively by many educational institutions around the world but India is still waking up to the benefits of TQM. Though, a few elite educational institutions in India have realised the importance of TQM and have utilised its philosophy to bring about improvement in the quality of their institution but still an overwhelming majority of educational institutions are yet to have their first tryst with quality and the philosophy of TQM.

Finally, it is important to realise the fact that "Quality is essentially a product of intensive investment of capital, talent and hard work. Quality cannot be superficially achieved. Quality is not a chance, but a choice. Quality, again, is not an accident but a design. Quality is not a destination but a continuous journey." (Shejwalkar, 1999)

REFERENCES

Acaro, J.S. (1997). *Quality in Education-An Implementation Handbook.* New Delhi: Vanity Book International.

Ali, M. and Shastri, R.K. (2010). Implementation of Total Quality Management in Higher Education. *Asian Journal of Business Management.* Vol. 2, No. 1, pp. 9-16, (Feb, 2010).

Brennan, J. and De Varies, P. (Ed.) (1997). *Standards and Quality in Higher Education.* London: Jessica Kingsley Publishers.

Crumrine, B., and Runnels, T. (1991). *Total Quality Management in Vocational-Technical Education.* Oklahoma: Moore-Norman Vo-Tech Center.

Elliot, J. (Ed.) (1993). *Reconstructing Teacher Education: Teacher Development.* London: The Falmer Press.

Garvin, D. (1988). *Managing for Quality.* New York: Free Press

Hogg, R.V. and Hogg, M.C. (1995). Continuous Quality Improvement in Higher Education. *International Statistical Review.* Vol. 63, No. 1, pp. 35-48. Mexico: International Statistical Institute.

Hoy, C., Jardine, C.B. and Wood, M. (1999). *Improving Quality in Education.* London: Falmer Press.

Kaufman, R. and Zahn, D. (1993). Quality Management Plus: A Continuous Improvement of Education. California: Corwin Press Inc.

Lomax, P. (1996). *Quality Management in Education.* London: Hyde Publications.

McCormack, S. (1992). TQM: Getting It Right the First Time. *Training and Development.* Vol. 46, No. 6 (June 1992): 43-46.

Mukhopadhyay, M. (2005). *Total Quality Management in Education* (2nd ed.). New Delhi: Sage Publications.

NAAC (2004). *A Decade of Dedication to Quality Assurance*. Bangalore: NAAC.

NAAC (2007). *Quality Assurance in Higher Education*. Bangalore: NAAC.

National Council of Education, Research and Training (2005). Position Paper of National Focus Group on Teacher Education for Curriculum Renewal. Accessed via www.ncert.nic.in

Powar, K.B. (2005). *Quality in Higher Education*. New Delhi: Anamaya Publishers.

Sallis, E. (1996). *Total Quality Management in Education*. London: Hyde Publication.

Seymour, D. (1992). *On Q: Causing Quality in Higher Education*. New York: American Council on Education/Macmillan.

Seymour, D., and Collett, C. (1991). *Total Quality Management in Higher Education: A Critical Assessment*. Massachusetts: GOAL/QPC.

Sohal, A.S., Terziovski, M., (2000). TQM in Australian Manufacturing: Factors Critical to Success. *International Journal of Quality and Reliability Management*. Vol. 17, No. 2, 158–167.

Stella, A. (2001). *Quality Assessment in Indian Higher Education: Issues of Impact and Future Perspectives*. New Delhi: Allied Publishers Limited.

Sutcliffe, W., and Pollock J. (1992). Can the Total Quality Management Approach Used in Industry Be Transferred to Institutions of Higher Education? *Vocational Aspect of Education*. Vol. 44, No. 1, 11-27.

Tenner, A.R. and DeToro, I.J. (1992). *Total Quality Management: Three Steps to Continuous Improvement*. Massachusetts: Addison-Wesley

Trow, M. (1994). *Academic Reviews and the Culture of Excellence*. Seminar paper for the Office of Chancellor of Swedish Universities, Stockholm

Witcher, B.J., (1990). Total Marketing: Total Quality and Marketing Concept. *The Quarterly Review of Marketing*.

18

Quality Management in Higher Education: Issues and Practices

Mohammad Yusoof

Environments in Higher Education Institutions are dynamic. These environments are frequently defined as turbulent and dynamic. National and International forces are among the driving forces of these environments of Higher Education of individual countries and Higher Educational Institutions. Due to the nature of Higher Education Environments, the issue of quality management remains firmly on the agenda of national governments, institutions, academic scholars and individual programmes of study.

There is a lot of progress in quality management of Higher Education through research and debate. Still there is no consensus on the quality of Higher Education. This is due to complex and multi facet nature of quality construct. Hence measurement and management created various issues and challenges. This also turns to led countries and institutions to adopt a number of quality management practices most of them drawn from the industry. Though Higher Education is an international business, but most of the research conducted by individual institution or by individual country. The environment in Higher Education is a major construct of the quality in individual Higher Education Institution. The environment of Higher Education may vary country to country due to Nature of Higher Education or public policy or demand of the Higher Education. There are a number of forces which affect the environment of the Higher Education. These forces which affect the environment of Higher Education are:

Political Forces

1. initiatives to widen public access.
2. development of more public HEIs.
3. strict governmental control over HE curriculum and management.
4. unified or centralized system for government control.

Economic Forces

1. limited funding per student.
2. reliance on private sector funding.
3. reliance on tuition or international student fees.

4. rising costs per student.
5. increase in number of private HEIs.
6. greater emphasis on globalization.

Socio-Cultural Forces

1. greater demand for student places.
2. greater diversity of student populations.
3. greater diversity of provision.
4. pressure for greater accountability or value for money.

Total Quality Management (TQM)

Total Quality Management (TQM) is a management philosophy developed for industry. The aim of TQM is to improve the quality of production. TQM, focus on enhancing the quality of the production system for a quality product with zero defects. TQM is the system which also see the improvement in production system a never ending cycle.

TQM is a closed loop system control. It was originally developed by Edward Deming after World War II to improve the quality of product. It was adopted and developed Japanese industrial leaders after World War II, to improve the quality of product. Americans did not use TQM until 1950 seriously. Japanese renewed their business activities and industry, and successfully managed to control the world market by 1980. TQM is a set of practices that focus on the regular improvement, fulfilling the customer needs and lowering rework. It is also the increased involvement of employees and more teamwork, the process redesign, competitive benchmarking, constant measurement of outcomes, long rang thinking, team based problem solving and closer relationship with suppliers.

Chronology of Quality Development

Pre–1900	Quality as an integral element of craftsmanship
1900–1920	Quality Control by foreman
1920–1940	Inspection based quality control
1940–1960	Statistical process control
1960–1980	Quality assurance/ total quality control
1980–1990	Total Quality management
1990–2000	TQM, the culture of continuous improvement
2000–Present	Organization wide Quality management

The issue of quality in Higher Education has been on agenda for decades. As Higher Education has its links in industry/ vocation, the employers always question the quality of Higher Education and Research. Educators from Higher Education maintained That TQM could also be applied to education especially to bring educational reforms and to reduce waste resources and increase productivity. Total quality management (TQM) is a quality improvement body of methodologies that are customer based and service oriented. It is a structured system for creating organization-wide participation in planning and implementing a continuous improvement process. It begins with a clear understanding of the organizations vision, mission, values and customers. It is the integration of team activities across divisions/departments to achieve organizational goals. TQM is a set of practices that focus on the regular improvement, fulfilling the customers' needs, and lowering rework. It is also the increased involvement of employees and more teamwork, the process redesign, competitive benchmarking, constant measurement of the outcomes, long-range thinking, team-based problem solving, and closer relationship with the suppliers.

There are several different theories at work guiding TQM practices.

Deming's Theory: William Edward Deming (1900-1993) was an American statistician, professor, author and consultant. Perhaps he was best known for his work in Japan. Deming's theory of Total Quality Management rests upon fourteen points of management he identified, the system of profound knowledge, and the Shewart Cycle (Plan-Do-Check-Act). Deming's system of profound knowledge consists of the following four points. Deming advocated that all managers need to have a System of Profound Knowledge, consisting of four parts:

1. *Appreciation of a system*: understanding the overall processes involving suppliers, producers, and customers (or recipients) of goods and services.
2. *Knowledge of variation*: the range and causes of variation in quality, and use of statistical sampling in measurements.
3. *Theory of knowledge*: the concepts explaining knowledge and the limits of what can be known
4. *Knowledge of psychology*: concepts of human nature.

Crosby's Theory: Philip Bayard "Phil" Crosby, (1926-2001) was a businessman and author. He contributed to management theory and quality management practices. He is also credited with TQM movement. Crosby initiated the Zero Defects programme.

Crosby's response to the quality crisis was the principle *of doing it right the first time* (DIRFT).

Crosby identified fourteen points/principles of quality improvement. The four major principles are:

1. The definition of quality is conformance to requirements (requirements meaning both the product and the customer's requirements)
2. The system of quality is prevention
3. The performance standard is zero defects (relative to requirements)
4. The measurement of quality is the price of non-conformance

His belief was that an organization that established a quality programme will see savings returns that more than pay off the cost of the quality programme: "*quality is free*".

Joseph Juran's Theory: Joseph Moses Juran (1904-2008) was a management consultant in management firm. He is principally remembered as an evangelist for quality and quality management. Joseph Juran contributed *Quality Trilogy (Juran trilogy)* to the management theory. The quality trilogy (Juran trilogy) includes of quality planning, quality improvement, and quality control. If a quality improvement project is to be successful, than all quality improvement actions must be carefully planned out and controlled. Juran identified ten steps to quality improvement programme.

Juran is widely credited for adding the human dimension to quality management. He pushed for the education and training of managers. For Juran, human relations problems were the ones to isolate. Resistance to change or, in his term, cultural resistance-was the root cause of quality issues.

Ishikawa's Theory: Kaoru Ishikawa (1915-1989) was a Japanese university professor. His theory influenced quality management theory. He is best known in North America for the Ishikawa or cause and effect diagram (also known as fishbone diagram). The Ishikawa is used in the analysis of industrial process. Dr. Kaoru Ishikawa also developed a theory of how companies should handle their quality improvement projects. Ishikawa takes a look at quality from a human standpoint. He points out that there are seven basic tools for quality improvement. These tools are:

- *Pareto Analysis* – Pareto analysis helps to identify the big problems in a process.
- *Cause and Effect Diagrams* – Cause and effect diagrams help to get to the root cause of problems.
- *Stratification* – Stratification analyzes how the information that has been collected fits together.
- *Check Sheets* – Check sheets look at how often a problem occurs.
- *Histograms* – Histograms monitor variation.
- *Scatter Charts* – Scatter Charts demonstrate relationships between a variety of factors.
- *Process Control Charts* – A control chart helps to determine what variations to focus upon.

QUALITY MANAGEMENT MODELS IN HIGHER EDUCATION

A number of Higher Education Institutions have tested quality management models. These models are drawn for industry. This approach has number of benefits in managing quality. Since to the environment of education is not as environment of industry, there are limitations also in implementation these models. As mentioned earlier, TQM has potential to encompass the perspectives of different stakeholders. Hence TQM is the comprehensive approach to quality management. Other models also have been tested within higher education.

Other models those have been tested within higher education are as following:

1. European Foundation for Quality Management (EFQM) Excellence Model

The European Foundation for Quality Management (EFQM) Model is based upon nine criteria for quality management. There are five enablers (criteria covering the basis of what a company does) and four results (criteria covering what company achieves). The result is a model that refrain from prescribing anyone methodology, but rather recognizes the diversity in quality management methodologies. Eight fundamental concepts of excellence of EFQM:

I. *Focus on Results*: pleasing company's stakeholders with results achieved by stakeholders is a primary focus.
II. *Focus on Customer:* It is vital that a company's quality management leads to customer satisfaction.
III. Constancy of Purpose and Consistent Visionary Leadership
IV. *Purpose and Facts from The Management Focus*: Management breaks down everything into systems, processes and facts for easy monitoring.
V. *Training and Involving Employees*: Employee should receive professional development opportunities and be encouraged to remain involved in the company.
VI. *Continuous Learning*: everyone should be provided with opportunities for learning on the Job
VII. *Developing Partnerships*: It Is Important to encourage partnerships that add value to the company's Improvement process
VIII. *Social Responsibility of the Corporation*: The Company should always act in a way where it is responsible towards the environment and society at large.

2. Balanced Score-card

The balanced scorecard is a strategic planning and management system that is used extensively in business and industry, government, and nonprofit organizations worldwide to align business activities to the vision and strategy of the organization, improve internal and external communications, and monitor organization performance against strategic goals. The balanced scorecard was originated by Drs. Robert Kaplan (Harvard Business School) and David Norton as a performance measurement framework that added strategic non-financial performance measures to traditional financial metrics to give managers and executives a more 'balanced' view of organizational performance.

Kaplan and Norton describe the innovation of the balanced scorecard as follows:

> "The balanced scorecard retains traditional financial measures. But financial measures tell the story of past events, an adequate story for industrial age companies for which investments in long-term capabilities and customer relationships were not critical for success. These financial measures are inadequate, however, for guiding and evaluating the

journey that information age companies must make to create future value through investment in customers, suppliers, employees, processes, technology, and innovation."

Perspectives

The balanced scorecard suggests that we view the organization from four perspectives, and to develop metrics, collect data and analyze it relative to each of these perspectives:

i. The Business Process Perspective
ii. The Customer Perspective
iii. The Financial Perspective
iv. Strategy Mapping

3. Malcolm Baldridge National Quality Award

The Baldridge Award is the only formal recognition of the performance excellence of both public and private US organizations given by the President of the United States. It is administered by the Baldridge Performance Excellence Programme, which is based at and managed by the National Institute of Standards and Technology, an agency of the U.S. Department of Commerce. This award may be given annually across six eligibility categories – manufacturing, service, small business, education, health care, and non-profit. The Baldridge National Quality Programme and the associated award were established by the Malcolm Baldridge National Quality Improvement Act of 1987 (Public Law 100–107).

The Baldridge Criteria for Performance Excellence serve two main purposes:

(a) to identify Baldridge Award recipients that will serve as role models for other organizations and
(b) to help organizations assess their improvement efforts, diagnose their overall performance management system, and identify their strengths and opportunities for improvement.

4. ISO 9000 Series

The International Organization for Standardization (ISO) is an international organization. The purpose of ISO is to establish agreement on international quality standards. In 1987 the International Organization for Standardization (ISO) published its first set of standards for quality management called ISO 9000. It has members from 91 countries, including the United States. By receiving ISO 9000 certification, companies demonstrate that they have met the standards specified by the ISO.

In December 2000 the first major changes to ISO 9000 were made, introducing the following three new standards:

ISO 9000:2000–Quality Management Systems–Fundamentals and Standards: Provides the terminology and definitions used in the standards. It is the starting point for understanding the system of standards.

ISO 9001:2000–Quality Management Systems–Requirements: This is the standard used for the certification of a firm's quality management system. It is used to demonstrate the conformity of quality management systems to meet customer requirements.

ISO 9004:2000–Quality Management Systems–Guidelines for Performance: Provides guidelines for establishing a quality management system. It focuses not only on meeting customer requirements but also on improving performance.

These three standards are the most widely used and apply to the majority of companies. However, ten more published standards and guidelines exist as part of the ISO 9000 family of standards.

ISO 14000 Standards: In 1996 the International Standards Organization introduced standards for evaluating a company's environmental responsibility. These standards, termed ISO 14000, focus on three major areas:

- Management systems standards measure systems development and integration of environmental responsibility into the overall business.
- Operations standards include the measurement of consumption of natural resources and energy.
- Environmental systems standards measure emissions, effluents, and other waste systems.

With greater interest in green manufacturing and more awareness of environmental concerns, ISO 14000 may become an important set of standards for promoting environmental responsibility.

5. Business Process Reengineering

Business Process Redesign is "the analysis and design of workflows and processes within and between organizations". BPR may be defined as "the critical analysis and radical redesign of existing business processes to achieve breakthrough improvements in performance measures."

Davenport and Short (1990) prescribe a five-step approach to BPR:

a. Develop the Business Vision and Process Objectives:
b. Identify the Processes to be redesigned:
c. Understand and Measure the Existing Processes:
d. Identify IT Levers:
e. Design and Build a Prototype of the New Process:

6. SERVQUAL

SERVQUAL or RATER is a service quality framework. SERVQUAL was developed in the mid 1980s by Zeithaml, Parasuraman and Berry. SERVQUAL means to measure the scale of Quality in the service sectors.

SERVQUAL was originally measured on 10 aspects of service quality: reliability, responsiveness, competence, access, courtesy, communication, credibility, security, understanding the customer and tangibles. It measures the gap between customer expectations and experience. The basic assumption of the measurement was that customers can evaluate a firm's service quality by comparing their perceptions with their expectations.

The simplified RATER model however is a simple and useful model for qualitatively exploring and assessing customers' service experiences and has been used widely by service delivery organizations. It is an efficient model in helping an organization shape up their efforts in bridging the gap between perceived and expected service.

The five gaps that organizations should measure manage and minimize:

Gap 1 – also known as the management perception gap is the difference between expected service by customers and the management's perceptions of the consumer's expectations.

Gap 2 – also known as quality specification gap. It is the difference between management perception and the actual specification of the customer experience – Service design and performance standards are pre-requisites for bridging this gap. Managers need to make sure the organization is defining the level of service they believe is needed.

Gap 3 – also known as the Service delivery gap. It is the difference between customer driven service design and standards and service delivery.

Gap 4 – also known as market communication gap. This is the gap between the delivery of the customer experience and what is communicated to customers.

Gap 5 – also known as the perceived service quality gap. This is the gap between a customer's perception of the experience and the customer's expectation of the service.

BENEFITS OF QUALITY MANAGEMENT MODELS

Strategic approach to quality management is the key benefit of all the quality management models. There are other distinct tangible benefits also associated with different quality management models. Some of the benefits of Quality Management models are as:

- Integrates TQM with strategy and links goals with processes through self assessment.
- Encourages disciplined thinking about tangible and intangible aspects of academic activities.
- Identifies key processes and operational aspects required in design and delivery of courses in line with customer voice.
- Demonstrated improvements include customer service, university processes, staff and faculty morale, course quality and personnel hiring.
- Integrated map of management issues valued and useful to secure confidence of stakeholders.

- Useful as a basis of self-assessment.
- Tests relationship between enablers/results.
- Scorecard used to manage rather than just monitor performance.
- Focus on performance management and evaluation.
- Staff understand performance targets.
- Improved budgeting, resource allocation and reward systems.
- System can increase educational quality.
- Evident in operational elements; strategic and budget planning, careers, outreach and information services.
- May be immediate and long standing.
- Quality certification can improve inter-departmental working condition, student enrolment, and staff/supplier satisfaction.
- Continuous improvement achieved through preventative action.
- Cost effective method for accountability.
- Enables organization to become improvement driven through re-focusing core processes to improve both productivity and service levels.
- Takes a broad number of stakeholder views into account.
- Quality Management System has significantly enhanced the use of data for quality assurance purposes.
- Enables assessment of internal and external stakeholders views which is important in a competitive environment.

LIMITATIONS OF QUALITY MANAGEMENT MODELS

Despite the benefits of quality management models, there are limitations also in Higher Education particularly. Since quality management models are borrowed from industry, there is dilemma of applying business models to the Education. Some of the limitations are as:

- Difficulty in transferring TQM principles developed for industry to Higher Education environments including defining outputs; autonomy of academic staff; bureaucratic and fragmented structures; application to complex course structures; definition of student roles within Higher Education (customer or co-producer).
- More relevance to academic service functions than teaching quality.
- Challenges regarding leadership skills and institution-wide strategic planning.
- Lack of acceptance and application of TQM in Higher Education.
- Less scientific control is possible in Higher Education when compared to manufacturing.
- More relevant to service functions.
- Dilemma of applying business language to public sector.
- It can be 3 to 5 years before benefits are evident.
- Challenges regarding managerial skills and top level commitment in Higher Education.

- Lack of integration between EFQM and national Higher Education quality control mechanisms.
- Performance indicators require careful identification specific to situation and can be dysfunctional unless grounded in strategy.
- Scientific control less achievable in higher education than in manufacturing.
- Student culture impacts upon perceived importance of different elements of Higher Education and thus on perceptions of quality.
- Performance indicators related to management processes but do not address education quality.

CONCLUSION

The environment of the Higher Education is driven by national and international forces i.e. political, economic and socio-cultural factors. Different environments in Higher Education Institutions nationally or internationally, make the quality management as a firm agenda. The quality management models which are borrowed from the industry are applied in modified form. These models have their benefits and limitations as well. There is improvement in quality by applying these models in Higher Education. Since Higher Education is an International Business, it need that the quality management models must have consensus to be applied into the Higher Education.

REFERENCES

Abdullah, F. (2006), Measuring Service Quality in Higher Education: HEDPERF Versus SERVPERF, *Marketing Intelligence and Planning*, 24(1), 31–47.

Arif, M. and Smiley, F. (2004), Baldridge theory into practice: a working model, *International Journal of Educational Management*, 18(5), 324–328.

Baker, R. (2002), Evaluating Quality and Effectiveness: Regional Accreditation Principles and Practices, *Journal of Academic Librarianship*, 28(1), 3–7.

British Standards Institution (1990), Quality Systems, Parts 1–3 1987; Part 4, BSI, London.

Crosby, Philip B. (1979), *Quality is Free*, Mentor Books, New York.

Crosby, Philip B. (1984), *Quality without Tears*, McGraw-Hill, Singapore.

Deming, W. Edwards (1982), *Out of the Crisis*, Cambridge University Press, Cambridge.

Deming, W. Edwards (1994), *The New Economics*, MIT, Cambridge, Mass European Foundation for Quality Management, www.efqm.org.

Ishikawa, Kaoru (1989), *Introduction to Quality Control*, Chapman Hall, London.

Juran, J.M. (1989), *Juran on Leadership for Quality*, Macmillan, New York.

Juran, J.M. and Gryna Frank, M. (ed.) (1988), *Juran's Quality Control Handbook*, 4th edn., McGraw-Hill, New York.

Maureen Brookes, Nina Becket (2007), Quality Management in Higher Education: A Review of International Issues and Practice, *The International Journal for Quality and Standards*.

NAAC (2007), A profile of National Assessment and Accreditation Council [online] http://naacindia.org/aboutus.asp (Accessed on 02 November 2012)

New Zealand Ministry of Education (2006), OECD Thematic Review of Tertiary Education Country Report: New Zealand, OECD.

Venkataraman, Sitalakshmi (2007), A framework for implementing TQM in higher education programmes Quality Assurance in Education, Vol. 15, No. 1, pp. 92-112 [online] Available from www.emeraldinsight.com/0968-4883.htm (Accessed on 02 November 2012)

World Bank (2001), Higher Education in Developing Countries – peril and promise, 17th December, The World Bank.

19

Quality Concerns in Higher Education in India

Ajit Kumar Bohet

Higher education is a powerful tool to build modern, value-based, knowledge based, culture based, and peaceful society which can lead the country towards becoming super power in the world. It is also considered one of the important and strong tools for the development of any country. Primary education is necessary for creating base, while, higher education is extremely important for providing cutting edge. Higher education contributes to the growth of nation by providing specialized knowledge and skill manpower.

India's higher education system is the second largest in the world, after the United States. The main governing body at the tertiary level is the University Grants Commission, which enforces its standards, advises the government, and helps coordinate between the centre and the state. Accreditation for higher learning is overseen by 12 autonomous institutions established by the University Grants Commission. Indian higher education system has expanded at a fast pace by adding nearly 20,000 colleges and more than 8 million students in a decade from 2000-01 to 2010-11. As of 2011, India has 43 central universities, 289 state universities, 130 deemed universities, 94 private universities, 5 institutions established and functioning under the State Act, and 50 Institutes of National Importance. Other institutions include 33,000 colleges as Government Degree Colleges and Private Degree Colleges, including 1800 exclusive women's colleges, functioning under these universities and institutions as reported by the UGC in 2012. The emphasis in the tertiary level of education lies on science and technology. Indian educational institutions by 2004 consisted of a large number of technology institutes. Distance learning and open education is also a feature of the Indian higher education system, and is looked after by the Distance Education Council. Indira Gandhi National Open University is the largest university in the world by number of students, having approximately 3.5 million students across the globe.

But in spite of all these developments and growth, quality of higher education remained the main concern for all the stakeholders in the education system i.e. students, parents, institution management, faculty members, policy makers and society as a whole because poor quality of higher education effects the overall progress of any nation. Indian higher education is far away from the global educational standard. India is nowhere in the recently released (year 2011) world universities rankings. India doesn't figure in world to 100 universities. The three rankings – Times Higher Education world University Rankings, Academic rankings of world universities compiled by Shanghai Jiao Tong University, and QS World University Rankings – are just out and none of our prestigious institutions of learning like the IITs and the IIMs make it to the top-200. While overall, US universities dominate all three rankings with its Harvard and Princeton, most of the other countries are ahead of India, including Thailand. IIT Bombay finds itself at the 225th position far beyond of 187th position in 2010, IIT Delhi is on 218th position and IIT Madras is on 281st position in the QS rankings. These data represents that Indian higher education does not stand anywhere among the world higher education institutions with respect to quality.

MEANING OF QUALITY IN EDUCATION

The quality in education need to be defined in the wider sense of the overall aim of education as the all round development of the individual and his commitment to social objectives; and viewed in this context, there is no doubt that vigorous efforts will have to be made to improve these to suit the changing needs of the country. It has become increasingly evident that the relevance of education, its significance, its validity for personal aspiration, its link with societal needs and goals, its efficiency and impact are the basic parameters of every educational system.

Quality in education can also be interpreted from a different viewpoint; it means educational standards are judged from examination results. An educational institution that shows high pass percentage is considered to be an institute of great quality.

CONCERN FOR THE QUALITY OF HIGHER EDUCATION

India needs multi-dimensional and broad-based quality education to maintain its leadership in the 21st century, therefore India should show the concern over the quality in education as the education in India is not competitive in terms of the quantity and quality with other countries. Quality in higher education is a burning issue which can be ensured through regular review of the function of the institutions either through self assessment or through outside agencies and by accrediting the institutions. The expansion of higher education over the years has also resulted in educational malpractices, which exist in the form of capitation fees being charged by the private institutions at the time of admissions in addition to the fees. The entry of large number of private institutions has also resulted in rapid increase in proceedings involving students, teachers, employees, management of higher educational institutions and universities and other stakeholders negatively impacts the quality of education and efficient function of the institutions. Also there has been spurt in activities of Foreign Educational Institutions operating in India since mid 1990s. While some of them are resorting to various mal-practices to appeal and attract students, particularly in smaller cities and towns. Many of these institutions have come up since there is yet neither a centralized policy nor the regulatory regime.

University Education Commission (1948-49) rightly felt the uneasy sense of the inadequacy of the higher education system particularly in terms of quality and standards. Reiterating the importance of quality in higher education and its sustainability, the Kothari Commission in (1964-66) remarked that "the situation of higher education was unsatisfactory and even alarming in some ways that the average standards have been falling and rapid expansion has resulted in lowering quality". We have to therefore, gear up the machinery of higher education to fulfill the aspirations of people and be conscious towards quality maintenance as well as its role to elevate the country to new heights. In his message, Dr. Radhakrishnan communicates "there is need for change in the perception and attitude of universities realizing that their field is wider, task is greater and goal is higher in building a strong and happy India." The universities are not merely places of conferring degrees and distinctions. They besides being places of learning, also centers of service and wholesome development of human personality of men and women turning them into fine human beings. This will demand for quality education at higher education level.

India needs to emphasize on quality education and following key issues for improving the quality of higher education in India:

National Knowledge Commission (2009) recommended that "The higher education system must provide for accountability to society and create accountability within. An expansion of higher education which provides students with choices and creates competition between institutions is going to be vital in enhancing accountability. It further stated that quality must be improved to avail all the benefits of higher education and for this some steps

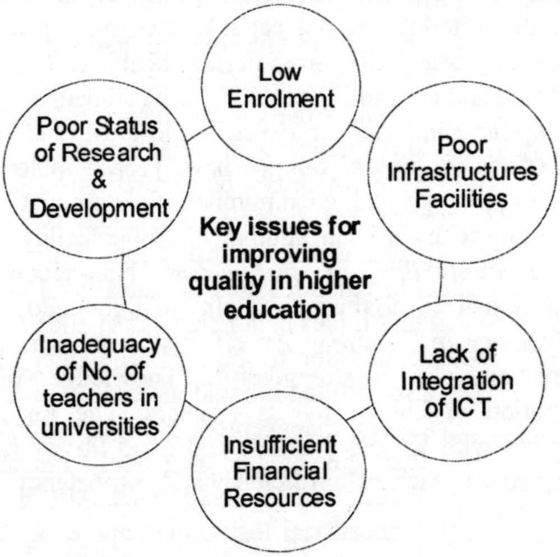

Fig. 1: Key Issues in Improving Quality of Higher Education in India

must be taken urgently like up gradation of infrastructure facilities, training of teachers, enhancement of ICT in higher education, improving transparency and accountability, increase in interaction and accessibility etc." thus, clearly stating the need and areas of quality improvement in higher education.

FACTORS INFLUENCING QUALITY IN HIGHER EDUCATION

Quality in education depends on several factors. A few of them include:

- *Politicization*: Politicization of higher education has posed a serious threat to the quality of higher education. Appointment of Vice-chancellors in many instances is being viewed politically. The challenge of education document indicated that depoliticization is not an early acceptable condition for the political parties in the country. (Min. of Education, 1985, p. 75)
- *Poor quality of intake*: In order to attract students for admission, the colleges go on awarding high grades/marks to undeserving candidates. The colleges/university departments admitting students on the basis of career marks get cheated in many situations and thus get poor quality of students.
- *Managerial Inefficiency*: generally, principals are appointed basing on the seniority and the managerial efficiency is not taken into account. There is no regular orientation programme for newly appointed principals. It affects the quality of education as they don't have the influential managerial skills.
- *Overcrowded Classrooms*: lack of adequate number of teachers and classrooms force many colleges to reduce their number of groups and merge them into larger groups making it possible for a teacher to carry out effective classroom interaction.
- *Inadequate Student Services*: Most of the higher education institutions today are not capable enough to provide services like conducting orientation programmes, health services, hostel facilities, guidance and counseling services to the students.
- *Inadequate material resources*: Most of the higher education institutions at present do not have proper material resources like building; play ground, good number of classrooms, infrastructure, and laboratory with sufficient equipments, toilet facility, and staffrooms.
- *Non-accountability of institutions*: Non-accountability of the institutions leads to the poor quality in higher education.
- *Inefficiency in Teaching*: An effective teacher needs to be lifelong learner and need to strengthen his knowledge voluntarily. A good institution is known by its teachers. The institution should be supplied with various journals and good library facility which will energize the teachers' proficiency and competency.

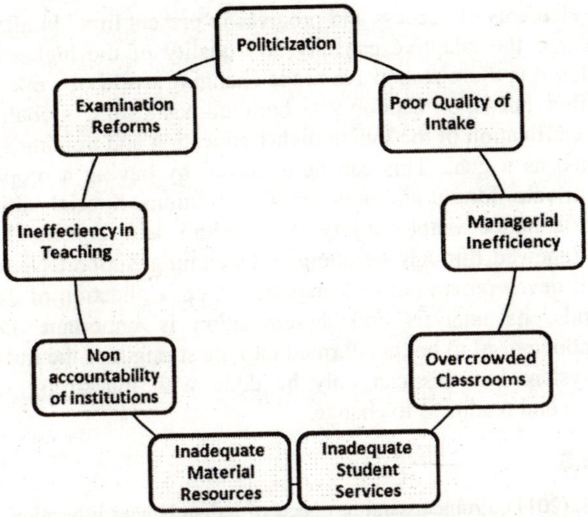

Fig. 2: Factors Influencing Quality in Higher Education

- *Examination Reforms*: Reforms in the examination system is the most common phenomenon in the recent past. Most of the researchers and academians are not satisfied with the present examination system. It may be true for years because the pitfalls in the evaluation system make the examination system ruin. The evaluation is not reliable. This can be changed by using the new methods of grading system and other various innovative methods.
- *Teaching Methods*: the curriculum framework should be such a way that it should provide new knowledge which is useful to the society and also provide the employability opportunities. The teachers should use qualitative teaching learning material and also aware of use of multimedia, IT and OHP.

There are other factors also which are affecting the quality of higher education such as motivation of the teachers and students, favourable environment for teaching-learning process, irrelevance of the curriculum leading towards the low employability etc. which needs to be improved for enhancing the quality of higher education in India.

CONCLUSION

Thus it can be concluded that education is the key to the progress especially higher education which provides the cutting edge and skilled manpower. But, quality of higher education is declining and is a matter of concern for all the stakeholders as well as for the whole nation. Indian higher education has expanded in quantity but lacking behind in terms of quality. India cannot progress until it higher education system is qualitatively strong enough because this poor quality is resulting in low employability, low performance of the specialized individuals, lack of innovative and creative ideas etc. which are the key elements of success and progress in present time. In all, there is a need to enlarge the adaptive capacity and quality of the higher education system so that it is more responsive to the changing world of work and meets the diversified needs of economy – both domestic and global. For that purpose diversification of the Indian higher education and training system has to be pursued as a goal. This can be achieved by having a proper mix of public and private, formal and non-formal institutions. Special initiatives are required to enhance employability. Curriculum and content has to be continually renewed through Teaching and Learning Support Networks and specific skill development network may be set up. Collection of data on job market trends, its analysis and dissemination is important. Drawbacks mentioned above need to be transformed into the strength of the Indian higher education system but this can only be done with the strong willpower, determination and readiness to change.

REFERENCES

Chaudhary, S. (2011), Problems and prospects of Indian Higher Education in the Age of globalization, *University News*, Vol. 49 (23).

Deka, B. (2000), *Higher Education in India*; Atlantic Publishers and Distributors, Delhi.

Dube, S.C. (1988), Higher Education and Social Change, in A. Singh and G.D. Sharma (ed.), *Higher education in India: The Social Context*, Konark Publishers Pvt. Ltd., New Delhi.

Premji, Azim (2004), Importance of Quality Education for the Development of the Nation; *Legal News and Views*.

Ranganathan, R. and Rao, SVL (2011), Reformation of Higher Education in India: Quality Concerns; *University News*, 49 (10) March 7-13, Delhi.

Report of Kothari Commission. (1964-66), MHRD, New Delhi.

Report of National Knowledge Commission (2009), MHRD, New Delhi.

Report to the People on Education (2010-11), MHRD, New Delhi.

Sehrawat, S.S. (2012), Quality Assurance in Higher Education; *University News*, 50 (26) June 25-01 July: Delhi.

Saleem, S. and Gawali, V.S. (2011), India needs Quality Education: *University News*, 49 (06) February 07-13, Delhi.

Singh, K.P. and Ahmad, S. (2011), Higher Education in India: Major Concerns, *University News*, Vol. 49 (29), Delhi.

Singh, K.P. and Ahmad, S. (2011), Issues and Challenges in Higher Education, *University News*, Vol. 49 (10), Delhi.

Singh, U.K. and Sudarshan, K.N. (1996), *Quality Education*; Discovery Publishing House: New Delhi.

UNESCO (2005), Education for All: the Quality Imperative; UNESCO Report 2005.

University Education Commission (1948-49): MHRD, New Delhi.

20

Quality Enhancement in Higher Education: A Global Perspective

Dheeraj Kumar Pandey and *Lokpati Tripathi*

Today, colleges and universities are facing major changes as they navigate the 21st century and make decisions that will not only impact higher education but will also contribute to our country's future competitiveness in the global marketplace (Dey, A., 2000). During the last sixty years after independence, higher education has expanded in India somewhat remarkably (John Morton, 2007). The number of universities and colleges has increased, there is an explosion in student numbers, the enrolments in higher education has swelled (John Morton, 2007). Today we have number of technological, management, medical science institutions, besides a large number of engineering colleges and agricultural colleges that are producing highly specialized human capital (UNESCO, 1998). India is regarded as having the second largest stock of educated and skilled manpower and the third largest reservoir of scientific and technical manpower in the world of nations with an estimated stock of about seven million (UNESCO, 2004). Today the world economy is experiencing an unprecedented change (Derek Bok, 2004). New developments in science and technology, media revaluation and internationalization of education and the ever expanding competitive environment are revolutionizing the education scene (Neil and William, 2000). A paradigm shift has been noticed in higher education now a days, from 'national education' to 'global education', from 'one time education for a few' to 'lifelong education for all', from 'teacher-centric education' to 'learner centric education' (Karen, Webber and Robert, 2008). These changes make new demands and pose fresh challenges to the established education systems and practices in the country (Jane *et al.*, 2009). Because of interdependence and integration of world economy in recent years, the Indian higher education system has a new role and a challenge to provide to the nation and the world at large, skilled human power at all levels, having breadth of knowledge and confidence to effectively confront the social and economic realities. India, like any other knowledge economy, depends on the development of its educational sector. Higher education drives the competitiveness and employment generation in India (John Morton, 2007). However, research findings have shown that the overall state of higher education is dismal in the country. There is a severe constraint on the availability of skilled labour. There exist socio-economic, cultural, time and geographical barriers for people who wish to pursue higher education (Bhattacharya and Sharma, 2007). The issue of accessibility to quality higher education needs to be addressed in the light of the vast economic and social disparities, cultural and linguistic diversities, and extremely uneven opportunities of learning at the school level together with the aspirations and capacities of the potential students (Douglas, 2001). Therefore, the question of access to higher education needs to be addressed at the local, regional, national and international levels from trans disciplinary, inter-disciplinary and discipline-specific perspectives (Neil and William, 2000). Education is the driving force of economic and social development in any country. Considering this, it is necessary to find ways to make education of good quality, accessible and affordable to all, by taking some necessary measures in this respect (Derek Bok, 2004).

WHAT IS QUALITY?

The concept of quality has been drawn from industry. Not very long ago, education and industry functioned independently of each other and displayed a very contrasting ethos and values. Quality is an elusive attribute of values, which cannot be easily measured or quantified (Steve, William, Cathy, and Festus, 2008). Webster's Dictionary describes it among the other things as 'degree of excellence' and 'superiority in kind'. In reality it is a relative concept that means different things to different people (Peter, 2010: Henaff, 2006). Ishikawa's definition of quality narrowly interpreted, quality means quality of product. Broadly interpreted, quality means quality of work, quality of service, quality of information, quality of process, quality of division, quality of people, including workers, engineers, managers, and executives, quality of system, quality of company, quality of objectives, etc. To control quality in its every manifestation is our basic approach (Peter, 2010). Thus in the field of education, while addressing quality, the focus of the students may be the facilities provided, of teachers and the teaching/learning process, of the management and parents on the score or grades achieved, and of prospective employers on the nature of the output (George, 2003) Quality has both absolute and relative connotations (Douglas, 2001). The concept of absoluteness in quality props up the morale of the higher education system at the delivery end i.e. institutional, and at the receiving end i.e. students. Quality dimensions seem to have two implications, i.e., functionality of the output and meeting the basic standards (Peter, 2010). Hence, the quality of a higher education system may be seen from the point of view of norms and standards, which may evolve depending on the need of the hour (Catherine, Crouch and Mazur, 2001). In the 21st century, it is crucial to identify the relative norms for different components of a higher education system. The alternative dynamics for teacher preparation and the sustaining quality in teacher input, like: Curriculum design and development; Curricular practices vis-à-vis emerging principles of pedagogy; Evaluation of learners performance and progress vis-à-vis curriculum evaluation; and, Quality management practices become crucial (Houston, 2010). Approaches to quality in higher education in most countries have started with an assumption that, for various reasons, the quality of higher education needs monitoring (Ewell, 2010). At root, governments around the world are looking for higher education to be more responsive, including:

- Making higher education more relevant to social and economic needs (Neil and William, 2000);
- Widening access to higher education (Ebner, Kickmeier and Holzinger, 2008);
- Expanding numbers, usually in the face of decreasing unit cost (Derek Bok, 2004);
- Ensuring comparability of provision and procedures, within and between institutions, including international comparisons (National Knowledge Commission: Report to the Nation, 2007).

Quality has been used as a tool to ensure some compliance with these concerns. However the rationale and policy often tend to be worked out after the decision to undertake an audit, assessment or accreditation process has been made. Thus approaches to quality are predominantly about establishing quality monitoring procedures.

PRINCIPLES OF QUALITY THAT INDIAN HIGHER EDUCATION CHERISHES

The best practices are those which improve the entire operations of the institutions and decide the standard of quality. The identifications of the best practices depends on many variables, all these variables must be considered while identifying the best practices (William and Steve, 2005). In the globalized World, the State-protected educational system cannot withstand the pressure without making itself competitive (Derek Bok, 2004). There seem to be four reasons why new policy initiatives should be taken by the Government in this connection. They are: (i) that the economic returns of primary education far exceed the returns of higher education; (ii) that the private returns on higher education far exceed the social returns; (iii) that the State funding for higher education is insufficient in countries like India (UNESCO, 1998); and (iv) that since private sector benefits the most from higher education, it is only just that it should make a decisive contribution (Karen and Robert, 2008). Whether or not one accepts the Government's rationale, new strategies need to be developed for the survival and well being of the higher education system in the present scenario (UNESCO, 1998).

There are various interpretations of what exactly constitutes acceptable quality: e.g., an institution's provision should be "fit for purpose"; should make effective use of resources; should offer its stakeholders value for money; etc. (Burbules, 2000). but it is increasingly agreed that it is important to promote improvement of quality, not just to ensure that quality is maintained. This shifts the emphasis from quality assurance to quality enhancement. Some key quality principles that Indian higher education cherishes are:

- Quality is directed at the satisfaction of post-secondary students as customer (Derek Bok, 2006).
- Quality means "meets the requirements of post-secondary students (Neil and William, 2000).
- Quality applies to every product of the institutions (Burbules, 2000).
- Quality should be a profitable investment in the institutions as an instrument of producing highly specialized scientific and technical manpower in the world (Derek Bok, 2004).
- Quality requires change in an institution's culture (Henaff, 2006).
- Quality requires top management leadership (Phillip and Crumbley, 2003).

QUALITY ENHANCEMENT IN HIGHER EDUCATION

Quality enhancements is an inclusive concept and a collective enterprise. It involves everyone who teaches, support and guides students and the managers and administrators of HE institutions (James, 2001). It takes taking deliberate steps to bring about continual improvement in the effectiveness of the learning experience of students and the opportunities that are available to students. It includes significant strategic initiatives and many small things that people do to try to make things better (Huber and Hutchins, 2005). According to Learning and Teaching Support Network (LTSN), the core aspects of the student learning experience are:

- The curriculum – its structure, aims, intended learning outcomes and types of assessment (Derek Bok, 2006).
- Institution's educational provision and relevant training and development activities for staff and students (Derek Bok, 2006).

The promotion and support of effective learning – to include types of teaching and learning; provision of student support services, library and IT facilities; measures to involve students in monitoring and enhancing the 'Quality enhancements (QE) in higher education is a deliberate process of change that leads to improvement. It provide a chance for departments to highlight what they were doing to develop staff, promote innovation and share good practices (David Glenn, 2010).

HOW CAN WE ENHANCE QUALITY IN HIGHER EDUCATION

Adapting Best Practices to Improve Quality: Increasing competition, demands for accountability, and higher volumes of available information are changing the methods of how institutions of higher education operate in the mid-1990s (Karen, Webber and Robert, 2008). For higher education to enact substantial and sustainable changes in efficiency and productivity, a new way of thinking or paradigm that builds efficiency and a desire for continual learning must be integrated into institutional structures (Srikanthan and Dalrymple, 2007).

Benchmarking in Higher Education: The strategy of benchmarking is important both conceptually and practically, and is being used for improving administrative processes as well as instructional models at colleges and universities by examining processes and models at other schools and adapting their techniques and approaches (Welsh and Metcalf, 2003). It has been described as a method of teaching an institution how to improve. As with other quality concepts, benchmarking should be integrated into the fundamental operations throughout the organization and be an ongoing process that analyzes the data collected longitudinally (Steve, William, Cathy, and Festus, 2008). Benchmarking attempts to answer the following questions:

- How well are we doing compared to others?
- How good do we want to be?
- Who is doing it the best?
- How do they do it?
- How can we adapt what they do to our institution?
- How can we be better than the best?

Among the improvement strategies and techniques such as Total Quality Management (TQM), Continuous Quality Improvement (CQI), and Business Process Reengineering (BPR), benchmarking has emerged as a useful, easily understood, and effective tool for staying competitive (Welsh and Metcalf, 2003).

Internal Institutional Audit: Internal institutional audit is a process that institutions undertake for themselves to check that they have procedures in place to assure quality, integrity or standards of provision and outcomes across the institution (Scott, 2006). The main aim of an institutional audit is to improve the procedures and consequences of a system taking into account students learning experiences and the curriculum with the aim of strengthening an institution to reach desired goals (Welsh and Metcalf, 2003).

Access and Equity: India has the second largest system of higher education, next only to USA, the total number of students hardly represent 6 per cent of the relevant age group, i.e., 18-23, which is much below the average of developed countries, which is about 47 per cent (Karen, Webber and Robert, Boehmer, 2008). The fact of the matter is that the system needs to be expanded to a much greater scale to serve the needs of the Indian youth (National Knowledge Commission: Report to the Nation, 2007). Thus, access, equity, accountability and quality should form the four guiding principles, while planning for higher education development in India in the twenty-first century (Ebner, Kickmeier, and Holzinger, 2008).

Economics of Higher Education: Access to higher education needs to be widened in the country, both within the formal system and through other effective innovative measures, such as a truly open system and networking of Universities (Ebner, Kickmeier, and Holzinger, 2008). It is now imperative on the part of Indian Universities to generate their own resources to a large extent (National Knowledge Commission: Report to the Nation, 2007). This could be done through several methods, like raising tuition fee and collecting capitation fee, both of which having severe limitations; and others like, launching courses for foreign students, obtaining donations from philanthropists, etc., which have a good potential (Hamermesh, 1994). Some alternative ways e.g. research grants from industries, donations for admissions etc. which were found to be inadequate. It was observed that an organized structure for higher-education fund raising and creating a culture of giving are the only possible solutions (Jane *et al.* 2009).

Reorientation of Higher Education: Educational opportunities and traditions that Indian Universities have built up, since independence have been able to produce graduates, capable only of pursuing limited careers, but, in the new globally competitive environment that is emerging in the country, the Indian student is now required to develop a multifaceted personality to cope up with the rapid changes in the world at large (UNESCO, 1998). This calls for the development of body, mind and spirit, through the educational processes in the institutions of higher education (National Knowledge Commission: Report to the Nation, 2007). The issue has significant implications in the sense that it demands a redefinition of the aims of higher education (James, 2001).

Professional Ethics and Value Education: The rapid developments in science and technology and the challenges of globalization are posing additional challenges to the education system in the country [Capper (ed.), 2011]. This is also the time when parental care to the children is on the wane. The adverse effects of the media on the mental development and moral values of the younger generation are being felt increasingly in all spheres of life [Cocking, (eds.), 1999]. Gross consumerism has distorted the outlook of persons into one of equating possessions with richness. Exploitation of natural resources is proceeding without reference to sustainability. The hiatus between the rich and the poor is getting wider. While the education system needs to keep pace with the scientific and technological developments in terms of building the skills and knowledge, it also needs to address the more fundamental issues of the social and moral consequences of such unregulated activities [Leicester, & Modgil (eds.), 2003]. In this context, there is now a growing demand to lay greater emphasis on education to inculcate, nurture and develop values, particularly among the youth of the country (Report of Radhakrishnan Commission, 1948-49).

Evaluation and Assessment Systems: During the last 50 years, higher education in India has made great strides leading to the Indian higher education system becoming one of the largest systems in the World. Unfortunately, it is the Indian experience that this expansion in quantity has overshadowed the quality of higher education (National Curriculum Frame Work, 2005). Lately, a chorus of criticism is heard from various well-meaning quarters about the deteriorating quality of higher education

(Programme of Action: New Education Policy, 1986). It is well known that one of the important components of higher education is the manner in which students' academic performance is evaluated. A concerted debate has been going on to determine the best system of assessment to be followed by the Universities in the twenty first century (National Curriculum Frame Work, 2005). A great degree of diversity has been observed in terms of assessment and grading of the students in the University system at present (Report Education Commission, (1964-66). It is desirable that a certain optimum degree of standardization in the examination system and in the assessment of students is put in place before grades are awarded to them (Teacher Education Curriculum: A Framework, 1978).

Quality Assurance in Higher Education: In an environment of global competitiveness it is important that Indian products of the higher education institutions are as competent as graduates of any· other country, not only in their scholastic attainments, but also in terms of the value system and richness of their personality (Peter, 2010). Unless the quality and standard of Indian higher education institutions is enhanced zealously and sustained at a high level through innovation, creativity and regular monitoring, it seems to be difficult for the Indian academics/professionals to compete in the World scene (Houston, 2010).

Assessment and Accreditation: Many institutions of higher education in the country are excellent in the sense that their infrastructure, resources, faculty, programmes of teaching and research are almost as good as the best in the advanced countries (National Knowledge Commission: Report to the Nation, 2007). But, the same cannot be said of the average institutions of higher education in the country. They do not come anywhere near the level of average institutions of higher education in the advanced countries (UNESCO, 2004). This vast gap in standards and facilities has been a cause of constant anxiety and concern to the policy planners of higher education in India (National Curriculum Frame Work, 2005). This calls for suitable assessment and accreditation mechanisms to be available in the country to ensure the quality and standard of the academic/training programmes at higher educational institutions (National Knowledge Commission: Report to the Nation, 2007). The assessment has to be continuous and the process has to be transparent to gain the acceptance of the society at large (Braskamp and Ory, 2004).

Sustaining Quality in Higher Education Institutions: The quality of these components may also differ from institution to institution (Harcleroad, 2006). Therefore, sharing of the experiences among institutions on quality issues may generate ideas for evolving norms and strategies for their quality assurance of management processes, curricular inputs and practices and the evaluation system as well (Welsh and Metcalf, 2003). Of late, various developments have been witnessed relating to quality assurance mainly through the intervention of information and communications technologies (ICT) in education, like networking of the open learning system with traditional Universities, interdisciplinary interactions at intra-institutional and inter-institutional levels, networking of institutions globally, data based management of higher education, changing the orientation of institutions by incorporating self financing in their financial management, assessment and accreditation of higher education institutions and creation of different statutory and regulatory bodies at the national level (Douglas, 2001).

By Changing the Core Aspects of the Students' Learning Experience: In recent years, the Indian Higher Education System has become fully aware of the need for quality. Quality and Excellence could not be attained overnight. Taking it into account students learning experiences and the curriculum with the aim of strengthening an institution to reach desired goals, the following changes are required:

- The curriculum – its structure, aims, intended learning outcomes and types of assessment (Derek Bok, 2006);
- The promotion and support of effective learning – to include types of teaching and learning; provision of student support services, library and IT facilities; measures to involve students in monitoring and enhancing the institution's educational provision; and relevant training and development activities for staff and students (Kezar, 2005).

INDIAN INITIATIVES FOR QUALITY ENHANCEMENT IN HIGHER EDUCATION

India, like any other knowledge economy, depends on the development of its educational sector. During the last sixty years after independence, higher education has expanded in India somewhat remarkably (John Morton, 2007). The number of universities and colleges has increased, there is an explosion in student numbers, the enrolments in higher education has swelled. Today we have number of technological, management, medical science institutions, besides a large number of engineering colleges and agricultural colleges that are producing highly specialized human capital (UNESCO, 1998). In an environment of global competitiveness it is important that Indian products of the higher education institutions are as competent as graduates of any other country, not only in their scholastic attainments, but also in terms of the value system and richness of their personality (Peter, 2010). Unless the quality and standard of Indian higher education institutions is enhanced and sustained at a high level through innovation, creativity and regular monitoring, it seems to be difficult for the Indian academics/professionals to compete in the World scene (Houston, 2010). In recent years, the Indian Higher Education System has become fully aware of the need for quality. In this respect, UGC, the governing body of Indian higher education, has taken upon itself this onerous task and has succeeded in some extent in maintaining the quality of higher education. It has launched many schemes, which have made some impact in the higher education system viz.

1. Innovative Programmes including Emerging Areas

2. International Cooperation
3. Identification of Universities and Colleges with Potential for Excellence
4. Networking of Universities and Colleges
5. Faculty Improvement Programme
6. National Eligibility Test (NET)
7. Schemes for Strengthening of Research
8. Programmes for the development of Engineering and Technical Education
9. Programme for the Development of Management Education
10. Programme for the Development of Computer Education and Up-gradation/Augmentation of Computer Facilities
11. Accreditation System.

Undoubtedly, during the last sixty years after independence, higher education has expanded in India somewhat remarkably (John Morton, 2007). However, the number of universities and colleges has increased but the research findings and survey reports reveal that the overall state of higher education is dismal in the country. Many institutions of higher education in the country are excellent in the sense that their infrastructure, resources, faculty, programmes of teaching and research are almost as good as the best in the advanced countries (National Knowledge Commission: Report to the Nation, 2007). But, the same cannot be said of the average institutions of higher education in the country. They do not come anywhere near the level of average institutions of higher education in the advanced countries (UNESCO, 2004). But in Indian context, educational opportunities and traditions that higher education institutions have built up, since independence have been able to produce graduates, capable only of pursuing limited careers, but, in the new globally competitive environment that is emerging in the country, the Indian student is now required to develop a multifaceted personality to cope up with the rapid changes in the world at large (UNESCO, 1998). This calls for the reorientation and redefinition of the aims of higher education (Selby, Lucas, 2002). In recent years, the Indian Higher Education System has become fully aware of the need for quality and has taken some measures for enhancing quality in higher education but they have been proved in sufficient to improve quality in higher education.

BARRIERS TO QUALITY IN HIGHER EDUCATION

Some major barriers to quality enhancement in higher education are listed below:

- Higher education programme structure and duration that make access and persistence difficult (Ebner, Kickmeier and Holzinger, 2008);
- Pedagogy and supports that do not meet learners' need (Neil and William, 2000);

- Alignment of higher education institutions and of courses and transferability of credits that slow progress to credentials (Eric Kelderman, 2008);
- Higher education system and procedures are traditional they are not supporting or inhibiting the pursuit of quality (William and Steve, 2005);
- Higher education institutions culture, faculties' attitudes, values and beliefs are not conducive to the pursuit of quality (Braskamp and Ory, 2004);
- Organizational climate and design doesn't support or inhibit quality achievement (Selby, 2002);
- Higher education institutions management system is also traditional. It doesn't allow easily to accept any new and innovative trends that are the need of the hour (Burbules, 2000).

CONCLUSION

Today, the world economy is experiencing an unprecedented change (Derek Bok, 2004). New developments in science and technology, media revaluation and internationalization of education and the ever expanding competitive environment are revolutionizing the education scene (Neil and William, 2000). India, like any other knowledge economy, depends on the development of its educational sector (John Morton, 2007). Many institutions of higher education in the country are excellent in the sense that their infrastructure, resources, faculty, programmes of teaching and research are almost as good as the best in the advanced countries (National Knowledge Commission: Report to the Nation, 2007). But, the same cannot be said of the average institutions of higher education in the country. They do not come anywhere near the level of average institutions of higher education in the advanced countries (UNESCO, 2004). Educational opportunities and traditions that Indian Universities have built up, since independence, have been able to produce graduates, capable only of pursuing limited careers, but, in the new globally competitive environment that is emerging in the country, the Indian students are now required to develop a multifaceted personality to cope up with the rapid changes in the world at large (UNESCO, 1998). This calls for making the whole higher education system oriented towards meeting the requirements and satisfaction of post-secondary students as customer as well as it should be more relevant to social and economic needs of the country (Neil and William, 2000). In recent years, the Indian Higher Education System has become fully aware of the need for quality. Quality and Excellence could not be attained overnight. Organized and focused efforts e.g. adopting best practices to improve quality in higher education, reorientation of higher education, benchmarking in higher education, internal institutional audit, access and equity, economics of higher education, professional ethics and value education, evaluation and assessment system, quality assurance in higher education, assessment and accreditation, sustaining quality in higher education institutions, by changing the core aspects of the students' learning experience etc. are needed to achieve this goal.

REFERENCES

Bhattacharya, D.B. and Sharma, A.C. (2007). Being to Rank Colleges by Measuring Graduates' Job Success. *The Chronicle of Higher Education,* Sept. 19, 2007, pp. A1, A14-16.

Birnbaum, R. (2008). How Colleges Work: The Cybernetics of Academic Organization and Leadership. Jossey-Bass.

Braskamp, L.A. and Ory, J.C. (1994). *Assessing Faculty Work: Enhancing Individual and Institutional Performance*. Jossey-Bass.

Burbules, N.C. (2000). Universities in Transition: The Promise and the Challenge of New Technologies. *Teachers College Record,* Vol. 102, No. 2, p. 271.

Capper (ed.), (2011). Case studies of innovations in teacher training and technology. Washington, DC: The World Bank, retrieved on September 20, 2011, from *http://www.the3tconnection.org/SingaporePrintingVersion.pdf/.*

Catherine H., Crouch and Eric Mazur (2001). Peer Instruction: Ten Years of Experience and Results. *American Journal of Physics,* Sept. 2001, pp. 970-977.

Cocking, R.R. (eds.). (1999). *How people learn: Brain, mind, experience, and school.* Washington, D.C.: National Academy Press.

David, Glenn (2010). Rating Your Professors: Scholars Test Improved Course Evaluations. *The Chronicle of Higher Education,* Retrieved on April 27, 2010 from, www.chronicle.com/article/ Evaluations-That-Make-the-G/65226/

Derek, Bok (2004). *Universities in the Marketplace: The Commercialization of Higher Education,* Princeton University Press.

Derek, Bok (2006). Our Underachieving Colleges: A Candid Look at How Much Students Learn and Why They Should be Learning More. Princeton University Press.

Dey, A. (2000). Who Actually Paid for My Education? Retrieved on November 07, 2012 from http://www.deeshaa.org/who-actually-paidfor-myeducation

Don, Houston (2010). Achievements and Consequences of Two Decades of Quality Assurance in Higher Education: A Personal View From the Edge. *Quality in Higher Education.* July 2010, p. 177.

Douglas, C. Bennett (2001). Assessing Quality in Higher Education. *Liberal Education.* Spring 2001, p. 40.

Ebner, M., Kickmeier-Rust, M. and Holzinger, A. (2008). Utilizing Wiki-Systems in Higher Education Classes: A Chance for Universal Access. Universal Access in the Information Society. Retrieved on November 5, 2012 from http://www.springerlink.com/content/01898k53u2041651

Eric, Kelderman (2008). Tuition Rises as Spending on Instruction Slows. *The Chronicle of Higher Education,* May 9, 2008, p. A14.

George, D. Kuh (2003). What Are We Learning About Student Engagement from NSSE. *Change.* Mar-Apr. 2003, p. 24.

Hamermesh, D.S. (1994). Facts and Myths about Refereeing. *Journal of Economic Perspectives,* 8(1), p. 153.

Harcleroad, F.F. (2006). Accountability, Quality, Quality Assurance, and Rewards for Institutional Faculty. Retrieved on Dec. 12, 2008, from http://www.sheeo.org/account/Harcleroad%20final.pdf.

Henaff, N. (2006). Higher Education: The Quality of Education and Its Evaluation. Retrieved on November 5, 2012 from http://www.vn.refer.org/confrasie/conf7/docs/nolwen_henaff_en.pdf

Hubball, H., Clark, A. and Beach, A.L. (2004). Assessing Faculty Learning Communities. *New Directions for Teaching and Learning,* No. 97. p. 87.

Huber, M.T. and Hutchins, P. (2005). *The Advancement of Learning: Building the Teaching Commons.* Jossey-Bass.

James, J. Duderstadt (2001). Engineering for a Changing World: A Roadmap to the Future of Engineering Practice, Research, and Education. University of Michigan Press.

Jane *et al.* (2009). Trends in College Spending: Where Does the Money Come From? Where Does it Go? *A Report of the Delta Project,* 2009. Retrieved on Feb. 13, 2009 from www.deltacostproject.org.

John, Morton (2007). *Engineering Skills: The Threat From China and India?* paper presented at the meeting of European Engineers Forum, Hanover, England, April 2007.

Karen, L., Webber and Robert, G. Boehmer (2008). The Balancing Act: Accountability, Affordability, and Access in American Higher Education. *New Directions for Institutional Research, S2,* Winter 2008, p. 79.

Kezar, A. (2005). What Do We Mean by 'Learning' in the Context of Higher Education? *New Directions for the Study of Higher Education, No. 131.* Jossey-Bass, p. 49.

Leicester, C. Modgil and Modgil, S. (eds.) (2003). *Education, culture and values.* Vol. II, London: Falmer, p. 99.

Mangieri C. and Collins, Block (eds.) (2011). *Creating Powerful Thinking in Teachers and Students.* Fort Worth, TX; Holt, Rinehart & Winston.

National Curriculum Frame Work (2005). New Delhi: NCERT.

National Knowledge Commission: Report to the Nation (2007). MHRD, Govt. of India. Retrieved on November 3, 2012 from Available at http://knowledge commission.gov.in/reports/report07.asp

Neil, Howe and William, Strauss (2000). *Millennials Rising: The Next Great Generation,* Vintage Publishing.

Peter, Ewell (2010). Twenty Years of Quality Assurance in Higher Education: What's Happened and What's Different? *Quality in Higher Education,* July 2010, pp. 173-175.

Peter, Selden (2010). Rating Student: Ratings of Professors. *Education Digest,* Oct. 2010, p. 70. Retrieved on November 4, 2012 from *www.asq.org/edu/index.html*

Phillip, R. Olds and Larry, D. Crumbley (2003). Higher Grades = Higher Evaluations: Impressions Management of Students. *Quality Assurance in Higher Education, No. 11,* Sept. 2003, p. 172.

Programme of Action: New Education Policy (1986). MHRD, Govt. of India: New Delhi.

Report of Education Commission (1964-66). *Education for National Development.* New Delhi: Govt. of India.

Report of Radhakrishnan Commission (1948-49). New Delhi: Govt. of India.

Scott, J.C. (2006). The Mission of the University: Medieval to Post-modern Transformations. *The Journal of Higher Education,* Vol. 77, No. 1, p. 39.

Selby, J.D. and Lucas (2002). *Aligning Hierarchical Goals in an Organization: The Path from Training to Performance.* Ph.D. dissertation (Engineering Management), Old Dominion University.

Srikanthan, G. and Dalrymple, J.F. (2007). A Conceptual Overview of a Holistic Model for Quality in Higher Education. *International Journal of Education Management,* Vol. 21, No. 3, p. 173.

Stenhouse, L. (1975). *An Introduction to Curriculum Research and Development.* London: Heinemann.

Steve, Duncan, William, Swart, Cathy, Hall, and Festus, Eribo (2008). A Quantitative Analysis of the Quality of Human Performance Among University Students. *American Journal of Educational Studies, No. 1,* Nov. 2008, p. 14.

Teacher Education Curriculum: A Framework (1978). New Delhi: NCTE.

UNESCO (1998). World Conference on Higher Education for the Twenty-First Century:

UNESCO (2004). EFA Global Monitoring Report 2005, *Education For All: The Quality Imperative*, Paris: UNESCO.

Value Education in Indian Schools: Experiences and Strategies of Implementation (2003). New Delhi: NCERT, pp. 56, 63, 79, 92, 132, 154, 201.

Vision and Action, Commission II: Quality of Higher Education, Final Report, Retrieved on November 2, 2012 from http://portal.unesco.org/ education/en/file_download. php/8e7bc55cc8d95504234f5f4c0d11cc94CommissionII-E.pdf.

Welsh, J.F. and Metcalf, J. (2003). Cultivating Faculty Support for Institutional Effectiveness Activities: Benchmarking Best Practices. *Assessment and Evaluation in Higher Education,* Vol. 28, No. 1. p. 33.

William, Swart and Steve, Duncan (2005). A Methodology for Assuring the Quality of Human Performance. *International Journal of Computer Integrated Manufacturing,* No. 18, Sept. 2005, pp. 487-497.

Woods, J.Q. (1999). Establishing a Teaching Development Culture, in Menges, R.J. (ed.), (1999). *Faculty in New Jobs: A Guide to Settling in, Becoming Established, and Building Institutional Support.* Jossey-Bass, p. 268.

21

Improving Quality in Higher Education: A Challenge

C.S. Shukla

The term *'Quality of Education'* is, today, a much misunderstood term. Generally, people talk about it in a rather vague or limited sense. They think of it merely in terms of percentage of passes in examination and percentage of marks obtained by individuals in university examinations and tests for entry in I.A.S. or State Services and foreign universities. Quality of education is much more than this. Like beauty or good health, quality of education is the sum – total of intellectual and moral health or excellence of the student. It is the working of several factors – internal as well as external.

A proper and comprehensive understanding of 'Quality of Education' is possible only when we identify and analyze its various elements or implications such as the following:

- Quality of Educational Goals or Functions.
- Compatibility with the Social Context.
- Quality of university management/college management.
- Quality of Academic Climate.
- Availability and Utilization of Funds.
- Quality of Teachers and Teaching.
- Quality of Efficiency of Examination System.
- Political will and Support for Higher Education.
- Quality of Curriculum.
- Quality of Interactions.
- Quality of Accountability and Autonomy.
- Expectations of the Clients of the Educational System.

The quality of higher education depends on several social, economic, cultural and technological factors as also on philosophical and administrative factors. Future possibilities and future hurdles and threats will determine the quality of future higher education. Thus the theme of quality of Future Higher Education in India being very complex, it is not possible for any one scholar, howsoever competent he might be to do full justice to it.

GOALS OF HIGHER EDUCATION

Yogiraj Aurobindo had held that the greatest developmental challenge before the modern man is to become a 'Superman'. He should be endowed with a larger cosmic vision. He should be in a position to realize his divine potentialities and possibilities and try to become socially, morally and spiritually awakened and at countable and active.

Sri Sathya Sai Baba, the greatest spiritual Master of the modern times, has held, "Education should foster morality, righteousness and character. The tremendous amount of knowledge that man has acquired in the field of sciences and technology contributes only to the superficial civilization, what man requires today is not superficiality but internal beauty of the heart. The internal beauty of the heart springs from transformed into a mere man, he has to be transformed into an ideal man. He further says: Attaining high marks is not the aim of education. Education is meant to broaden the mind. Education and discrimination should go hand in hand. The prosperity of the nation depends on the progress of you (students) make in the field of Education. The future of the nation depends on the students."

In his illuminating keynote address "Man, Society and Education: Some Questions Concerning a Preferred Future" presented to the National Seminar on 'Alternatives in Education' (Indian Institute of Advanced Studies, Simla, 2-7 Nov., 1976, eminent sociologist Professor S.C. Dube had rightly stated as under:

"In the final analysis we have to return to the question of the quality of life. The minimum needs of the two-thirds of world – food, clothing, shelter, health, education and culture have to be met first. Simple joys of life are as lofty as intellectual ideas."

We have been hearing about these lofty goals of education for several years about, we have not yet tried to shape and reform our higher education in India accordingly. Most of the educational institutions are still laying their sole emphasis on academic performance at any cost, and they are not really concerned about the moral, social, spiritual and related finer goals or functions of life and education. The manifest or accepted and professed goals of these institutions glibly mention all these, but in reality the latent functions of higher education are in the centre stage. Most of institutions do not try to develop futuristic perceptions, FFRI (Future Focused Role Image) and futuristic values in their students. Most students sole concern is selfish gain to achieve vertical motility in their personal careers and make money. Hardly any one of them is really concerned about sieving the society or becoming a superman as Aurobindo had en visage. It appears that this trend of the pursuit of higher education for selfish gains will all the more prosper in the future years and so the quality of higher education in future is not likely to improve in the real sense of the term.

WHERE INDIA STANDS TODAY?

What are the world trends today, and where do we as a nation stand? This is not known to or understood by most of the university and college Teachers,

There are so many assessments as such available today in many recent books and articles but not many teachers are even bothered to know them. An excellent realistic analysis of our national context, *vis-à-vis* the contemporary world trends has been made in a recent article '*Nation at Fifty: Competing Visions of Our Future*' by Gurucharan Das, a Former CEO and Vice-President of Proctor and Gambles Worldwide, in 1996.

After more than six decades of our national independence, it is a good time to pause, look beyond the horizons of current events, and examine where we are heading in the 21st Century. There appear to be two tendencies of some consequence, which are going to define our future. The first is the relentless push of the global economy and communications, supported avidly by our rapidly growing middle class. Domestically we will see the irrestible spread of competitive markets and social democracy. The primary occupation of the people will be with a rising standard of living, with social mobility, with the peaceful pursuit of middle-class values and culture influenced increasingly by the homogenous floral culture.

The second is the growing consciousness of religious identity, which is leading to fundamentalist and separatist attitudes. It is the part of the revival of religion and the de-secularisation of our society. This tendency encourages conflict, instability, divisiveness, rigidity and irrationality.

The Two Trends

Which of these two trends is likely to prevail? Or will our society evolve uneasily from a constant clash of both these forces?

Like the rest of the world, India too is headed in the direction of some form of democracy, whose peace will be occasionally punctured, by religious extremism.

The irony of liberalism is that it gives the individual free space in order to fashion his life, but he, unfortunately, is unable to cope with the free space and fills it with trivial objections. Without a God of ideology, bourgeois life is reduced to the endless pursuit of cars, VCRs, dishwasher arid channel surfeit. Increasingly the reference point is the self, one becomes self absorbed in a world of physical security and rational consumption. Even when it comes to exercise one prefers to jog rather play team sport, without a higher moral purpose there are no heroic acts to perform.

Is this dull, banal and bleak life that we look forward in India in the 21st Century?

India will resist becoming dull and bleak because of the powerful hold of religion. Although we may compress the economic time table and become prosperous in the next 25-30 years. I believes we will not lose out on religiosity quite as rapidly, if at all. Religion has a powerful place in Indian life and the persistence of God will thus be our strongest defense. The second trend, ironically, has a silver lining because it will protect us from the weakness of the first trend. The challenge is to keep religion a private matter.

We have, thus, good reasons to expect that the lives of the majority of Indians in the 21st century will be free, more humane and prosperous than their parents and grandparents lives."

All those who are concerned about ensuring quality of our higher education in future must take note of this analysis and try to see what best they can do in this national context.

UNIVERSITY MANAGEMENT

The quality of education in any university is very largely determined by the quality of its management and administration. We know that in India today, all state universities are experiencing too much interference by ruling politicians and local political goons. It is widely known that there exists a virtual anomie (formlessness) in the management and administration of the Indian universities. In most of them – Central as well state ones – the chief functionary i.e., Vice-Chancellor is appointed not on grounds of academic merit, integrity or administrative acumen, but usually on the grounds of caste politics, religious politics, nepotism, corrupt practice of appeasements of certain communities or pressures of undesirable leaders or the like. In many cases by sycophants, relatives, favourites of Governors/Chancellors, Chief Ministers, Ministers, get appointed to such high position. When such persons become Vice-Chancellors, what hope is left that they will try to raise the quality of education in their University and colleges? In the states of U.P., Bihar, Rajasthan, Karnataka etc. in recent years many such people have been appointed as Vice-Chancellors on such undesirable grounds. There have been lots of disturbing news in the national dailies about the inefficiency and corrupt practices rampant in the Universities of these states. *The Hindustan Times* had carried the news about the U.P. Universities 'Chaos reigning high in versifies' on 18 July 1997 – most of the VCs were then appointed by the Governor Romesh Bhandari as Chancellor under the pressure of politicians. In Rajasthan in 1997 the then Vice-Chancellor, a political appointee, was unceremoniously removed after his corrupt practices were exposed. So many Vice-Chancellors have been indulging in grave malpractices and corruption at the behest of their political Godfathers and under the pressures of their coterie. Even in Central universities, such appointments are not always fair and appropriate. Most VCs function as dictators or politicians,

This trend is likely to continue and prosper in the coming years as a lot of political instability is likely to be there in future years – both at the centre and in the states, and politicians are habituated to appoint their favourites anyhow. Therefore, the quality of higher education will, it appears, not improve in future years, most of the universities are administered on the basis of groupism, favouritism, unfairness towards juniors, suspicion and the like. They do not inspire teachers to contribute their very best to enhance the quality of education.

ACADEMIC CLIMATE IN INDIAN UNIVERSITIES AND COLLEGES

The very concept of university as an institution of higher learning implies that there should be free, uninhibited exchange and flow of ideas, views and opinion in an atmosphere of mutual goodwill and Harmon and there should be quest for excellence. There should be participant democracy and none should be allowed to remain alienated. There should be human and intellectual values to guide the thinking 'and behaviour of those working in them. Scholars often quote Newman, Pandit Nehru, Zakir Husain, Radhakrishnan and so many great personalities to drive home the point that universities must be ideal places for the pursuit of excellence in learning and life. Unfortunately, most of our universities have failed match up to these high expectations, for we find them to be hotbeds of politics, indiscipline, and all kinds of mischief, violence and crudities

Most of the teachers in universities and colleges do not study and prepare for their classes earnestly and properly. They do not have much aptitude for learning and teaching. They do not wish to keep abreast with the latest developments in their subjects. They do not wish to participate in discussions, and they are shy of doing any creative and innovative work. Most of them lack the skills basically necessary for their profession like typing, taking proper notes, communication in preparing bibliographies etc. Very few of them ever read new books and journals in the libraries. Most of them are unenthused, dull and quite out of date in their knowledge.

We are now observing that information technology has arrived in India with a big bang during the last few years. Today computers, Internet, Fax, e-mail etc. are being used in offices, business houses, industries, and even in homes. But most of our university and college teachers have not yet started using them. Those teachers who are not able to learn to use these new tools of learning and communication will soon become outdated and they are very likely to be ignored as inefficient and backward teachers. There is no future for them. It is very much likely that in just 5 years, it might become a compulsory condition for appointment as a teacher of higher education institution and for enrolment for Ph.D. research that the candidates must be proficient in the use of computers. Those who cannot change in the light of the advancements in information technology and explosions of knowledge taking place will have no proper futuristic perceptions of their roles as university or college teachers. They will be treated as backward teachers and they will receive a crude cultural shock. Academic Colleges have so far not realized this and teachers are not getting proper re-orientation in regard to their future role performance. The UGC is making only some half-hearted measures to improve things, but the resource crunch is pouring cold water on its ambitious schemes to revitalize teachers.

AVAILABILITY AND UTILIZATION OF FUNDS

The economy of our nation is in a precarious condition. This is going to be worsen in the coming years. It will affect the quality of higher education. We cannot even think of how much it will go down because of lack of funds. Even now the situation is very gloomy. For many years our universities and colleges have not been getting sufficient funds for libraries, laboratories, workshops, seminars and conferences and publication of researches. The budget grant of almost every university is utilized in the payment of salaries to the extent of 95 per cent; with the remaining 5 per cent funds how much can they do for the improvement of the quality of education?

During the last 10 years, a number of universities and colleges in Delhi and else-where have been motivated or pressurized to generate funds for themselves by starting income-generating courses. This trend has caught up. Now privatization is the latest fad in the Indian action. The days are not far when some of our Central and State universities might be auctioned to the HRIs or local entrepreneurs so that the government may in place of having to spend on them reap profits from them and the problem of indiscipline and lack of accountability, malpractices and inefficient are solved. Who cares if in future poor students won't be able receive higher education in regular colleges and universities?

Already there is a pinching shortage of funds for our libraries, laboratories, workshops, research projects etc. Hardly one per cent of our teachers of our universities and college are able to attend any seminar or conference due to financial constraints. It is likely that the situation will still worsen in the future years and that will further deteriorate the quality of higher education in India, Moreover, higher education is now not priority no. 1 with the central and state governments.

TEACHING

In most of the universities and colleges teaching is not done in quality manner. When it is so, how can there be quality of education? While there is lot of talk on innovations in teaching methods, curricular reform and the like, by and large teaching continues to be traditional teacher-directed instead of being learner-directed. We have still separate departments of subjects. Despite a lot of talk of interdisciplinary departments, researches and teaching, very little of these have fructified so far. Authorities are not really interested or keen for the improvement of teaching in the higher institutions of education.

Few of them have ever thought it fit to go to the departments and discuss with the teachers as to what they are teaching, what difficulties and limitations they are facing, how they (VCs) can help and facilitate their role – in functioning and the quality of teaching and learning can improve in the university. Many of the Vice-Chancellors are not academic persons. Most of them are too much obsessed with bureaucratic procedures and day-to-day fire-fighting operations in the campus to find time to do so. Teachers, by and large, remain alienated as ever.

The academic climate of most of the universities and colleges in India is very sterile. There are very few departmental seminars, Guest lectures, exchange of experiences and views, give and take of books and materials, and no encouragement to junior colleagues is given by the senior teachers, There is no one to check the lethargy and inactivity of teachers. Rotation of Headships in universities and colleges, whatever its advantages may be has not really resulted in the improvement of quality of education. Our Teacher Unions' contribution to the raising of the quality higher education is dismal, and minimal. While sycophants and favourites and members of the boss' inner circle snatch all inducements and rewards, hard-working, sincere and dedicated teachers are generally not looked after and properly rewarded in any manner. In the institutions of higher learning in India, as the proverb goes 'horses and donkeys all are driven alike'. Many highly qualified teachers prefer to go in for administrative posts leaving aside their teaching jobs.

This scenario is likely to prevail in future years at least for 10 more years. There is not much hope for the future, unless drastic measures are taken to improve and innovate, and proper motivation and reorientation is provided to teachers. Offering contract jobs to teachers, having the systems of the evaluation of teachers, work by their students and the like might, be adopted in our future universities. Honesty in appointments must be there in future. It is unimaginable how future universities will be able to select teachers on the basis of the undesirable considerations of religion, caste, friendship and the like.

RESEARCH

While it is fact that thousands of students are being awarded M. Phil and Ph.D. Degrees by the Indian Universities each year and some of them are remarkably meritorious work, the bigger fact than this is that most of the researches are generally repetitions, futile, bogus, and they do not add anything to the existing fund of knowledge and to the good of the locality or the region and even to the caliber of the candidates concerned. Not all teachers are competent to guide research. Not all candidates are capable of doing research, yet the craze to do Ph.D. research has been created by the UGC. There is a well established informal practice of appointing Ph.D. examiners on mutual give and take basis, "You oblige me, and I oblige you". Examiners are often appointed on the basis of religions, caste, regional affinities and from among trusted friends. In many cases, most of the theses of a university department or theses under one teacher go for evaluation to one particular university department or the teacher, whether a person is expert in the area or not, all sorts of theses may be sent to him and he can easily examine them and give favourable reports as is expected of him. If ever an external examiner conscientiously decides to recommend revision or rejection of the theses, he is immediately labeled as unfriendly or 'enemy' and no more theses are sent to him. There are many Heads, Deans, and Seniors among professors, whose own Ph.D. theses have not been considered fit to be published and who have not done any creative or research work after doing their Ph.D. years back. Even the high bureaucratic authorities of apex educational councils and other by institutions like the NCERT, NCTE, ICSSR, CSIR and the like are seen accepting Ph.D. examinership offers from their friendly Heads in the Universities.

EXAMINATIONS

Examination is the most crucial, aspect of higher education. During the last fifty years, there have been a lot of discussion and throwing up of suggestions on examination reforms – Question Banks, Internal assessment, Objective type questions, transparency in examinations, multi-question papers and the like, but very little reform has taken roofs so far. Often, even first rate candidates can get III division or even fail and a candidate deserving third division may be awarded first division marks. In the name of re-checking nothing is virtually done in many universities. The re-evaluations almost always result in increase of so many marks. The reliability of examination system is thus still very doubtful. Under Delhi High Court orders the Central Board of Secondary Education Examination scripts were carefully scrutinized and 10 per cent serious errors have been discovered in them as has been reported in national papers in February 1999. When question papers in UPSC and State PSCs can leak out, how can universities lag behind? Deans and Vice Chancellors in some universities have been involved in examination scandals and recent examples are from Delhi University, Rajasthan University and some of the universities of Kerala and Karnataka. Many teachers do not feel shy in awarding even up to 95 per cent marks to their own students or favourites although they themselves might not get such high marks in the same papers if they were examinees. Many universities have of course good track record of conducting fair examinations, but in many others copying is a serious problem. Some politicians opposed anti-copying act in UP, as if copying is the birthright of a candidate. In these sensitive years when human rights of all sorts of groups are being so spiritedly talked about, how can university students right to copy be denied! If these trends continue (indications are that they will continue at least till 2015), then we should better only pray to God "God save our University Examination System!"

LACK OF POLITICAL WILL

There is lack of political will to make the universities run efficiently and have quality education. This is clear from so many trends – many worthless people are often appointed as Vice-Chancellors, Principals and teachers at all levels; inbreeding in appointment of teachers at all levels; intruding in appointment of teachers and research scholars is growing in all universities; politicians influence appointments, promotions, examinations, and admissions; chancellors themselves also violate established rules regulations and age bar in appointing their own relatives and favourites as Vice-Chancellors and the UGC cannot do anything; politicians encourage and help teachers to agitate and do all sorts of strikes; they support their students in student elections; their patronized student leaders have to be given admissions in the institutions. In order to curb indiscipline in the universities now the reformist trend is to appoint unacademic people like IAS, IPS and Military Officers as Vice-Chancellors. This trend is catching up. In many universities of the states like Rajasthan, Haryana etc. IAS officers have been appointed as VCs and Registrars, also, but the results here have not been good, they too are not conducive to the enhancement of quality of education. Today, the trend is that the Union HRD Ministry bureaucrats disregard the recommendations of UGC, Universities disregards the recommendations and order of UGC, colleges disregard the norms suggestions of the universities, and students and teachers do not follow the instructions of their principals and all their superior authorities and do what they please. They have always some friendly politician and present or ex-MP to support them.

EPILOGUE

Higher education is now becoming costlier day-by-day. The trend of privatization will make it all the more costly each year in the coming decade. This will deprive many poor and lower and middle class students to receive higher education in good colleges and universities. This will creates class differences and sparks of many agitations. Already many groups are clamoring for reservations and special privileges and rights. The woes of our higher education institutions will surely increase. Most of our educational administrators and teachers are not seriously aware of these sociological realities and contemporary trends and they do not have any proper futuristic perception. They have not started preparing scenarios of their probable and preferred futures, they have no FFRI and they have no perception of what Indian society and education there if, many of them are ignoramus or just 'frogs in the well', quite oblivious of the global trends, and lots of thinking and activity that other nations are doing in regard to the 21st century. Futurology has not yet become a subject of study in our schools, colleges and universities. All these trends show that we are going to face a severe future shock. It seems that very soon most of our higher education institutions are going to turn into academic ghettos, slums and isolated poor backward villages. We may have some very enchanting island of excellence but most of the institutions will continue to be poor in their resources functioning and overall quality of education. This depressing scenario throws up a great challenge before all the reference groups. They must see that the existing deficiencies and problems are removed, institutions are well provisioned and all possible reforms, innovations and futuristic boost are there in higher education institutions in India.

REFERENCES

Aggarwal, J.C., *Development and Planning of Modern Education*, Vikas Publishing House Pvt. Ltd., New Delhi, 2011.

Aggarwal, J.C., *Landmarks in the History of Modern Indian Education*, Vikas Pubiishing House Pvt. Ltd., New Delhi, 2012.

Kalam, A.P.J. and Rajan Y.S., *India: 2020 A Vision for New Millennium* Penguin, 1998.

MHRD, DOE, *National Policy on Education*, Govt. of India, New Delhi, 1986.

MHRD, DOE, *Programme of Action* – National Policy on Education 1986, Govt. of India, New Delhi, 1992.

Menon, PN, Work Ethics and Faculty Accountability, *University News*, September, 1996.

NCF, *National Curriculum Framework* NCERT, New Delhi, 2005.

Shukla, C.S., Development of *Educational System in India*, International Publishing House, Meerut, 2012.

Shukla, C.S. *Teacher in Emerging Indian Society*, Dhanpatrai Publishing Company Pvt. Ltd., New Delhi, 2012.

22

Enhancing Quality in Higher Education

Shyamasree Sur

"Internationalization" is not an altogether unknown phenomenon in higher education in India and other developing countries. Students have, for many decades, gone abroad for higher studies and professionals have gone out to teach or do research. Foreign faculty has come to our shores for teaching and managing institutions. Foreign books and journals have been an indispensable source of knowledge for our university students and teachers. Thus, teaching and learning, research and institution building have all been influenced by some form of internationalization or other.

The unprecedented expansion of the private sector and the entry of foreign education providers in India's higher education arena have caught the regulatory authorities off guard. There is as yet, no coherent regulatory framework to monitor or accredit these new players. Whether their quality, standards and related management practices are of an acceptable level is a matter of conjecture.

QUALITY ENHANCEMENT IN HIGHER EDUCATION

Study abroad by students is still the most visible mode of internationalization. The Organization for Economic Co-operation and Development (OECD) countries dominates. The United States (US) leads in this regard with 6,00,000 visiting students. China alone has 3,50,000 students studying abroad. India and China account for the largest proportion of foreign students in the US. China is a country where much progress has been made in terms of internationalization and where the pursuit of a deliberate strategy to achieve it is under way. China leads in the export of students for study abroad. China government is investing in the development of 38 world class universities to upgrade the access to and quality of higher education. Compared to the developments in China and other countries, India's forays into internationalization have been modest. These include the liberalization of foreign exchange for those who wish to study abroad, easing of restrictions on foreign investment and a limited number of collaborative programmers with foreign providers. The key Indian players that taken advantage of the new policies are from the private sector. Public universities have not been active on this front so far, nor do they have the resources to take such initiatives.

This is, however, no effective and coherent strategic or regulatory framework to monitor and assess these activities. As a result, internationalization has been dominated by foreign and Indian institutions which are not in all cases known for their high standards and educational quality.

Though the higher education sector is relatively small in relation to future needs, its record in terms of quality and standards of performance leaves much to be desired. In global rankings of universities, very few Indian institutions find a place. The shanghai world rankings of the top 500 universities/institutions include only three Indian Institute of Technologies (IITS) and one Indian Institute of Management (IIM), and that too, at the lower end. *The Times* global rankings of the top 100 also find a mention of just a couple of Indian Institutions. In terms of published papers (an indicator of research output), India has slipped from the 8th place in 1985 to the 14th in 2006. Thus though we have a few outstanding colleges and other higher education institutional standards of quality and excellence. According to some observers, the entry of self-financing private colleges in a big way has exacerbated this problem. This in turn, has negative implications for the acceptance of our degrees and of the graduates of the system in other countries and markets.

TOTAL QUALITY MANAGEMENT

Before understanding the term 'Quality enhancement', we have to understand first the Total Quality Management. Quality Management is an art of long term management to achieve excellence. It provides organization with sustainable qualitative management development and continuous process of the Management system for consumer satisfaction. In this Total Quality Management the term 'Total' signifies everyone in the system should be involved in quality management in the transformation process. Transform management and organization for betterment keeps as a door open making universe appear as a global village. Organizational level meets the external customer requirement and interacts with society process level bridges the gap between external and internal customer requirement. Performance or job level integrates the internal customer requirement i.e. students. What kind of education, syllabus or curriculum and how is the job done through teachers etc. passed down to students.

Transformation is required at all levels but paradox is universal pivot for development and distribution of knowledge, are least bothered about quality. Most of the institutions are not ISO qualified because the focus is on tradition but does not want improvement with eyes and minds to open traditional approach.

The institutions are state controlled to autonomous i.e. state monitored.

- There is lack of authority to implement values to authority.
- In 10th Five-Year Plan, UGC implemented laws are not following.

University Governance Mechanism or Administrative Governance is a way by which the entire administration is governed or controlled. It is a complex, impartial, transform mechanism process relationship and set of rules are accepted as constituent legitimate authority through which stake holders of the institutions expect their institutions, exercise then rights and obligations and mediate differences towards achieving to object of system.

(1) Organizational sustainability
   a) Strategic focus
   b) Financial viability
   c) Risk Management
(2) Compliance
   a) Acts, statuses, ordinances
   b) Financial rules.
   c) Governance of apex regulatory bodies.
(3) Quality Management
   a) Transparency in University Administration.
   b) Transparency in Financial Governance or disclosure.
(4) Achieving objectives of higher education.
   a) Equity, relevance and quality of higher education.
   b) Integrating efficient and honest human resources.
   c) Undertaking effective research and development act.

AIMS OF QUALITY MANAGEMENT

- Competition to create educated work force to do the best job in the market.
- Finance control.
- Managing type of risks, external and internal.
- Certifying rules and regulations which have to be ensure that they are complied with.
- Section 12B must be maintained.

PREPARATION FOR IMPLEMENTATION OF TOTAL QUALITY MANAGEMENT

(1) Redefining the organization structure, role and accountability to improve and work in innovative areas.
(2) Redefining the definition of quality:
   - Institutions must understand the requirement of time and expectation of stake holders.
   - Institutions must re-orient human of physical facilities to produce industry ready cultivated work force for the society.
   - It must reconstruct the quality policy and transmit it into different layers of administration.
(3) Redefining the performance chain and co-ordination amongst the internal and external customers or stake holders of institutions. The customers or stake holders are required to be identified properly as co-ordination or relationship amongst internal and external stake

holders. It is a pre-requisite to make total quality management a truly meaningful proposition. The performance indicators regulated to be properly established, regulated and audited.

(4) Redefining the Management ethics of academic institutions: Ethics are reflected in culture and valves of organization. It must follow properly developed ethical code of conducts, stake manner, how the employees of university or institution behave.

(5) Redefining financial governance and autonomy of the institution: The financial governance ensures optimal utilization of resources by channeling it into the most remunerative or rewarding channels. There must be adequate financial autonomy given to tae academic department to enable them to function properly.

(6) Redefining Training and learning process and resources: Introduction of total Quality Management calls for introduction of institutional practical skill development, motivational and professional transferring process to improve attitude of employees. It ensures total involvement attitude of work force to move in same frequency level.

(7) Redefining involvement of teaching, administration and non-teaching employees of organization: Improvement of every unit in the organization is pre-requisite of total quality management. In developing country it is very difficult to apply because of existence of prominent class difference in society. The only way to get rid of it is implementation of motivational process to the confidence level.

(8) Going through SWOT analysis: SWOT analysis = Strength + Weakness + Opportunity + Threat analysis.

It helps to assess the institution actual position or standing in the global perspective. Strength, Weakness, Opportunity threats, good relationship among employees are part of higher education. It is an effective tool of self assessing management.

QUALITY ASSURANCE IN EDUCATION

Quality Assurance refers to the policies, attitudes, actions and procedures necessary to ensure that quality is being maintained and enhanced. Accreditation refers to an evaluation of whether an institution qualifies for a certificate status. The status may have implications for the institution itself leg permission to operate and/or its students leg, eligibility for grants and/or its graduates qualified for obtain employment.

In fact, the underlying purpose of accreditation is to determine the extent to which institutions are discharging their responsibilities for realizing their goals and for the quality of education provided to enable the students to attain standards. Thus accreditation is the process of examining institutional procedure for assuring quality and assessing the arrangements for effective implementation of strategies. There are two major purposes which accreditation serves. One is quality assurance; determining standard quality and performance for minimum acceptability in the interest of public; and the other is quality improvement: Providing the service that is designed to through an external review process.

PRINCIPLES OF QUALITY ASSURANCE

A common approach based on the following principles needs to be evolved such that: (a) The system should be transparent and it should encourage rather than constrain diversity and be sensitive to distinct mission of each institution; (b) External quality assurance process should be consistent with the existing practices such as to complement institutional process rather than duplicating or replicating then; (c) criteria and processes should be adoptable to a change in global environment and change in a communication processes; and (d) It should facilitate progressive improvement in standards. It should provide for rigorous external verification of quality assurance strategies through peer review. Quality assurance should cover the academic affairs of institutions, relating to courses, staff qualification, research, academic administration and decision making. Mechanisms, and services and facilities in support of academic processes. It is necessary that the system be able to deal with several different classes of institutions, which encompass non-university institutions, accredited by the councils.

In this backdrop, the framework of quality assurance and accreditation, as evolved by the institutions and regulatory bodies become important to realize the mandate of higher education institutions.

WEAKNESSES OF EXISTING SYSTEM OF QUALITY ASSURANCE

The existing system of quality assurance in higher education operates at a variety of level and compromises both long standing elements and recent developments towards national approach

CURRENT PRACTICES

The basic plans for QA framework lies in the establishment of Higher Education Institutes is main universities as self accreditation institutions through legislation and regulation and the accreditation of other higher education coerces by the statutory bodies academic bodies and governing councils have major responsibilities for the qualities of educational provisional including academic standard

A number of extender mechanisms for reviewing aspects of internal university activities are of long standing among the universities. These include the use of external examiners for higher tasks done is research and some honours degrees, The role of professional bodies and associations in accreditation professional courses as medical, law, management, engineering, agriculture, architecture etc. Peer review mechanisms in relation to research fund in and the use by the universities of a wide variety of internal / external review and reporting procedure for faculties, departments and whole institution.

MAJOR SHORT COMINGS

There are however, several weaknesses in current mechanisms:

(1) Lack of clear mechanism for ensuring comparable standards of judgment in different states and for different institutions.
(2) The criterion for recognition of a university sue as central, state, deemed to be universities, institutions of national importance etc. widely differ and thirty it needs to be reviewed.
(3) Transparency in the existing system of independent external or self accreditation universities.

RESPONSIBILITY OF QUALITY ASSURANCE IN HIGHER EDUCATION

The responsibility of quality assurance in higher education lies with the university Grants commission and statutory councils like All India council for Technical Education (AICTE) The UGC established in 1994 the National assassin and accreditation council (NAAC) that undertakes institutional evaluation of universities and colleges. For quality assurance in technical and management education. The AICTE set up, also in 1994, a National Board of Accreditation (NBA) which undertakes programme evaluation. The Distance Education Council, Indira Gandhi National Open University (DEC-IGNOU) has the responsibility of monitoring quality in distance education programme. The Govt. of India has set up a number of councils to monitor professional activity in different professional areas. The councils also regulate higher education in their respective areas.

These statutory councils are of two types: those with both funding and regulatory powers relating to education e.g. All India Council of Technical Education (AICTE), Council of Architecture (CA), Pharmacy Council of India (PCI), Indian Nursing council (INC), Bar Council of India (BCI), Dental Council of India (DCI), Medical Council of India (MCI), National Council for Teacher Education (NCTE), Central Council for Homeopathy (CCH), Central Council of Indian Medicine (CCIM), Rehabilitation Council of India (RCI), and Veterinary Council of India (VCI).

CONCLUSION

The foregoing problems are linked to a large degree to the weaknesses in the regulatory framework of higher education. This applies especially to the question of quality and standards. The overload on the regulatory authorities, enforcement failure, overlaps and conflicts due to political or other influences have all played a role in this outcome. There much confusion also about the role of these agencies and collusion due to political or other influences have all played a role in this outcome. There is much confusion also about the role of these agencies in the regulation of private and foreign providers.

India's higher education sector is currently facing serious challenges in respect of the need to expand student in take (access), upgrading quality and achieving excellence mobilizing the needed resources, and strengthening the regulatory function. All these are complex issues and there are no simple remedies that can solve them. Many commissions and working groups have made recommendations to deal with them. Nevertheless, progress has been slow with respect to all the four problem areas.

Internationalism entails exchanges between domestic and foreign parties interested in these activities. The more developed countries (OECD for example) have an interest in exporting educational services in which they hold an advantage. Developing countries, on the other hand are recipients of the services from the former. This is not to say that they cannot export services in which other countries are interested. Some developing countries such as china and India for example are attracting overseas students to their institutions. It means that eventually they may develop the capacity and incentive to engage in both the export and import educational services towards a strategy. India's strategy with regard to internationalization should be based on its potential to be an effective aid to the mitigation of the basic problems facing our higher education sub-sector. Liberalization policies that open up the sector to foreign investment and permit the unregulated entry of private players will have only a marginal impact on the sector's basic problems such as access and quality. Any way the progress has been slow in enhancement of quality in higher education with respect to all problems areas which India can certainly overcome.

REFERENCES

Agarwal, Pawan (2006): *Higher Education in India: The Need for Change*, ICRIER Working Paper (New Delhi), June.

National Conference on 'Internationalization of Higher Education: Issues and Concerns', NIEPA, 26-27 August, 2004.

Panchamukhi, P.R. (2008): *Globalization and Higher Education* (ed.), New Delhi: Academic Foundation.

Paul, Samuel (2009): Internationalization of Higher Education: Strategic Implication, *Economic and Political Weekly* (Bangalore).

23

Ameliorating Quality in Higher Education

Rajesh Agarwal

The common objectives of education can be as such enumerated as:

(i) Socialization of successive generations
(ii) Disseminating existent knowledge
(iii) Enriching/expanding the existent knowledge-pool by initiating research
(iv) Enabling social mobility

A sound education system, i.e. a quality education system, can initiate changes in the pattern of societal behaviour and social relationships, by bringing about a change in outlook and attitude of the individual. The consequent social changes and social development enables every individual to effectively participate in the activities of society and to make a positive contribution to the progress of society. Thus the education system is that foundation which is the best social leveler ensuring the sustained growth of any social system. In this context, higher education plays the important role of analyzing, interpreting and authenticating/enhancing the existent knowledge structure erected by the primary and secondary levels of education, via research and contemplation.

Historically, the system of higher education stems from the idea of the *university*, the latter itself emanating from the intellectual work of German philosophers – from Kant and Fichte to Schleiermacher and Wilhelm von Humboldt – and its concept was born in the nineteenth century, with the rise in national aspirations and. the consequent rise in the significance of nation-states. A tacit deal made between power and knowledge provided scholars with unprecedented institutional opportunities in return for their obligation to support the national culture/help in inculcating the national consciousness in citizens. Elaborative, in its modern beginnings the regulatory idea of the modern university was enlightened reason, then, in Schleiermacher and Humboldt, the idea was culture in the sense of cultivating oneself as a subject of the nation-state.

Since the advent of Globalization in the 1980's and its consequent diffusion, social disparity and social deprivation have become areas of concern because of their destabilizing potential in the social and political arena. Education is considered a basic element to invalidate the destabilizing tremors arising due to disparity and deprivation. Here, along with being a development goal by itself, education is also the main avenue of social mobility and, therefore, of ensuring development and escaping poverty. "Education is more than a right associated with full personal development. It is also a key factor in determining the opportunities and quality of life accessible to individuals, families and communities. There is a wealth of evidence which demonstrates that education has a positive impact on income and health, family structure (in terms of fertility and its members' participation in the economy, etc.), the promotion of democratic values and civilized co-existence and the autonomous and responsible pursuits of individuals." (ECLAC, 2005) However, with the spread of free-market economies and neo-liberal economic views, consequent to Globalization, all over the world, public higher education institutions, and the universities in particular, are under siege. The questioning of the nation-state and the gradual decomposition of the welfare state, via the globalization processes, has brought about a major revision in thinking about the role of the state in contemporary politics and economies. Capital, goods, technologies, information, and people cross borders in ways that were unimaginable only a few years ago. The power of the state as such is increasingly viewed as mere administrator, a "facilitator", rather than as a direct provider of growth or of social services. National identity ceases to be the social glue binding the citizens and their gregarious groupings and, therefore, its production, cultivation, and inculcation – the ideals that stood behind the idea of the university as conceived by its German intellectual founders – ceases to be a crucial social task. The decreasing role of the state goes hand in hand with the decreasing role of its modern ideological arm – the university.

In line with this the University seems no longer to be capable of maintaining its modern role as a cultural institution closely linked to the nation-state and the notions of Enlightenment/post-Enlightenment in Europe. In the globalizing world of today, references made to national culture as the rationale of the university, are non-convincing. The underlying question about spending will be whether, at the margin, higher education spending is contributing more than spending at the margin in other programmes affecting public schools, health care providers.

So the global direction taken by government s worldwide, with huge intellectual backups provided by international organizations, is to favour an increasingly market-oriented, financially independent system of higher education Institutions. (OECD, 1998; World Bank, 1997) This ruthless logic of consumerism brings forth the idea of "excellence in education", i.e. the most useful, best-selling, and rapidly attained education/knowledge (or merely certification). This is possible only in a 'corporation' like university bureaucratically governed, consumer-oriented and based on "academic capitalism". (Slaughter and Leslie, 1997) tasked with training specialists rapidly, cheaply, and efficiently – preferably very rapidly, very cheaply, and very efficiently.

This gives rise to some critical questions. What is the future of the university deprived of its Enlightenment-Culture-Nation oriented mission? Does the university really have to drift towards the model of a managed corporation, fighting in the marketplace with other similar corporate structures in search of consumers? Under these circumstances will the university be able to maintain its function of critical judgments pertaining to the society? Is higher education merely a private commodity or is it a public good? (Currie and Newson, 1998)

It is certain that in an era Globalization and the consequent intensification of global linkages higher education cannot be traditional or static as it receives competition from global universities and private educational institutions. The contemporary form of transnational education such as liberal education-migration policy, internet-based distance learning, branch campuses, educational franchising is expanding, providing opportunities for students to study and learn outside their country of origin.

In the Indian context, in lieu of India's membership of the World Trade Organization (WTO) and the General Agreement of Trade in Service (GATS), opening up of it's their education sector to foreign investment has been inevitable. This impetus to global integration and the advent of a '*knowledge economy*' in this media mediated, hyper competitive world, has boosted global-relativism leading to the expansion of what is possible for pupils with adequate/relevant education. Non-cognition of this expansion via sufficiently focused educational endeavours will result in the non-retention of the national talent-pool and to the flight of the indigenous intellectual and financial capital to foreign lands, in the search of better opportunities, to the detriment of the mother country. Thus, the growing demand of accessibility of Higher Education has laid the onus of infusion of funds in the educational sector on the governments. But limited financial resources have compelled governments to gradually shorten funding in the education sector. All this requires an increase in not only the quantum of education but also the quality of education in terms of a new orientation in academic credentials addressing the learners' choices, which has multiplied manifold.

Realizing these requisite conditionality of higher education, India has established approximately 407 Universities, 10377 Colleges for General Education and, 3201 Colleges of Professional Education in the Year 2004-05 (Reserve Bank of India, 2008). Efforts have also been made to renovate /rejuvenate the educational system by providing greater resources via public – private participation, permission to the entry of foreign educational providers and, the impetus to academics – in order to bridge the gap between demand and supply in education sector. These measures reflect the spirit of the economic reforms initiated in the 1990's and aim at aligning with the globalization process. The Foreign Educational Institutional Bill (FEI) allowing foreign direct investment in Higher Education, pending approval of the cabinet, along with the Right to Education Bill (RTE) are examples to the point.

However, the situation has not improved substantially, the reasons being:

- *Inadequate infrastructure* for imparting classroom education/ conducting research. The persistence of inadequacies in libraries and laboratories in terms of books/equipments available and optimum research atmosphere hampers quality development.
- *Inadequate scrutiny* by funding agency due to its preoccupation with assessing the utilization of money rather than the quality of the academic output.
- The institutional, acceptance *of mediocrity levels* in academics to absorb demand.
- *Low performance of teachers* due to the systemic failure. Despite substantive increase in the pay and perks of the teachers in order to attract talent, the non-availability of academic/ research resources in Indian languages, the near absence of academic/semi-academic journals in many social sciences where teachers/students can contribute, placement of greater value on academic degrees as compared to knowledge, arbitrariness in the choice of research without due consideration its relevance in furthering socio-developmental goals/market requirements leads to the low performance of teachers.
- Prevalence of *dud credentials* due to an increase in high-purchasing power armed, quality indifferent entrant aspiring status over competence and/or a tight job market where acquiring additional degrees apparently offers additional competitive advantage.
- Non-recruitment on *vacant faculty positions,* despite rapid increase in enrollments, due to procedural lacunas. At many of the institutions, politics has intruded into campus life, influencing academic appointments and decisions transcending levels. Student unrest and occasional faculty agitation further disrupts operations. Despite all this, the faculty administrators strive to provide teaching, coordinate examinations, and award degrees, with a semblance of normality. Appointments on vacant faculty positions can improve the state of affairs.
- India's *Gross Enrolment Ratio* for higher education at 12.4 per cent, in 2006, was well below the world average of 23.2 per cent, the Asian average of 22 per cent, and the developed countries average of 54.6 per cent – 81 per cent for USA; 54 per cent for UK; 49 per cent for Japan (Planning Commission, 2008).

  The NSSO (2007-08) data puts the Gross Enrolment Ratio for higher education even lower at 17 per cent.
- The total higher education outlay has remained consistently low. Thus, out of the total outlay of approximately ₹ 47,000 crores, during the 11th plan period, merely 39 per cent is expected to be spent. Even here the major share of this outlay – as much as 71 per cent – was allotted to the Universities while over 6,000 Under-

Graduate Colleges received only 29 per cent (11th Five Year Plan, 2007-12).

The National Knowledge Commission corroborates this by stating that the Government expenditure on education was a measly 3.6 per cent. Out of this approximately 0.37 per cent was spent on higher education. The OECD figures for the corresponding period for USA were 2.9 per cent and that of the UK were 1.3 per cent (Report to the Nation, NKC, 2005).

- The geographical imbalance created between the cities and remote areas in reference to educational investments has become alarmingly dangerous. Geographical locations like Hyderabad, Chennai, Pune, Noida, and Bangalore received significant educational investments at the cost of the villages/remote areas. This education-divide has increased migration and has blocked the youth of Indian villages from availing the advantages of globalization particularly the sophisticated education and research facilities This stifling of academics is leading India towards emerging as one of the largest exporter of students in the world, sending over 200,000 students and over 4 billion dollars, per year, to Universities across the world.

Remedial Actions

In light of these lacunas, remedial action can take the following course:

(i) All the concerned stake-holders/knowledge users in education should be given the *opportunity to participate* in curriculum/policy formulation albeit keeping some universal broad guideline (e.g. The NCERT National Curriculum Framework) in mind. This would encourage contemporary skill-development along with holistic character building.

(ii) Integrating *On-Job-Training* into learning frameworks would also help by not just improving employment outcomes but by reaffirming the practicability of the educational courses offered.

(iii) Adequate importance should be provided to indigenous/vernacular languages due to their utility in the comprehensive diffusion of knowledge to the lesser endowed, at the local levels. But *teaching of English language* should also be emphasized because English is the key which opens new vistas for accessing knowledge, employment outcomes and geographic mobility in a situation of homogenizing globalization.

(iv) An *alternative educational framework* which recognizes non-traditional areas of educational attainments, ignored by the established disciplines/specialties, in consultation with the user-groups, is also requisite. Thus, courses in natural resource management, technological up gradation of unorganized industry etc. should also be considered.

(v) *Distance education systems* should also be given due importance. These systems can provide more options of academic attainments/ improvements for the already employed but geographically disadvantaged ensuring their proper integration into the globalized markets.

(vi) Implementing more succinct/contemporary *means of supervision and regulation.* Here, the Gujarat government is experimenting with performance analysis of the government teachers by using technology (GPRS) along with a mix of incentives for learning outcomes and penalties for absence. Here, the Gujarat state government has initiated a pilot project in Narmada district, one of the most backward districts of Gujarat having low literacy to ensure full enrolment of all eligible students and to reduce dropout rate in primary schools. This project could be emulated in the higher education system too. The pilots being implemented by Bangalore based enterprise Software Solutions Lab (ESSL). A standalone fingerprint biometric machine with external uninterrupted power supply up to 12 hours will be installed in each primary school for recoding attendance of teachers as well as students. At the end of the month, the attendance data is transported to the Block-HQ in a portable memory device like a pen drive. This attendance data is processed with the help of a software application for getting pay rolls of teachers and other various reports.

(vii) *NGO's* should also be adequately considered in any initiative for ensuring contemporariness in educational systems. This requires a transformation in the institutional images only comprehending the dichotomy of either public or private educational institutions. The super 30 initiative of Bihar is a case to the point.

(viii) Establish a *strong linkage* between Indian Universities and Universities abroad.

(ix) Adoption of the *PPP model* to ensure adequate availability of educational institutions which would upgrade the status of the students from being hostages to being clients. Hirschman concept of Exit has special relevance in this context. The idea of Exit relates to the economic decision to leave an educational service provider due to the dissatisfaction with cost incurred and the benefits obtained. According to Hirschman it is the Low availability of good educational institutions that makes the use of Exit redundant which,(along with Voice: the political activity undertaken by an individual, while remaining within an organization, to maintain quality) in the absence of other compulsive tools of quality management, paves the way for the continual deterioration in the quality of education. The providers use such a situation to impose additional hidden costs on the community by emphasizing greater pomp and display or/and marketing; the response from the community, if any, being subdued and akin to a plea rather than taking the form of any concrete action, exerting pressure on the educational providers to improve services.

Higher education is the penultimate vehicle for harnessing a country's human resources for national development. The need of the hour is that the Indian higher education system should be able to provide the country with contemporary knowledge and skills necessary for the sustainable livelihoods and the systematic development of the local resources. For fulfilling this purpose the higher education institutions have to be made competitive, competent and compatible in line with the global changes. Equality of access is an equally vital consideration here. Foreign universities may be better endowed than Indian institutions in terms of infrastructure, financial resources, staff, reputation etc., but, obtaining admission/education in them is far more expensive and can be opted for by the wealthy only. This creates a wide gulf between students coming from different economic background. Inadequate cognition to these issues can and will jeopardize the capacity of higher education to produce the right people. It is therefore suggested that the government should ensure an appropriate budget and right allocation for higher education in the public sector, along with a fair controlling policy to monitor the quality of education and training provided in the private sector. A mandatory policy should be evolved to ensure a strong network /interface between the mediocre institutions and the institutions of excellence and also between the higher education institutions and industries. It is possible that by such an effort both an application-oriented education and employability could be effectively offered to meet out the challenges of globalization.

The actualization of the benefits of education esp., in light of the diminishing control of the nation-states, requires the universal diffusion of sensitivity. Globalized considerations to the issue of higher education and subsequent localized action taking the peculiar conditions/aspirations of the local community into consideration, by both the governing structure as well as the community it-self, is an essential requisite.

ANNEXURE

Table 1: Higher Education in India: 2000/01–2004/05

Year	*Colleges for General Education*	*Colleges of Professional Education**	*Universities*
2000-01	7929	2223	254
2001-02	8737	2409	272
2002-03	9166	2610	304
2003-04	9427	2751	304
2004-05	10377	3201	407

*Professional education includes engineering, technology and architecture, medical (Allopathy/ayurvedic/homeopathy/unani/nursing/pharmacy, etc.), teacher training Institutes.

Source: Handbook of Statistics on Indian Economy, Reserve Bank of India, 2008.

Table 2: Expenditure on Higher Education: 2000/01-2004/05

Year	*Higher Education Expenditure (USD Million)*	*% of Total Education Expenditure*	*% of GDP*	*% of Total Government's Expenditure*
2000-01	3587.50	20.52	0.89	2.96
2001-02	2946.51	17.93	0.69	2.31
2002-03	3404.47	18.55	0.70	2.34
2003-04	3766.05	18.03	0.68	2.22
2004-05	3656.89	18.96	0.69	2.18

Source: Central Statistical Organization, Ministry of Statistics and Programme Implementation, New Delhi, 2008.

REFERENCES

11th Five Year Plan, 2007-12, Vol. II, Planning Commission, GOI, Delhi, 2008.

Currie, J., and Newson, J., eds. Universities and Globalization: Critical Perspectives, Sage publications, 1998.

Handbook of Statistics on Indian Economy, Reserve Bank of India, Online version, 2008.

Hirschman, A., 'Exit, Vote and the State' *World Politics* 31 (1), Oct., 1978.

NSS 64th Round, GOI, Delhi, 2007-08.

Redefining Tertiary Education. Paris: Organization for Economic Cooperation and Development, OECD, 1998.

Report to the Nation, The National Knowledge Commission, 2005.

Slaughter, S., and Leslie, L.L. *Academic Capitalism: Politics, Policies, and the Entrepreneurial University*, John s Hopkins University Press, 1997.

The State in a Changing World: World Development Report, World Bank, 1997.

The United Nations Economic Commission for Latin America and the Caribbean (ECLAC), 2005.

24

Relationship between TQM in Education and Leadership Qualities of Teachers and Administrators

Deepti Rani Chaudhary

An excellent education system is an imperative for any human society to grow and develop. Although the products of education are not tangible and the returns cannot be measured directly, they are reflected in the performance of almost all sectors of the society. It is because education provides inputs for their functioning by way of knowledge, skilled and trained manpower. Indian society as focuses on removal of poverty and bring prosperity should give more attention to its education and invest more. If education is improved the whole society will improve and that is what has happened to Japan, America, Germany and many European countries.

The policy paper of the World bank (Education Sector, 1980) also describes education as follows:

Education is a basic human need to acquire a broad base of knowledge, attitudes, values and skills. It provides techniques to learn to respond to new opportunities to adjust to socio-cultural changes and to participate in social, cultural, economic and political activities. Education is an activity that sustains and accelerates overall development as it prepares and trains skilled workers at all levels to manage capital, technology, services and administration in every sector in the economy. It also facilitated the advancement of knowledge in pure and applied fields.

It can be concluded from above that development of a country dependent on the education and training of people and educated and trained people accumulate capital, exploit natural resources, and built social, economic, political and cultural organizations and modernize them to develop and maintain quality.

As education is so imperative for the development of a country, an attempt has been made here to elaborate the concept of TQM and its implications for education as a system.

CONCEPT OF TOTAL QUALITY MANAGEMENT (TQM)

Quality like beauty is elusive and difficult to define. By this term different people mean different things and also the meaning changes for the same person from time to time. The ISO defines quality as "The totality of features and characteristics of a product or service that bear on its ability to satisfy stated or implied needs." So Total Quality Management can be defined as a process of change with the following basic characteristics:

1. Focus on consumer expectation.
2. Prevention of problems
3. Building commitment to quality in workforce
4. Open decision making process
5. Decentralized management

TOTAL QUALITY MANAGEMENT IN EDUCATION

The concept of Total Quality Management is a multifaceted concept. It can be applied phase by phase from the grass root level. However the top level manager shall give the vision statement and quality policy. The vision statement should be SMART i.e., specific, measurable, attainable, relevant and traceable. The quality policy should have relevance to functional cost and value and it gives proper directions to the people in the organization to carry out their role efficiency.

The people in the education system should be empowered to take decisions at their own level. This may require some training and reorientation of the teaching and non-teaching staff. In this process people are given a chance to bloom fully and show their calibre. This will lead to innovation and change in the education system. System approach in education occupies important place. Different components of a system and educational institution as a system have been examined. It focuses on client orientation towards Total Quality Management.

There may be two kinds of clients when applying Total Quality Management in education:

1. *Internal clients*: Teachers, non academic staff, principal, manager and managing committee.
2. *External clients*: Parents community, the state government and the society.

Students in this concept occupy a unique position of belonging to both internal and external clients.

Total Quality Management represents a permanent shift in an institution's focus, away from short term expediency to a long term quality improvement. Constant innovation, improvement and change are stressed and those institutions that practice it lock into a cycle of continuous improvement, Khurran (2000) they make a conscious attempt to analyze what they are doing and plan to improve it.

TOTAL QUALITY MANAGEMENT IN HIGHER EDUCATION

Educational system is a complex system as it involves human beings as input to and output from the system. Students are input and customers too. But the

Total Quality Management tools and techniques can be adapted to build quality in higher education. Talwar (2010) quality assurance and accreditation in higher education is defined as systematic management and assessment of procedure adopted by higher education institutions or system to monitor performance and to ensure achievement of quality improvement. It is also to be underlined that in the process of education for quality of character development, good quality, character of the teacher is of supreme importance. TQM provides an opportunity for all educational institutions to get quality at each and every stage and provide different alternatives to manage in a holistic manner.

The need for Total Quality Management in higher education arises on account of the following:

- Ever growing number of students
- Increasing competition due to privatization of' education and access to education through internet
- Limited resources
- Inadequate involvement of students in teaching learning
- Lack of commitment among faculty and staff
- Lack of accountability
- Students not possessing requisite capabilities especially the generic skills of decision making, problem solving, creativity, independence adaptability, learning to learn etc
- Increasing cost per unit

In other words efficiency, effectiveness and quality of higher education at this stage are questionable. Sirvanci (2004) TQM has been adopted by many organizations worldwide, its implementation in non-profit organizations, such as higher education institutions, presents more challenges and difficulties than those encountered in business organizations. A critical step in TQM implementation is the process of customer identification, there are other issues such as leadership, cultural and organizational issues that tend to create difficulties for TQM implementation in higher education.

Owlia (1997) the role of Quality plays in higher education sector is becoming more important as the dominance of market orientation leaves no alternative for universities and college but to improve their quality while increasing efficiency.

Implementation of Total Quality Management in higher education requires a deep commitment, full involvement of people, top management support, fair reward and recognition policies and training of concerned people in the concept tools and techniques of Total Quality Management.

LEADERSHIP

Leadership has been described as the process of social influence in which one person can enlist the aid and support of others in the accomplishment of a common task.

1. Leader lives cordially with other members and take opinion of other members.
2. Leader is omnipotent.
3. Leadership of leader depends upon mutual agreements of members and also divide the members in groups.
4. Leader should honour the opinion of his critics.
5. Leader should decide according to the opinion of members together.

Leadership style preference: During the past several decades the sheer volume of theory and research devoted to leadership testifies to its prominence in your collective efforts to understand and improve organizations. Hoy & Wayne (1991, p. 251).

Dimensions of Leadership

Theory and research are replete with various frameworks of examining the important general dimensions of leadership behaviour. Most conceptualizations of leadership are multidimensional that is supporting at least two distinct types.

In his analysis, Chester I. Barnard (1938, p. 60) distinguishes between the effectiveness and the efficiency of cooperative action.

The persistence of cooperation depends upon two conditions:

- Its effectiveness.
- Its efficiency.

Of the various types of leadership described in industrial and social setup, the most common form of leadership classification is on the basis of the manner of exerting influence. From this point of view the two opposite poles are authoritarian and democratic leadership styles, as initially presented by Lewin, Lippitt and White (1939). Although some objectives have been raised to the use of value loaded terms 'Authoritarian' and 'Democratic' the fact remains, as observed by Krech, Crutchileld and Dallachey (1962) that the authoritarian – democratic is "Perhaps the most prominent and socially significant typology of leadership". The description given by Krech *et al.* (1962) served as the basis for the construction of items of the scale in the present study.

Chatterjee (2008) It describes that leadership is the process of evolving adaptive culture by relating to reality in new ways leaders are change artists. They bring about change by creating institutions and communities where people learn to relate to each other in novel ways. It also showed that wisdom traditions of the world shed light on fundamental values for personal and organizational excellence.

Significance of Study

The investigator herself is a teacher in education institution that is why she felt concern about the present state of affair. It is not necessary that a highly qualified person with high percentage of marks and with good research experience can be a good administrator on whom total quality management depends because they are being promoted from teachers with certain amount of experience and without administrative training. They can manage but quality of management is of what degree? In this modem era Total Quality Management is now attracting attention in the field of education. Different interpretations of Total Quality Management in industry however may result in contrasting outcomes. Main aim is improving the quality of the production system in order to produce a quality product with "zero defects".

This may lead to a teaching and learning process which focuses exclusively on achieving good examination results. This is contrasted with a second interpretation of Total Quality Management as a never ending cycle of improvement in the system. In the content of' education, this may lead to continually improving the quality of instruction in order to encourage students to become critical and creative thinkers in a fast changing technological world. Also investigator wants to investigate various aspects related with Total Quality Management in relation to leadership qualities of teachers and students (rural and urban background). The responsibility lies on teachers because teacher can produce the students who are the future teachers and administrators so Total Quality Management focuses on developing overall development of students, teachers and administrators. And also find the relationship of Total Quality Management with leadership qualities of students, teachers and administrators.

Objectives

1. To study the Total Quality Management in education of teachers in relation to their leadership qualities.
2. To study the Total Quality Management in education of administrators in relation to their leadership qualities.
3. To study the Total Quality Management in education and leadership qualities among teachers and administrators.

Hypotheses

1. There is insignificant relation between Total Quality Management in education of teachers in relation to their leadership qualities.
2. There is insignificant relation between Total Quality Management in education of administrators in relation to their leadership qualities.
3. There is insignificant relation between Total Quality Management in education and leadership qualities among teachers and administrators.

Delimitation

1. The present study is confined to the teachers of B.Ed. Colleges of Amritsar city
2. The present study is confined to the administrators of B.Ed. Colleges of Amritsar city.

3. The study is limited to main variables TQM, Leadership as determined by questionnaire.

Selection of Sample

For the present study a sample of 100 Teachers and 50 Administrators of B.Ed. Colleges have taken.

TOOLS

The tools used are:

1. Mukhopadhyay institutional profile questionnaire (MIPQ)
   By Marmar Mukhopadhyay
2. Leadership preference scale.
   By Bhushan, L.I. (1995)

ANALYSIS AND INTERPRETATION OF DATA

Hypothesis-I

"There is insignificant relation between Total Quality Management of teachers in relation to their leadership qualities."

Table 1: Showing Mean (M) and Coefficient of Correlation (r) of TQM in Education in Relation to Leadership Qualities Teachers

Group	*Variables*	*Sample*	*Mean (M)*	*Coefficient of correlation (r)*	*Level of significance*
Teachers	TQM	100	240.52	0.38	Significant
	Leadership		118.04		

Interpretation

It is evident from Table 1 that coefficient of correlation of TQM in education in relation to leadership qualities among Teachers is 0.38.

Discussion

Table 1 shows that 'r' value is 0.38 which indicates that there exist positive correlation between TQM in relation to leadership qualities among teachers. However the value of 'r' is greater than corresponding table value at 0.05 level of significant. From this we infer that there is insignificant relation in Total Quality Management in education in relation to leadership qualities among teachers.

So our hypothesis, "There is insignificant relation between Total Quality Management in relation to their leadership qualities of teachers," is Rejected.

Hypothesis-II

"There is insignificant relation between Total Quality Management in education in relation to their leadership qualities of administrators."

Table 2: Showing Mean (M) and Coefficient of Correlation (r) of TQM in Education in Relation to Leadership Qualities of Administrators

Group	*Variables*	*Sample*	*Mean (M)*	*Coefficient of correlation (r)*	*Level of significance*
Teachers	TQM	10*	131.8	– 0.13	Insignificant
	Leadership	10	130.9		

Interpretation

It is evident from Table 2 that mean and coefficient of correlation of Total Quality Management in relation to leadership qualities among administrators are 131.8, 130.9 and calculated 'r' value is –0.13.

Discussion

Table 2 shows that 'r' value is –0.13 which indicates that there exists negative correlation between Total Quality Management and leadership qualities among administrators. However the value of 'r' is less than corresponding table value at 0.05 level of significance. From this we infer that there is an insignificance negative relation in TQM of administrators.

So, our hypothesis, "There is insignificant relation between Total Quality Management in education in relation to the leadership qualities of administrators." is accepted.

Hypothesis-III

There is insignificant relation between total quality management in education and leadership qualities among teachers and administrators."

Table 3: Showing Coefficient of Correlation (r) of TQM in Education in Relation to Leadership Qualities for Teachers and Administrators

Group	*'t' value*	*Level of Significance*
Teachers	0.38	Significant
Administrators	–0.13	Insignificant

Interpretation

It is evident from the Table 3 that coefficient of total quality management in education in relation to leadership qualities among teachers is 0.3 and among administrators is –0.13.

CONCLUSION

From the above results it was inferred that the teachers have high leadership qualities and TQM. So the teachers can manage the quality educational system but the administrators showing significant relation in TQM and leadership which means that the administrators cannot alone influence the TQM of the institutions. So, teachers and administrators both are accountable for total quality management in education.

EDUCATIONAL IMPLICATIONS

The implications of the present study are:

1. Country's development depends upon quality. Today each company produces product with zero defect. So education system should be such which will produce total quality management and produce products (teachers and administrators) with zero defects.
2. Education system should stress on developing the democratic leadership among teachers and administrators, so that it can improve total quality management of the institution.
3. The leaders with ethical base can lead their responsibility in a better way. They will help people to be happy, maintain peace everywhere in society. They will free the people from frustrations and stress and help them to be happy and progressing. So in education leadership plays important role for total quality management of the institution.
4. In rural areas there is no quality of education so educational policies must be developed by administrators to improve quality of education in rural areas and also develop leadership qualities.
5. Teachers promote leadership qualities among students and thereby increasing total quality management among them, this can further help the teachers to manage relationships inside and outside the class.
6. Equal opportunities must be available to rural and urban students so that quality of education is improved.

REFERENCES

Allen, L.E., Frances, L., and Lowther, D.L. (2009), "The Role of Leadership in Statewide Student Laptop Implementation." *Journal of Educational Technology*. Vol. No. 1.

Arya, C. (2010), "Academic libraries in the light of Total quality Management." *A Weekly Journal of Education*, Vol. 48, No. 8.

Bass and Auolio (1997), "Relationship between Teachers job satisfaction and principals leadership style at secondary school stage." An unpublished M.Ed. dissertation, GNDU, Amritsar.

Bassi, T. (2009), "Assessing the quality of education across nations." *Journal of the Society for Educational Research and Development*, Vol. 25, No. 2.

Best, J.W. (1963). *Research in Education*. New Delhi: Prentice Hall of India.

Bhusshan, L.I. (1995), "A Manual of Leadership Scale." McGraw Hill, New Delhi.

Buzan, P. (2008) "Spiritual based leadership in business." *Journal of Human Values*, Vol. 14, No. 2.

Cantwell, J. (2003), A study of relationship of principal leadership, teacher interaction and school climate on three years of Pennsylvania system of school assessment test data, dissertation completed at center of education, Widener University, Chester.

Chattejee, D. (2008), "Wise ways: Leadership as Relationship," *Journal of Human Values*, Vol. 12, No. 2.

Clabough, P.R. (2006), "The study of relationship between leadership style, school climate and violence in middle schools." Retrieved from www.umi.com.

Gakhar, S.C. (2008), *Educational Management Theory; Policy and Practice*, Haryana: N.M. Publication.

Garrett, H.E. and Woodworth, R.S. (2008), *Statistics in Psychology and Education*, New Delhi: International Publishers.

Guilford, J.P. (1973), *Fundamental Statistics in Psychology and Education*, New York: McGraw Hill Book Company.

Gurr, Drysdale and Mulford (2005), "Relationship between Teachers job satisfaction on Principal Leadership Style at Secondary School Stage," an unpublished M.Ed. dissertation, GNDU, Amritsar.

Harnesk, R. and Abrahamsson, L. (2007), "TQM: An act of balance between contradictions." *TQM Magazine*, Vol. 19, Issue 6, retrieved from http://demo/emeraldinsight.com/insight/viewcontent se rvlet,jsessionid.

Hoy, K. Wayne (1991), *"Educational administration"*, McGraw-Hill book Co. Singapore, p. 251.

Joolideh, F. and K. Yeshodhara (2006), "Leadership between among high school teachers in India and Iran", *Indian Educational Review*, Vol. 44, No. 1 (84-85).

Koch, J.V. (2003), "TQM: Why is its impact in higher education so small?" *TQM Magazine*, Vol. 18, Issue 6 retrieved from http://demo/emeraldinsight.com/insight/viewcontainer.do?containertype= journal&container Id=10912.

Koul, L. (1984), *Educational Research*, New Delhi: Vikas Publishing House. Lachlan, E.D., Crawford, Paul Shutler (1999), "Total Quality Management in education and issues for the classroom teacher". *International Journal of Educational Management*, Vol. 13, Issue 2(67-73).

Meenu (1998-99), "Leadership style preference and organizational effectiveness of school principals". M.Ed. Dissertation unpublished submitted to GNDU Amritsar.

Padhi, N. (2005), "Application of TQM in open and distance learning: A strategic approach." http://www.ignou.ac.in./icdef2005/pdfs/theme3port/theme3-213.pdf.

Renu (2007), "SC Leadership in Panchayats in Punjab." Divener: A Research *Journal of Humanities and Social Sciences*, Vol. 4, No. 2.

Sidhu, K.S. (2004), *Methodology of Research in Education*, New Delhi: Sterling Publication.

Talawar and Kumar (2010), "Total Quality Management in Higher Education", *A Weekly Journal of Higher Education*, Vol. 48, No. 1.

Vinut Kumar, Kandujon, K.S. Kazana and Sunil Kumar (2009), "A Conceptual Analysis of the Concept TQM", *University News Magazines*, Vol. 47, No. 41 (15).

Wepner B.S. Doxfri, A. and Wilhite C.S. (2008), "The Leadership dimension of education dears", *Journal of Teacher Education*, Vol. 59, No. 2, Sage Publications.

25

Prospects of Internationalization of Higher Education, Estimable Assessment and Evaluation: Panacea for Quality Education

Ismat Jahan Siddique

Internationalization came as a revolution in the development of higher education, Now it is the demand of the hour to exchange students and faculty members for professional courses like Medical, Engineering and other courses, for this purpose universities are adopting various plans policies and strategies to internationalize education to cater the needs of globalization

UNESCO (2006) defined internationalization of Higher Education: "It is Higher education that takes place in situations where the teacher, student, programme, institution or provider and course materials cross-national jurisdictional borders. Cross-border education may include higher education by public or private and not-for-profit/for-profit providers. It encompasses a wide range of modalities in a continuum from face-to-face (taking various forms from students traveling abroad and campuses abroad) to distance learning (using technologies and including e-learning)."

Therefore it is a process of integrating an international perspective into the education. It needs an institutional vision to motivate people to change the whole to think globally and collaboratively. It is a way towards an ever-changing, diverse external environment that focused on global environment. Through internationalization of Higher Education we can co-operate and exchange in Education and Research. Competition in Higher Education is increasing day-by-day so there is need to improve communication, exchanges and partnerships, internationalization of curriculum, improvement in the teaching and learning processes then only we can say that it has become and indicator for quality in Higher Education.

The internationalization of higher education have two major dimensions. One dimension is merely domestic which refers to the international and intercultural dimensions of without ever leaving their home country. The second dimension refers to the mobility of the participants across national borders. It is also called cross-border education, and this type of education growing rapidly, particularly at the higher education level.

According to UNESCO report (2006) cross-border mobility of programmes is "a movement of individual education or training courses and programmes across national boundaries through face-to-face, distance or a combination of these. Foreign country provider or the affiliated domestic partner or both of them jointly award credits for the course." Franchising, double or joint degrees and various articulation models are popular methods of international programme mobility.

IMPORTANT MODELS FOR INTERNATIONAL PROGRAMME MOBILITY

1. *Franchise*: It means when a reputed institution allows another institution in another country to deliver programmes in that country. The more a reputed organization usually awards the qualification. Partners customize their arrangements for teaching, management, assessment, profit sharing and awarding of qualification each franchise. This dimension is in practice nowadays

2. *Joint Degree*: In this arrangement, institutions in different countries offer a programme jointly for which a student receives a qualification from each organization. Institutions customize arrangements for the programme provision and the basis for awarding the qualifications for each arrangement. U.S.A., U.K. Australia and India are following this joint degree programme

3. *Joined Efforts*: It is an arrangements between institutions of different countries allow students to gain credit for courses offered by all the providers. This allows students to gain credit for work done by a provider other than the provider awarding the qualification.

4. *Distance Education*: It is very common today, especially in India. In this arrangement, institutions deliver a programme to students in different countries through distance and online. It may include some face-to-face support for students through domestic study centers. The main reason of these collaborations is to improve acceptability of the programmes and their creditworthiness. Who awards the degree is important depending on the reputation of the institution. Recognition of qualification for employment or further study is the most important reason. From an academic point, these dimensions in higher education affect the country's higher education institutions intellectual enrichment, and stimulate teaching and research. From the cultural angle, it helps to understand the cultures of other cultures.

There are some important rationales for Internationalization of Higher Education Literature (De Wit, 2002) identifies four broad categories for rationales. They are as follows:

1. Political rationales, Include foreign policy, security technical assistance peace, Mutual friendship and understanding, National and Regional Identity and Mobility of Students.
2. Economic Rationale – it includes financial assistance, Growth and healthy competition, Educational demands and labour market
3. Social and cultural rationales, to create intercultural and social

understanding our universities and research work play very important role, Faculties and Students provide international environment.

4 Academic Rationales means improvement of the quality and international academic standards, valuable research, better teaching processes, institution building, profile and status, Improved Curriculum to meet the needs of the international standards

The Joint Committee on Standard of Educational Evaluation, USA suggested that system, used for personal evaluation, say for teachers, student-teachers or teacher-educators must have the following four basic attributes.

1. *Propriety*: This means that evaluation should provide for:
   - Sound Educational principles and effective performance on the job.
   - Formal guidelines in the manuals supplied to evaluate to make it consistent and equitable in terms of ethical codes.
   - Access to those only who are to review or use these reports.
   - Self-esteem, motivation for better performance and reporting in a considerate and courteous manner.
2. *Utilities* means making evaluation informative, timely and influential. It refers to
   - Identification of users and intended uses of teacher evaluation.
   - Encouraging development of human resources, teachers and teacher educators.
   - Conducting evaluation professionally for better acceptance of reports.
   - Follow up of evaluators for appropriate action and
   - Functional reporting which has to be clear, timely and accurate.
3. *Feasibility*: It refers to the practicability of evaluation system in a given context of setting. Resources and instructional time. It is based on.
   - Practical viability that is system for evaluation works with minimum disruption of instruction and is cost-effective for producing intended evidences.
   - Social viability meaning thereby that teacher evaluation system may be worked out on active collaboration with all those involve in the system and
   - Resource viability means the provision of adequate time and resource to make the system efficient and effective.
4. *Accuracy*: It refers to the evidences obtained during evaluation of teachers, which should not only be dependable and technically defensible but also lead to logical conclusion based on the data. Accuracy, however, demands.
   - Clear definition of performance objectives to determine valid criteria of assessment.
   - Identification and description of the work environment that influences performance.

- Use of measurement procedures leading to valid and accurate inferences.
- Use of measurement procedures yielding consistently reliable information about teacher performance and
- Fair assessment by providing safeguards against biased judgments.

Currently in teaching there is worldwide standards movement leading to the development of new accountability procedures and standards to assess teacher quality and performance. A National and International mapping of these developing teaching standards reveals a significant role for standard rating to culturally inclusive pedagogy, practices and understanding. The same specifics by the Newly Qualified Teaching Standards (NQTS) from England Specified that "Teachers must take into account ethnic and cultural diversity to enrich the curriculum and raise achievement for standard education". For better output there should be estimable evaluation does not mean related to students only but our professors and Faculty members should evaluate themselves is the following manner.

PERSONAL EVALUATION

- Command on Content
- Full Qualification
- Update Knowledge
- Use of New Technologies
- Equipped with Research
- Communication Skill
- Way of Interaction with students.
- Time Management
- Responsible Behaviour
- Work Ethics
- Code of Conduct
- Proper and timely Advise
- Quality of good Motivator
- No bias in Nature
- Professionalism in Teaching
- Good human Relationship

OTHER POINTS FOR QUALITY OF INTERNATIONALIZATION OF HIGHER EDUCATION

- Develop Competence in relating and using various types of teaching learning aids for effective teaching.
- Devise Minimum essential Instructional aids in relation to different units of teaching.
- Develop needed competence in the delivery of knowledge, skills and appreciation lessons at the elementary or secondary stage.
- Apply knowledge and understanding of theory in devising new

strategies of teaching, developing and using new teaching aids and communication techniques to meet new situations.

- Construct and use various types of tools and evaluation devices for appraising students' achievement and growth
- Identify the most talented, the slow learners and the under-achievers to meet their special needs through enrichment teaching.
- Manage the classroom problems that may arise during instruction, using relevant psychological and pedagogical techniques.
- Interpret summaries and report evidences that accrue from the use of various assessment devices, in the form of individual and class profiles.
- Analyze question paper, courses of studies in special areas of studies and content of units in terms of content elements.
- Formulate unit-wise objectives in terms of competencies in relation to content elements of units of teaching
- Internalize democratic and secular values and develop the same among children
- To judge individual strengths and weaknesses by the use of teaching tasks and use of skills

Sometimes teachers less willingness, inadequate qualification less, professional attitude, unfavourable working conditions, more work load less workload, role ambiguity, lack of motivation, personal attribute, less interpersonal relations with students, wrong policies for admission, inappropriate curriculum, society values etc. are some major hindrances in the way of Internationalization of Higher Education so we need some prospects factors for the enhancement for the education quality.

They are shown as follows:

PROSPECTS ENHANCING FACTORS

Input	*Process*	*Output*
1. Physical resources ➢ Building ➢ Library ➢ Laboratory	1. Academic ➢ Admission process ➢ Teachers' performance ➢ Award of Degree	1. Student ➢ Student achievement
2. Manpower resource ➢ Students ➢ Teachers ➢ Parents ➢ Coordination of each	2. Examination ➢ Scheduling and holding Exams ➢ Result declaration	2. Teacher ➢ Publication ➢ Research ➢ Paper presentation ➢ Published work (books) ➢ Resource persons ➢ Invited talks
3. Financial resources ➢ Budget ➢ Resource mobilization	3. Finance ➢ Expenditure ➢ Funds ➢ Scholarships ➢ Funds for mobility	3. Institution ➢ Invited faculties ➢ Resource faculty from reputed university ➢ Result

In the above discussed points it is important to suggest some points for the betterment of Internationalization of higher education to Indian government authorities. They may be in the following manner:

- Take suitable action to promote Indian culture abroad. This needs setting up a Committee for promoting Indian Education Abroad.
- Allow Indian Universities to open offshore campus abroad. Amend the University Grants Commission Act 1956 and the Acts of other statutory councils to include a specific provision allowing universities to open offshore campuses and export Indian education through the distance.
- Simplify the procedures about registration, entry test need, the issue of 'No Objection Certificate' and the issue and extension of visas.
- Indian Embassies and High Commissions abroad must play a role in providing information about higher education available in India. They should help in the conduct of fairs, entrance examinations and student recruitment.
- From an open-door policy for financing students.
- They recommended the creation of a central website to strengthen the information base and spread of information.
- Government and other statutory bodies' should grant greater autonomy and flexibility to universities to admit foreign students and to enter collaborative arrangements with foreign institutions.
- Create a Task Force including representatives of different bodies like the University Grants Commission, All India Council for Technical education and the Medical Council of India for admitting students to different professional programmes.
- The government should consider extending financing for international education. This will enable institutions providing financial aid to Indian students going abroad, to foreign students coming to India and to educational institutions wishing to develop infrastructures for international education.
- There should be a suitable means to watch the standard of education given by foreign universities.

Countries Sending the Most International Students to India (1988/89 to 2006/07)

	1988-89	*1998-99*	*2006-07*
1.	Kenya (2,332)	Kenya (639)	Iran (2,180)
2.	Sudan (1,692)	Nepal (574)	UAE (1,878)
3.	Jordan (1,247)	Bangladesh (461)	Nepal (1,728)
4.	Nepal (912)	Ethiopia (403)	Ethiopia (1,033)
5.	Malaysia (824)	Sri Lanka (368)	Saudi Arabia (771)
6.	Iran (553)	Sudan (245)	Kenya (621)
7.	Ethiopia (455)	Thailand (197)	U.S. (615)

	1988-89	*1998-99*	*2006-07*
8.	Sri Lanka (430)	Uganda (196)	Oman (608)
9.	Somalia (429)	Iran (108)	Yemen (598)
10.	Nigeria (339)	Vietnam (88)	Bhutan (531)
11.	Bangladesh (252)	Jordan (60)	Sri Lanka (466)
12.	Thailand (187)	Afghanistan (59)	Korea (452)

Source: Association of Indian Universities, 2000, 2007, 2009.

CONCLUSION

India is one of the world's largest markets for foreign universities. The country has a significant un-met demand for higher education access. Currently only 10 per cent of the age group receives university education, which is half the rate in China and well below the rate in most developing countries. Thus, foreign institutions have a huge opportunity for profitable growth in the Indian market. Now, nearly 150 foreign institutes offer courses with Indian university under a twinning arrangement – part of the course in India, the remaining abroad – that is allowed by the education department. A panel set up by the government to draw up a reform road map for the higher education sector recommended that only the top 200 foreign universities be allowed to enter the country. India is a key nation in debates surrounding Internationalization of higher education. The country's large number of young people, rapidly growing economy, and booming middle-class make it a favourite source country among host countries hoping to recruit internationally mobile students. And though India currently hosts a small number of international students, the country has the potential to host many more. Thus, India's importance in international student mobility is destined to grow. Currently, foreign provision in India is small and peripheral. Many institutions are keenly watching developments in India related to the new law for foreign providers, and there is a great deal of enthusiasm among foreign universities. India is seen as a huge market with immense potential. Foreign providers can not only create additional capacity but also energize local institutions, both by example and through competition. Thus, opening Indian higher education to foreign competition will strengthen it and boost Internationalization efforts.

The statement "If you do not have any goal you do not have anything to assess" explains the close relationship between goals, objectives and assessment and evaluation procedures. It is necessary for faculty to get feedback of the functioning of orientation, curriculum, instruction, academic advising and teaching method in order to get good institutional results. It is rightly said, "Any curriculum remains dead unless, it is quickened with the right kind of method and the right kind of teacher" (Secondary Education Commission).

As far as input assessment and evaluation is concerned, it is helpful to know the characteristics of entering students, their abilities judged by the placement testing, learning potential, abstract reasoning, critical thinking, epistemological and moral development and technological understanding. The above information will be helpful to faculty members and administrators in designing the educational programmes, keeping in mind the psychological climate of the campus to improve the institutional quality. Internationalization of Higher Education sector is very expensive so every nail should be fitted properly to get desired results.

India's strategy with regard to Internationalization of higher education should be based on its potential to be an effective aid to basic problems facing. So far, the liberalization policies have induced foreign providers to focus only on certain technical and professional fields of study that can earn them good market returns. In contrast to these modes, it is better to design a strategy that taps foreign universities and institutes of acceptable quality to work together with Indian universities/institutes to improve both access and quality because "A person can enlighten himself through education process to diminish the darkness of ignorance."

For this we need our prospects of Internationalization of Higher Education and Evaluation procedure to be improved, only then we can say that "Under Internationalization the world is our oyster or perhaps our garden in which we sow the seeds from the fruits of our academic Labours, powerful knowledge, proven best practices and established system of scholarships, administration and inquiry" (Knight 2008).

REFERENCES

Association of Indian Universities (2009), International students in Indian Universities 2006-2007, New Delhi, Association of Indian Universities.

American Council on Education (2003), Internationalizing the campus, A User Guide ACE Washington.

Atlbach, Philip Reisber, Lizard and Rumbley, Laura (2009), Trends in Global Higher Education, Boston College, Boston.

Bhandari, R. and Chow, P. (2008), Open doors 2008: Report on international *educational exchange.* New York: Institute of International Education.

Cronin, J.M. and Horron, H.E. (2009), Will higher education be the next bubble to burst?

Dhar, I. (2008, May), Foreign education providers in India: Report on collaborative *arrangements.* UK-India Education and Research Initiative (UKIERI).

Gupta, A. (2006), January-March. India's soft power. *Indian Foreign Affairs journal,* 45-57.

De Wit, H. and Knight, J. (1997), Asia Pacific countries in comparison to Europe and North America: concluding remarks. In Knight, J.; de Wit, H., Ed., *Internationalization of Higher Education in Asia Pacific Countries.* European Association for International Education, Amsterdam, Netherlands.

IAU Newsletter (2001), Internationalization of Indian Higher Education. International Association of Universities, *Newsletter*, Vol. 7, No. 3.

Knight, J. (2003), *Internationalization of Higher Education: Practices and Priorities.* International Association of Universities Survey Report.

Knight, J. (2006), Higher Education Crossing Borders: A Guide to the Implications of the General Agreement on Trade in Services (GATS) for Cross-border Education. UNESCO.

Knight, J. (2008), *Higher Education in Turmoil*. Sense Publishers.

Knight Jane and DE Wit, Hans (1999). Quality and Internationalization of Higher Education, OECD, Paris.

Palomba, Catherine A. and Trudy W. Banta (1999), *Assessment Essentials: Planning, Implementing and Improving Assessment in Higher Education*. San Francisco: Jossey-Bass, USA.

Pickett, S. and Turlington, B. (1992), *Internationalizing the Undergraduate Curriculum: A Handbook for Campus Leaders*. Washington, DC: American Council on Education.

UNESCO (2009), World Conference on Higher Education: The New Dynamics of Higher Education and Research for Societal Change and Development, Paris.

http://chronicle.com/arricle/Will-Hi Education-*Be-the/444001*

Chronicle o/Higher Education 55(37), A56. Retrieved November 9, 2009 from

26

Promoting Quality in Higher Education

Megha Juyal and *Mithilesh Topal*

Jawahar Lal Nehru once said, "A university stands for humanism, for reason, for the adventure of ideas and for search of truth. It stands for the onward march of human race towards even higher objectives. If all is well with the universities, all is well with the nation".

Higher Education is a very important sector for social, economic and scientific development of the country. Higher Education is no longer a luxury, it is essential for survival. The mission of Higher Education is to educate, to train, to undertake research and to provide service to the community. With the globalization in the 21st century, the scope and demand of Higher Education is increasing day by day. The new paradigms in Higher Education involve creation of world class intellects and training of skilled manpower without compromising on quality.

The progress of the country is not possible without converting it into a knowledge society. With the globalization and liberalization, the country has to develop its Higher Education System to respond to the challenges arising out of the rapid changing environmental factors, including global competition, to cater to the developmental needs competitively and strategically. This seems to be a herculean task which requires consistent efforts on the part of every stakeholder of the education system.

PRESENT STATUS OF HIGHER EDUCATION

Indian Higher Education system is the third largest in the world after US and China. At the time of independence there were 20 universities 500 colleges with 0.1 million enrolled students. There are 610 universities with about 5,21,843 teachers and 23,76,718 students at present. The exponential growth in Higher Education sector has compromised with the quality of education. The fact is that after India's independence the Higher Education System seems to be inclined towards the access to the large section of the society. This 'quantity' focus has resulted in the development of a mass production system with little focus on 'quality'. The quantity approach, which has successfully worked for long, is now in question!

The following figures and rankings of India clearly indicate the pitiable plight of Higher Education System in the country:

1. The proportion of Indian population, in the age group of 18-24, that enters the world of Higher Education is around 7 per cent which is one half the average of Asia.
2. India holds 48th position in the global competitiveness ranking of World Economic Forum.
3. It is placed at 126th position in the world in terms of specialised research and training services.
4. The quality of management schools makes us at 115th position among 131 countries.
5. We are at 120th position in providing internet access to colleges.
6. On some other related parameters like quality in scientists and engineers, university – industry interaction and quality of scientific institutions, the country stands at 111th, 131st, and 130th position respectively.
7. No Indian university except IIT Mumbai (187th position) stands in the list of top 200 academic institutions of the world. India's counterpart Japan has a credit of 10 universities in the list while China has 6 and Korea has a credit of 5 institutions in the list.
8. In terms of publications of scientific research in the worlds, India's ranking from 8th position in 1980s has nose – dived to 21st position in the new millennium.
9. Our GDP expenditure on Education has dipped down from 1 per cent in 1971 to 0.4 per cent in 2011. On the contrary, the countries like US, France, Germany and UK spend about 4-8 per cent of GDP in Higher Education.
10. Companies across industries are complaining of insufficient graduates that they consider them "unemployable". According to a report by NASSCOM, only 10 per cent of fresh graduates in India are employable. Approximately, only 23 per cent of MBA graduates and 10-25 per cent technical graduates are readily employable.

WHAT IS QUALITY?

We are now transiting to a knowledge society where the quality and relevance of education play a crucial role in India's development. Over the last decade, the quality of education has become an important concern the world over. Global organizations like UNESCO and UNICEF have published their own account of quality, taking into consideration learning achievements as well as developmental goals for education that is guided by an overall vision of human well being.

According to Oxford dictionary (2000), quality has been defined as the 'the standard of something when it is compared to other things like it; how good or bad something is: hence the degree or grade of excellence etc. possessed by a thing'. Quality can't improve by itself. Relevance of education, standard of teaching, administration, curricula, research and evaluation, utilization of infrastructure are some keys issues which are essential for quality improvement. These have also been emphasised in Challenge of Education – A policy perspective, NPE (1986), Ramamurti Committee Report, 1990 (Towards an enlightened and Humane society) POA 1992, NKC (2005), Committee to advise on Renovation and Rejuvenation of Higher Education in India (Prof. Yashpal, 2009).

REASONS OF CONCERN

The quality of Higher Education in most of our universities and colleges require substantial improvement. The following problems are common enough to be a cause of concern:

1. *Lack of clarity in the norms for private partnership*: the private sector came in the scene when Government was unable to bear the burden of Higher Education alone. But due to lack of funding pattern, incentives and regulatory oversight, there is a decline in the quality of private educational sector.
2. *Obsolete curricula*: The curricula have not kept pace with the times. Global Higher Education has undergone a paradigm shift from National to Global level, from teacher centered to learner centered. But Higher Education in India has not responded to either global or national needs. It preserves the curriculum inherited from Britain, which has lost its significance in the present scenario.
3. *Summative Assessment*: There is no significance of presentations, projects, seminars during the academic year. The assessment rests solely on the annual examination. Learning and creativity are at a discount in a system of assessment that places a premium on memory rather than understanding.
4. *Ineffective teachers*: The work culture is not conducive to anything beyond the classroom for it is caught in a 9:30 to 1:30 syndrome. A country can have the best policies, infrastructure, curriculum, high enrolment, but the responsibility of imparting quality education ultimately rest on good academicians. Earlier poor salaries of the teachers were the reason stated for their poor performance. Today, in contrast high salaries are available but the commitment is still less. The status of teachers has deteriorated in the last few decades due to expansion of the educational system, lowering standard of teacher education, negligence of duty by many teachers and changed social value system of the society.
5. *Funding shortage and disparities*: Public funded Higher Educational institutions have been subjected to severe resource crunch. In order to meet their ends, they have to increase their intake capacity with insufficient infrastructure leading to rapid decline in quality and efficiency.
6. *Lack of initiative by the government*: Due to lack of political will and resources, the government take minimum efforts in the development of the Higher Education.

7. *Low standard of Research*: It is only namesake. It involves more of plagiarism rather than innovative work
8. *Poor administration*: It is supposed to be the major organ for sustenance of a system for achieving quality. There are many slippages in schedule so much so that the exams are delayed by 6-12 months. One of the weakest links between policy, planning and practice is the lack of proper data and research base for the purpose of policy making and implementation. Often, the decisions taken are based on general understanding. This may be close to reality but often overlook the crucial aspects which one learns through a deeper analysis of the problem.
9. *Archaic Management System*: Many universities continue to follow the age old hierarchical system of governance with centralized control, rigidity in administration and an organized structure which lacks flexibility. There is little scope for innovation and creative talents. There is absence of new forms of management that encourage speedy decision making, networking, team effort and collective responsibility are necessary to meet the challenges.
10. *Unaccountability*: There is no accountability either on the part of the teacher or taught or administration. It is so because there is no reward for performance or punishment for non performance.

SUGGESTIONS FOR QUALITY IMPROVEMENT

The following pro active steps need to be taken that would foster quality in Higher Education:

1. *Incentives*: The time has come to think of salary differentials within and between universities for talented faculty members. The student – teacher ratio of 1:15 in 2006-07, which rose to 1:22 in 2007-08 has to be reduced.
2. *Information dissemination*: Higher Education institutions should place their basic information relating to their financial situation, physical assets, faculty positions to the public domain so that the public can make an informed choice.
3. *Accountability*: The Higher Education System must provide for accountability vis-à-vis the outside world and create accountability within the system.
4. *Competition*: An expansion of Higher Education which provides students with choices and creates competition between institutions is going to be vital in enhancing accountability.
5. *Motivated students*: Higher Education should not be synonymous with earning another degree. Only those candidates who are genuinely interested in seeking Higher Education should be encouraged to join college or university.
6. *Prompt administration and management*: Universities have to be managed more and more by market driven forces such as managerial

efficiency, cost effectiveness, executive leadership, strategic planning and control. The academic calendar should be crisp and academic session deadlines should be met in time.

7. *Clarity in norms for PPP (Public Private Partnership)*: Good quality of Higher Education can only be provided if clearly defined regulatory and ethical mechanisms govern the system.

STRATEGIES FOR ENHANCING QUALITY AND EXCELLENCE IN HIGHER EDUCATION

A large number of calibrated initiatives have been covered in 11th and 12th Five year plan to promote and nurture excellence across institutions of Higher Education. They are as follows:

1. *Regulatory Reforms*: Under the recommendations of NKC and suggestions of Yash Pal Committee; the initiative was to address the issue of multiplicity and regulatory bodies in order to make Higher Education better governed. The following legislative proposals have been developed in this context:
   a) The Educational Tribunals Bill, 2010.
   b) The Foreign Educational Institutions Bill, 2010.
   c) The National Accreditation Regulatory Authority For Higher Educational Institutions Bill, 2010.
   d) The Prohibition of Unfair Practices in Technical Educational Institutions, Medical Educational Institutions, 2010.
   e) Higher Education and Research Bill, 2010.

   Moreover, all the regulatory bodies like AICTE, UGC, DEC, NCTE should be replaced by an apex regulatory body – National Commission on Higher Education and Research (NCEHR). This body would be independent of the influence of the government and all stakeholders.
2. *Curricular Reforms*: Admission through a common entrance exam with due weight age to applicant's past academic record. Implementation of Semester system, Continuous and Comprehensive Internal Assessment and choice based credit system. Revision of curricula at least once in three years.
3. *Making Institutional and Programme Accreditation Mandatory*: Accreditation should be done discipline wise rather than of the whole university or college. This procedure will give a clear picture to the candidate to choose a particular department in a college. National Accreditation Authority is proposed for specific disciplines on the same lines.
4. *Attracting Quality Faculty, Promoting Faculty Mobility and Continuous Faculty Development Programmes*: The 12th Five Year Plan will envisage effective implementation of the brain gain policy where initiatives will be taken to attract and retain quality faculty coupled with mobility. Facilitation of faculty movement from one

institution to another for a period of 6 months to 2 years during exchange programmes. Increasing the Academic Staff College (ASC) from present 66 to 100 for faculty development programmes.

5. *Student Mobility*: It is an integral component of quality enhancement which involves opening admission to students of other states and countries.
6. *Evaluation of Teachers by Students and Peer Assessment*: It is recommended that peer assessment, teachers' and students' assessment and self appraisal need to be implemented with serious thought by all the institutions.
7. *Establishment of Navratna Universities*: The salient features of a Navratna University could be:
   (i) The number of programmes and departments offered in the university.
   (ii) The rate of expansion during the last five years.
   (iii) Number of students seeking admission.
   (iv) Plurality and demographic diversity of faculty and students.
   (v) Number of SAP departments, CAS advancements, National facilities.
   (vi) Number of research projects carried out.
   (vii) Number and quality of impact factor journals, Average H Index.

INTERNATIONAL COLLABORATIONS

1. *National Mission on Education through Information and Communication Technology (NMEICT)*: It was launched with the aim of making educational institutions technology savvy by providing digital campuses, video conference classrooms, Wi-Fi connectivity in hostels etc.
2. *Promotion of Autonomous colleges*: The UGC has to review and renew its efforts to achieve a target of 50 additional autonomous colleges during 12th Five Year Plan.
3. *Strengthening and expanding initiatives and e-resource facility*: A national Educational Resource Portal needs to be created and the data of all educational institutions of the country should be made available on the portal. Moreover all state universities as well as centrally funded institutions should avail the e-resources funded by the UGC through NFLIBNET.
4. Research facilities:
   (i) *Maximizing the utilization of research facilities of National Institutes and laboratories*: The 12th Five Year Plan should encourage collaboration between National Research Laboratory and selected universities through fellowship/scholarship supported programmes.
   (ii) *Strengthening Research facilities for science teachers in State universities and colleges*: Research opportunities will be

provided to the science teachers in order to upgrade their knowledge.

(iii) *Research fellowship*: Awarding fellowship will now be extended to colleges and universities covered under the SAP/CPE and UPE programmes.

(iv) *Curbing plagiarism*: In order to curb plagiarism, mandatory installation of relevant software in all libraries by UGC funding and introduction of compulsory check of all the thesis before they are evaluated would bring in enormous scientific ethics and will control plagiarism.

5. *Reforming the self financed teaching programmes*: Conversion of self financing course offered by state government and government aided colleges as government approved courses subject to the condition that these institutions strictly adhere to government's rules and regulations.

CONCLUSION

Education is known to be an effective catalyst for social development and economic growth as it empowers not only the individual but also the community and society at large. It is the index of human development.

With globalization and sensitization, there has been an unprecedented growth in Higher Education sector. The implementation of Right To Education Act 2010, will further increase the number of Higher Education aspirants. Government institutions can no longer sustain the burden of Higher Education. A mismatch between the demand and supply has led to a compromise in the quality of education. With the entry of private sector in Higher Education, the quality has further deteriorated from bad to worse. It is necessary to emphasize here that education is not a money spinning business, but it's a noble cause! Various committees are set up and recommendations have been made for quality education. However their implementation is so gradual and half hearted that the quality is lost in the long run! Since time immemorial, Indians have proved their worth in the world. Indian Higher Education can still make a remarkable position in the world only if quality goes hand in hand with equity and access! Three aspects have to be emphasized in order to maintain the quality standards. Firstly, stringent measures have to be taken secondly, strict adherence to the rules and regulations and thirdly, to be true to our conscience.

REFERENCES

Chauhan, S.P.C. (2008), Higher Education: Current Status and Future Possibilities in Afghanistan, Bangladesh, Bhutan, India, Maldives, Nepal, Pakistan, and Sri Lanka.

Draft Report of Working Group on Higher Education for the XI Plan, Planning Commission, Government of India (2007-12).

Kaul, S. (2006), Higher Education in India: Seizing the Opportunity. *Working Paper* No. 179, ICRIER, New Delhi.

Thorat, S. (2006), Higher Education in India: Emerging Issues Related to Access, Inclusiveness and Quality, Nehru Memorial Lecture, University of Mumbai

Knight, J. (1999), Internationalization of Higher Education. In *Quality and Internationalization in Higher Education*. IMHE Publication.

Knight, J. and Hans de Wit (1999), An Introduction to the IQRP Project and Process. In *Quality and Internationalization in Higher Education.*

http://www.criticalthinking.org/pages/higher-education/431

27

Legacy of Indian Education and Human Development: Rethinking the Ideals of Higher Learning in Global Context

Mohammad Shaheer Siddiqui

Higher education does not mean to study in a university rather it is the application of knowledge in the higher stages of life for the achievement of higher ideals. The above prayer from the ancient treasure of *Rig-Veda* is related to the aspirations of a person after the accomplishment of formal education. These aspirations are universal and human beings all through the ages have entertained them. We all dream to enjoy an enlightened, successful, healthy and virtuous life. The Vedas accept life in fullness which is well balanced and free from excessive want. '*Daridrata*' (poverty) is a curse and so are greed and the Vedas define it as poverty of mind, body and ideas. Only when life is lived on altruistic principles, one can achieve peace, tranquility and happiness.

HIGHER EDUCATION IN ANCIENT INDIA

"Since ancient times, India has been a centre of excellence in the field of higher education. Nalanda, Vikramashila and Takshashila were few of the oldest universities in the world and were the most renowned seats of higher education during their time. Students' from far off countries came to study in these universities. Today India has one of the largest higher education systems in the world and also some world-class institutions for higher education. The present system of higher education dates back to Mountstuart Elphinstone's minutes of 1823, which stressed on the need for establishing schools for teaching English and the European sciences. Subsequently, the universities of Calcutta, Bombay and Madras were set up in 1857, followed by the university of Allahabad in 1887." (NIC, Govt. of India). In ancient India there was a well established system of higher education. Also in medieval India higher education was imparted at various centers of learning. Sufi Khanqahs were the renowned places for higher learning.

LEARNING IN HIGHER EDUCATION

Higher education is concerned with the applied aspect of knowledge. Psychologically learning is concerned with three levels of man's potential to learn; Cramming, Understanding and Reflective. At primary level cramming makes the child habitual to educational process, at secondary level all the previous experiences of the learner are used to teach him the current piece of knowledge and to sharpen the understanding capacity. Finally the transition period between adolescence and adulthood is concerned with reflective level when a learner is able to reflect his views to the extent of his understanding. This level is the beginning of higher education. Learning in higher education means the attainment of reflection ability through the application of knowledge.

In ancient India when a student left the 'Gurukul' after completing 'Brahmacharya Ashrama' he had attained the age of 25 and was declared eligible to enter into 'Grihastha Ashrama'. It clearly indicates that 'Gurukuls' were also the centers of higher education. Hermitages were the popular places of higher learning. Indian saints developed a scientific social system of life. The whole life struggle was planned to fulfill the four major aims of life called 'Purushartha' viz. 'Dharma', 'Artha' 'Kama', and 'Moksha'. In ancient India philosophers distinguished four broad stages of 'ashramas' in an individual's growth:

1. ***Shaishava:*** In this stage the child is entirely concerned with play and primary education.
2. ***Brahmacharya:*** This stage is devoted entirely to education and training as a disciplined scholar.
3. ***Grihastha***: This is the important stage where the individual is concerned as a householder doing his duties to his family and society.
4. ***Vanaprstha***: This is the last stage which will come around the retirement age from active life and he has to devote himself to pursuing ontological and abstract studies.

The content, method and structure of education are generally addressed to develop ten functions of man. As intellectual, moral, spiritual, social, economic, political, physical, domestic, aesthetic and recreational.

PREPARATION BEFORE HIGHER LEARNING

Knowledge was divided into *Apara* and *Para.* Latter being the highest knowledge should not be imparted to a learner who is not prepared. Higher education refers to the attainment of highest ideals. Upanishads suggest some preparatory conditions before imparting this kind of knowledge.

When Indra went to Prajapati in quest of the knowledge of the Supreme Self, he was asked by the latter to observe *brahmacharya* (Mundakopnishad

Ch. 8-7-2). Six disciples of Pippalada were also asked by the rishi to live in *brahmacharya* for one year before they were permitted to put any question. It may be noted that special stress on *brahmacharya* was laid by ancient teachers because subtleties of the Supreme Knowledge remained incomprehensible unless one fully observed the vow.

Another condition is '*Tapas*'. The Maitrayani declares that 'Supreme Knowledge' should not be given to one who has not practiced *tapas.* Six disciples of Pippalad were asked to practice tapas for one year. (Prashnopnishad 1-1-2). Bhraguvallu of Tatriyopnishad says, "*Tapas* is the means of attaining Brahmvidya (Highest Knowledge of Cosmic soul)." One cannot comprehend Supreme Knowledge (adhigamah) or significance of Karman who has not practiced *tapas* (Maitrayani 4-3). Sankaracharya interprets *tapas* in the above mentioned context as 'total discipline of body, mind and senses.' The Svetasvatara Upanishad says that the knowledge of Brahman is rooted in *tapas* (Cp. 1-16, 6-21). The Mundaka declares: "those who are wise, peaceful in mind, who live in the forest in penance (*tapas*) and faith (*sraddha*) verily attain the path of the Sun, that world where that immortal, imperishable Being is" (1-2-11).

Thus, *tapas* is one of the essential conditions of studentship. It is the means for attaining Supreme Knowledge or Brahma. The object of tapas is realized by twofold discipline-by a discipline of body, as well as the discipline of mind.

Yoga is another preparatory condition for attaining higher education. It is "calmness of the senses and the process of introversion" (Kathopnishad). It says that at the time of practicing yoga an aspirant should be very vigilant because when one becomes vigilant he attains fulfillment and when careless, ruins himself. (Kathopnishad 2-3-11)

It is necessary that pupil should be free from all the prejudiced thinking and motivated to achieve knowledge. Sometimes prejudiced concepts hamper the learning at higher stages.

To Sankaracharya, "Develop (*Sadhana Chatushtay*) four qualities if you are the real seeker of knowledge:

1. ***Viveka:*** Developing the ability to realize the truth and discriminate between real and unreal. Everything except 'Brahma' is perishable and hence unreal. Viveka is developed spiritually not merely by the readings of scriptures.
2. ***Vairagya:*** It is the detachment from those desires and actions which are not sanctioned by 'dharma', according to 'karmayoga' philosophy of Gita. It is also control of mind which is not possible without 'astangyoga'. (*Yoga Vashistha*)
3. ***Shatguna:*** It is the acquisition of six virtues:
   a. *Sama* (Calmness of mind)
   b. *Dama* (Self control or the control of sense organs)
   c. *Uparati* (Concentration of mind with the help of yoga and escape mind from the undesirable activities of sense organs)

d. *Sraddha* (To have faith with conviction in Teacher and his teaching)
e. *Titiksha* (To be bold enough to bear the results of the actions of self and to learn self-control. It is the virtue of tolerance)
f. *Samadhana* (Intellectual concentration with all the calmness of mind to solve a problem)

4. ***Mumukshuta:*** The firm determination and full hearted efforts towards goal are required to achieve the target. It is the purity of intention and efforts. It requires complete efforts and dedication with faith in Guru.

Vedanta prescribed a refined philosophy of life and hereafter and unveils the means to realize the Highest Knowledge. It is not confined to the blind belief that an only reading of the scriptures is the sufficient exercise to realize the Ultimate Reality.

Higher Education in Islam is also concerned with the application of acquired knowledge and Sufism is the best manifesto of Higher Education in Islam. Sufi Education System in Medieval India provides a universal code of conduct based on values and virtues, fear, love and knowledge. A Sufi personality is the result of utmost purification of heart (tazkia).

Firstly, the fear of Allah, as regards one's responsibilities, is emerged in heart; all the deeds will run correctly by self realization. Today's system of education does not create a sense of responsibility in students. 'Alert for Accountability' due to fear of God, is the motivating force in Sufi educational process.

Secondly, Love is the essence of Sufism. If a person fulfils his duties due to the fear of God, he will receive the love and blessings of Allah and general public will admire his sense of responsibility too. Divine Love changes the fear of God into a different way which becomes universal.

Thirdly, Knowledge adorns the personality of that student who holds above two traits. Two traits save the pupil from all kinds of threats and perils to knowledge acquisition.

Sufi System of education begins with the purification of heart from all the prejudices. Sufi education is '*Tazkia*' (Refinement) of heart from all types of confusions, worldly fear, prejudices and misconceptions so that the heart may be filled with high level of motivation and receptive ability. As Lord Krishna did at Kurukshetra: the heart of Arjun was made free from confusion, in the same way Sufi System does it at every step of knowledge acquisition. Thus Sufism, like Upanishadic System, also deals with the process of purification of heart and inculcation of traits and virtues before imparting higher education in order to avoid the wastage.

THE LEGACY OF HUMAN DEVELOPMENT

Ancient Indian Education aimed first at the preparation of personality for the attainment of Higher Education. Enhancement of Traits was the primary requirement of educational practice. The pedagogy of Vedanta is not a set pattern of teaching method for all the students. The above discussed traits and steps are the precondition to start with. The Guru first purifies the body and mind then he shows the ways to purify and fill the spirit with the knowledge of Truth. Educational Process does not start all of a sudden like yearly session. Take the example of six seekers who came to Risi Pippalad to ask questions regarding Mystic knowledge. The Rishi did not reply all at once and directly on the spot rather he said, "*Stay here a year longer with penance, abstinence and faith; then you may ask questions according to your pleasure, and if we know them, we shall tell you all.*" (Prashna Upanishad). We can learn 2 things from above statement:

1. Faith in Guru is fundamental condition which is nourished by self discipline and humbleness in behaviour. The aggressive attitude, dogmatic arguments and impatient behaviour obstruct the ways to acquire knowledge.
2. Arrogance of knowledge eats the entire fruits of knowledge. In spite of having the ocean of knowledge in the breast, the Risi says with humbleness, *"If we know."* This indicates that absence of arrogance is actually the pre-condition of knowledge acquisition.

Prophet Mohammad (S.A.W.) also says, "Arrogance (takabbur) destroys a man as fire eats up the wood". (*Hadith Sahih Bukhari*)

Table 1 shows the fifteen means for attaining knowledge and traits for human development as are described in Upanishads. Sankaracharya accumulate these fifteen steps for the seeker of higher knowledge, as the means to reach this goal.

Table 1: Means for Attaining Knowledge and Human Development

Sr.	*Sanskrit Term*	*Meaning*
1.	Yama	Self Restraining of senses
2.	Niyama	Fixed Observances
3.	Asana	Yogic Postures for developing body and mind
4.	Tyaga	Renunciation from evil thoughts and deeds.
5.	Mauna	Silence from unnecessary arguments
6.	Vijnana-desha	A solitary place, Space:
7.	Kaala	Time and its importance
8.	Mulabandha	Restraining the root of evils and drowsiness
9.	Dehasamya	Balancing the Physical Body
10.	Drik-sthiti	Steadiness of Vision
11.	Pranayama	Control of Vital Energy
12.	Pratyahara	Withdrawal of mind from sense object
13.	Dharana	Concentration and steadfastness of mind
14.	Dhyana	Meditation on one thought and detachment from all other thoughts.
15.	Samadhi	Spiritual absorption for achieving self realization and knowledge.

Above means are abounded with a number of human traits. Each stage of higher education is related to human development in many ways. For example *Yama, the first stage* is the observance of ten principles: (Restraint of Senses for developing) non-violence, truthfulness, non-stealing, continence, kindliness, equanimity of mind, speech and body, forgiveness, firmness of mind, moderation in eating, purity of mind and body (*Shandilya Upanishad*). Similarly Sufism requires the following traits to develop in students for higher learning. Sufi Masters suggested a list of 10 primary traits in a student.

Table 2: Traits in a Student in Sufi System

Sr.	*Arabic Term*	*Meaning*
1.	Ikhlas	Purity of intention
2.	Sidq	Truthfulness
3.	Haya	Mortification
4.	Hurriyat	Freedom from desires
5.	Zikr	Remembrance
6.	Fatoot	Altruism / Philanthropy
7.	Khulq	1. Good Behaviour
8.	Ghaiyrat	2. Shame
9.	Khalvat	3. Seclusion
10.	Istiqamat	4. Firm concentration

A Student in Sufism is expected to flourish in him the above traits. The process of reformation and reconstruction works on the 'principle of exoneration. In this process the normal and existing 'flaws' in the personality go on diminishing and 'inner' or 'self' goes on improving by various practices as 'Tauba' 'Zuhad' and 'Zikr'. (Repentance, Purity and Recitation). This process of refinement is called 'Tazkia'. Higher Education is concerned with reflection level. Heart is like the mirror which receives knowledge and reflects it in behaviour. If inner heart is not refined and polished with such traits, one cannot reflect the radiance of knowledge.

The task of education is to generate virtues in student and values in the contents under study. The generation of Social, Political and Economical values is concerned with the curriculum and process of education. Pupil can adopt the values and virtues to understand and apply them in his life. Some of the virtues, based on the educational philosophies of Sufism and Vedanta, are given below:

Table 3: Sufi Code of Conduct for Teachers and Students (Selective)

Sr.	*Arabic Term*	*Meaning*
1.	Tawakkul	Trust in Almighty God
2.	Tazkia	Self Purification
3.	Sabr	Patience: Tolerance and no prompt and show of knowledge.
4.	Adab	Humility and softness in conduct.
5.	Haya	Shame on wrong doings and fear God in doing prohibited deeds.
6.	Farz	Sincerity and loyalty for his obligations towards God

Sr.	Arabic Term	Meaning
7.	Tawazo	Hospitality and fraternity towards everyone without distinction.
8.	Tauba	Repentance over self-weaknesses and sins.
9.	Faqih	An expert of the subject and content.
10.	Khalvat	Far away from debates and arguments in useless affairs, seclusion.
11.	Sukoot	Silence or to save from verbosity and excess talking.
12.	Faham	Wisdom and power of comprehension.
13.	Amal	Application of knowledge in his own deeds

HIGHER LEARNING IN GLOBAL CONTEXT

The application of knowledge is the pivot of modern development in all the arenas of life. Science is just information if we do not apply it. The applied aspect of Science is called 'Technology'. Needless to say that technology is the driving force behind modernization and internationalization of all the socio-economic activities. Education is no exception. Thus application of knowledge in behavioural terms is the concern of Indian Education System since centuries. It developed through the ages. During medieval India, the Sufism reflects the best manifesto of applied knowledge.

Ancient India adopted a holistic view of the education. The idea of future should also take into consideration the basic human values, ethical and cultural, and also the various roles the individuals will be required to play in the society as a citizen, worker, technician, manager, and a member of a family. It is also needed today in our higher education system that "it should be moulded to develop the personalities of the individuals, so that they could realize their responsibilities as citizens of the country, as factors in the production process and as inheritors of human civilization. This is possible only through a well-disciplined and integrated education. If the system recognizes only one aspect of it and neglects the others, it will only produce only such freaks and pagans, hippies, escapists, disenchanted youth and narrow-minded scientists." (Chalam, 1993)

From School to University we just get the Education of mind and body neglecting the education of heart. Our dogmatism at present lies in our blind support to pragmatic approaches in education at the cost of spiritual requirements in life. There is rush for 'market value' in this era of globalization, greed and glamour of 'Devi Moneta'. Education is a commodity to be valued on the bases of 'market demand of courses'. The result is agony, frustration and violence because heart and soul are lost and mind gets training in trades not in traits. We know that war begins in mind; the condition becomes more catastrophic when mind is literate and filled with the information of science and technology. Take the instances of major crimes and scandals just during last ten years; highly educated were engaged in wrong doings.

Education of heart and soul is much required today. Take an extract from the paper on 'Education for Peace' by NCERT (2006). A teacher had a dream in which she saw one of her students fifty years from today. The student was angry and asked a number of questions complaining of the irresponsible teaching and unripe education. What pinches more is the following extract. "With ever greater anger, the student shouted, 'You helped me extend my hands with incredible machines, my eyes with telescope and microscopes, my ears with telephones, radios and sonar, my brain with computers, but you did not help me extend my heart, love and concern for the human family. Teacher you gave me half a loaf."

Whatever we claim as quality of education in the name of infrastructure, number of teachers, pile of certificates, and circulation of free books, it is in fact the quantitative aspect in terms of demand and supply. Quality is concerned with the outcome of educational process not by counting the first divisions, rank holders etc. but quality of education can be best measured by observing decreasing trends of crimes, corruption, superstition and hatred on the one hand and increasing breezes of love, fraternity, patriotism, inter-religious harmony, unity, peace and efforts to maintain the dignity, pride and happiness of the Nation, on the other. All these elements are concerned with heart. If Education of heart is promoted in higher education then it is possible.

CONCLUSION

The legacy of Indian Education is extremely rich. It extends its reflection in higher ideals in all the arena of life, social, economic and political. Ancient education is no doubt a treasure of knowledge and those values which are utmost important to lead the life of a human being. It further enriched itself with the amalgamation of Islamic ideals of education during medieval period. Madarsas were the centers of initial education and learning in the theoretical aspects but Sufi Khanqas and Shrines were the places of higher learning where theories put in to application. This is the main task of higher education in which one is concerned with the applied aspect of knowledge. It may not be possible to cite an instance showing that a student is getting degrees and diplomas in either 'Gurukuls' or 'Sufi Seminary' as we see today, rather there was a plan for educating a man till his last breath. Knowledge was not based on a thing like reading a particular book or discussion but knowledge was a sort of development of human being inside and killing the animal instincts. It was for biological development, psychological growth and spiritual advancement. Preparation before attainment of knowledge was utmost important. Purity of body, mind and heart was primary condition for higher learning. Vices in thoughts were considered as viruses for education thus process of contemplation was integral to realize the fruits of higher learning. Sufism also concentrates on 'Tazkia' before any learning. This legacy of Indian Education is ever global in context of human development because problems of life are same in every era of advancement. Upanishads present a beautiful blend of worldly and spiritual knowledge. In search of Higher Knowledge the teacher does not distinguish between himself and his student. *Kathopnishad* describes this beautiful relation as:

- *Sahana vavatu:* May God protect us (Teacher and Pupil) both.
- *Saha nau bhunaktu:* May He nourish both of us in learning.
- *Saha viryam karavavahai:* May we work together and increase each other's energy and glory.
- *Tejasvi navadhitamastu:* May we both be vigorous by study and learning.
- *Ma vidvisavahai:* May we never hate each other or never be jealous of each other's progress.

Cultural and social progress is unthinkable without mutual cooperation, love and coordination in educational process between teacher and pupil. Such are the ideals of higher learning in Indian Heritage of Education. Modern system of education is on the edge of suffering on the part of human values and peaceful co-existence. Unrest of mind and mental violence are the major diseases among the new generation of pupils. Indian Legacy of education concentrated on human development for peaceful coexistence, universal fraternity, Love and attainment of Spiritual Advancement. It is much required today.

REFERENCES

Altekar, A.S. (1957), *Education in Ancient India.* Varanasi: Nand Kishore and Bros.

Bhattacharya, H. (1956), *The Cultural Heritage of India.* Kolkata: Ramakrishna Mission.

Challam, K.S. (1993), *Educational Policy for Human Resources Development.* New Delhi: Rawat

Chatterjee, C. (1957), *Vedantic Education.* Lucknow: Gauranga Cultural Research Institute.

Kabir, Humayun. (1961), *Indian Philosophy of Education.* New York: Asia Pub. House.

Kalam, Abdul, A.P.J. (2003), *Ignited Minds.* New Delhi: Penguin.

Manhas, M.S. (1923), *The Holy Vedantic Life*. Delhi: B.R. Publishing Corporation.

NCERT (2006), Position Paper, National Focus Group on Education for Peace, New Delhi:

Nicholson, R.A. (1976), *The Studies in Islamic Mysticism*, New Delhi: Idara Adabiyat.

Radhakrishnan, R. (1984), *True Knowledge*, Delhi: Ravindra Printing Press.

Radhakrishnan, S. (1927), *Indian Philosophy*, Vol. I and II. London: George Allen and Unwin Ltd.

Rizvi, S.A.A. (1986), *A History of Sufism in India, Vol. I,* New Delhi: Munshiram Manoralal.

Sharma, D.S. (1961), *The Upanishads, An Anthology.* Bombay: Bhartiya Vidya Bhavan.

UNESCO (2001), Learning the Way to Peace. A Teachers Guide to Education for Peace.

28

Quality Accreditation of Education in Odisha: The Impact Factor of NAAC

S.K. Swain and Biswajet Ray

In the increasingly competitive global context, knowledge is gaining prominence in all aspects of life probing the maxim, "Knowledge is Power". The information communication technology, globalization, market oriented-education, and knowledge revolution are the crux of the quality education that brings prosperity and progress of the nation in the socio-economic, scientific and cultural scenario of the world.

Higher education institution, as the centre of learning, finding and research is fetched with a number of emerging issues, challenges and opportunities. This is one of the most important areas of education where the topic highlights and shares some common contributions in the total quality assurance of education in this present information age.

India is proud of being one of the prestigious nations of higher education during the past centuries. The centres of higher learning like Nalanda and Takshyasila during Buddhist era flourished abundantly from east to west where scholars came from all over the world for higher learning. During medieval period, Muslim rulers provided higher education through madrasas aiming at materialistic prosperity and propagation of Islamic culture and religion. India, under British rule, received education through the instructions laid down by the Company from time to time. As a result, many differences occurred among anglicists and orientalists in India about the structural and cultural development of education. But, after declaration of Wood's dispatch in 1854, it created a landmark revolution in the educational panorama of India and as a consequence the universities of Calcutta, Bombay and Madras came into existence. At present there are 659 registered universities and university level institutions which include public (National, state owned and autonomous) and private universities and 33,023 colleges in India. The students enrolment has 1,84,96,800 (77,49,000 girls) in 2011-12. In higher education the present student-teacher ratio is almost 21:1. It is estimated that the total number of teachers in universities and colleges is about 8,48,750. India has the third largest education system in the world after the United States of America and China.

HIGHER EDUCATION SCENARIO IN ODISHA

The Department of Higher Education looks after education at the university, post-graduate, graduate and higher secondary levels. It also promotes vocational education, professional courses and provides grants to institutes for development studies. In 1947, there were only 12 colleges in Odisha. But at present, there are 2323 general colleges including 99 govt. colleges, 618 govt. aided colleges, 1026 non-government unaided colleges, 166 block grant colleges, 381 self financing colleges and 33 other department colleges. Out of these colleges, 34 colleges have got autonomous status. Before independence, there was only one university in Odisha. At present there are 12 state universities, 01 central university, 01 state private university, 02 deemed universities and 03 institutes of national importance (IIT/NIT/NISER). The state Government has permitted for the establishment of Sri Sri University, ICFI University, and Sambalpur University Institute of Information and Technology in the state. The government has agreed to establish the Xavier University of Management, Amrita Viswa Vidyapitham University and Odisha State Open University in the State. Besides this, 16 more proposals for the establishment of universities in the private sector are there under active consideration of the state government.

QUALITY ASSURANCE IN EDUCATION: THE CONCEPT

Education without substantive quality can be judged as a man without mind. In the contexts of global policy, global society and global economy, each and every nation is seriously thinking of heightening the degree of quality in the system of education. Therefore, quality assurance is now debated seriously from different angles of vision.

The quality in terms of "conformance requirements of the customers" (Crosby, 1979), define 'fitness of use' (Juran, 1988). Similarly, Barry define, "quality is the process of continuous improvement and is not something absolute but relative. The key to quality improvement is to focus on process and not the product or the outcome" (1996). Accordingly, five different approaches are identified to define quality:

- In terms of exceptional
- In terms of consistency (zero defect)
- Getting right the first time
- Making quality a culture
- As fitness for purpose (Green and Harvey, 1993).

Every element in education and higher education implies complexities as input process and human being as its output (product) process. So, education is the means to achieve higher living standards for personal and social development through the application of new techniques and technologies to overcome the complexities which individual faces in real life. Higher education has special value in the emerging knowledge society. It contributes directly as well as indirectly to the 'wealth of nation'. Therefore, the future of the country depends on the massive expansion of education having best quality particularly at higher education level.

Quality assurance in higher education in Odisha has become a distant dream due to a number of factors like lack of qualified teachers, poor teacher-student ratio, finance, accessibility, equity, modern equipments, research and extension facilities, consultancy service, lack of modern techniques and technologies. As a result of which teaching-learning process, poor governance, other support service, and less links with national and international organizations are becoming the emergent factors for difficulties. One of the most important factors is the mushrooming growth of institutions without basic requirements. It becomes a stumbling block on the path of progress and ensuring quality. At this juncture, reengineering the traditional and conventional education system through enhancement of quality with a committed assurance method is becoming the need of prime time.

THE ROLE OF NAAC IN PROMOTING QUALITATIVE DEVOLVEMENT IN HIGHER EDUCATION

In order to face challenges posed by Liberalization, Privatization and Globalization (LPG) in India through GATT and WTO agreements, institute of higher education have to become competitive, compatible and accountable for which assessment must be done through external agency like NAAC. Colleges even situated in remote areas of our state have been sensitized to the quality movement started by NAAC. This effort accelerates the process of making colleges as the quality centres of higher education. With entry of free trade economy LPG (Liberalization, Privatization and Globalization) in India in 1991 onwards, the road of higher education system of affiliated colleges started getting halts and breakdowns due to the entry of foreign universities and fast growth of information and knowledge through IT revolution. At this juncture, NABHE (National Accreditation Board of Higher Education) was set up in 1992 by the UGC to measure the quality of higher education in India which paved the way for the formation of National Assessment and Accreditation Council (NAAC).

In pursuance of the Government policy for Higher Education (1986) and PoA (1992) the external agency called National Assessment of Accreditation Council (NAAC) was established by the University Grants Commission (UGC) with full support from the Ministry of Human Resource Development, Govt. of India in September 1994 under section 12ccc of the UGC Act of 1956.

Agenda: The prime agenda of NAAC is to assess and accredit institutions of higher learning with an objective of helping them to work continuously to improve the quality of education.

Vision: To make quality in defining element of higher education in India through a combination of self and external quality evaluation, promotion and sustenance initiatives;

Mission: To arrange periodic assessment and accreditation of institutions of higher education of units and thereof, or specific academic programmes or projects;

To stimulate the academic environment for promotion of quality of teaching-learning and research in higher education institutions;

To encourage self-evaluation, accountability, autonomy and innovations in higher education;

To undertake quality-related research studies, consultancy and training programmes, and

To collaborate with other stakeholders of higher education for quality evaluation, promotion and sustenance.

National Consultative Committees: NAAC functions through its General Council (GC) and Executive Committee (EC).and other academic, advisory and administrative sub-committees inviting senior academicians of undoubted integrity from all over India as members. There are different strategies of NAAC for quality assurance of higher education institutions.

Process: There are four stages in the process of assessment and accreditation.

(i) On-line submission of a Letter of Intent (LoI) for all institutions and institutional Eligibility for Quality Assessment (IEQA) format for Affiliated/Constituent colleges that are seeking Assessment and Accreditation for the first time.
(ii) Preparation and submission of a Self Study Report (SSR) by the institution.
(iii) Site visit by the peer team.
(iv) Final decision of NAAC.

First stage approach has been introduced by NAAC w.e.f. 1st April 2007 under new methodology. Similarly, in the new methodology, the institutions are graded for each key aspect under four categories, viz., A, B, C and D, denoting Very Good, Good, Satisfactory and Unsatisfactory respectively, as it is revealed in Table 4.

Criteria: NAAC visualizes the holistic approach being practiced by a college in order to understand the values through seven criteria. Here, seven point criteria with key indicators used by NAAC are detailed Table 1.

Table 1: Criteria of NAAC

I.	**Curricular Aspects** • Goal Orientation • Curriculum Development • Programme Options • Academic Flexibility • Feedback Mechanism	II.	**Teaching-Learning and Evaluation** • Admission Process • Catering to Diverse Needs • Teaching-Learning Process • Teacher Quality • Evaluation of Teaching • Evaluation of Learning • Evaluation Reforms
III.	**Research, Consultancy and Extension** • Promotion of Research • Research Output • Publication Output • Consultancy • Extension Activities	IV.	**Infrastructure and Learning Resources** • Physical Facilities • Maintenance of Infrastructure • Library as Learning Resource • Computer as Learning Resource

	• Participation in Extension • Linkages		• Other facilities
V.	**Student Support and Progression** • Student Profile • Student Progression • Student Support • Student Activities.	**VI.**	**Organization and Management** • Goal Orientation and Decision Making • Organization Structure, Powers and Functions of the Functionaries • Perspective planning • Human Power Planning and Recruitment • Performance Appraisal • Staff Development programmes • Resource Mobilization • Finance Management
VII.	**Healthy / Innovative Practices/** • Total Quality Management • Innovations • Value Based Education • Social Responsibilities and Citizenship Roles • Overall Development • Institutional Ambience and initiatives.		

THE GRADING SYSTEM OF NAAC

NAAC followed Star System and Nine-point scale system up to March 2007 and Cumulative Grade Point Average (CGPA) System from April 2007 which are reflected in Table 2, 3 and 4 as follows:

Table 2: Grading according to the Star System

Grade	*Instructions Weighted Score in % (Upper Limit Exclusive)*
A*****	>=75
A****	70-75
A***	65-70
A**	60-65
A*	55-60

Table 3: Grading according to Nine-Point scale up to 2007

Grade	*Institutional Score (Upper Limit Exclusive)*
A++	95-100
A+	90-95
A	85-90
B++	80-85
B+	75-80
B	70-75
C++	65-70
C+	60-65
C	55-60

Table 4: Grading according to the Cumulative Grade Point Average (CGPA) Grading from April 2007

Letter Grade	*Range of CGPA*	*Performance Descriptor*
A	3.01-4.00	Very Good (Accredited)
B	2.01-3.00	Good (Accredited)
C	1.51-2.00	Satisfactory (Accredited)
D	< = 1.50	Unsatisfactory (Not Accredited)

QUALITY INSTITUTIONS IN ODISHA: THE ROLE OF NAAC AT A GLANCE

Odisha has made significant progress in higher education in terms of number of higher educational institutions but not in quality of higher education. Quality has become the buzz-word on campuses of higher education and the NAAC, almost a household name. In its short span of existence, the NAAC has formulated the guidelines and procedures for assessment and accreditation and conducted a large number of awareness programmes to familiarize the institutions with the process.

The State Quality Assurance Cell has an important role in ensuring effectiveness, efficiency and accountability in universities and colleges of Odisha. It promotes quality awareness, recognizes quality achievements of educational institutions and provides a forum of sharing successful strategies. The cell also provides a framework for designing, implementing, assessing and managing the quality of educational institutions in the state. As per the NAAC guidelines, assessment and accreditation process has been exercised through the joint ventures of NAAC and the institution being assessed in Odisha. The Directorate of Higher Education, Odisha functions as a good liasoning agency between the NAAC eligible colleges and universities. This is made mandatory for assessment and accreditation of all government and aided educational Institutions. NAAC has become a pre-requisite for higher education institutions to get financial support form the UGC.

NAAC has so far accredited and graded 07 universities, and 204 colleges in Odisha up to July 2012 which is reflected in Table 5.

Table 5: NAAC Performance of Odisha (up to July 2012)

Universities		*Colleges*	
Number	Grade	Number	Grade
03	A	12	A
01	B++	08	B++
02	B+	23	B+
01	B	82	B
		40	C++
		13	C+
		26	C

*At the time of accreditation both nine points and CGPA scale system are used in rating the NAAC accredited universities and colleges in Odisha.

Out of 204 colleges, two colleges have been reaccredited recently by NAAC.

FINDINGS

Odisha has made significant progress in higher education in terms of quantitative expansion but it lacks behind qualitative achievements. One of the studies conducted by NAAC after assessing a number of institutions, it was found that the curricula followed are outdated and have not been revised for one or two decades. Our educational system is extremely rigid and highly compartmentalized. There is no academic flexibility in curricular renderings. Curriculum over the years has become socially irrelevant for which it needs revisions.

Teaching-learning process is one of the main indicators of quality in higher education. It was found that in majority of institutions, there is crushing faculty shortage. The method of teaching is not student-centric rather teacher-centric. Teaching is only imparted through lecture method. Experiments, project and practical methods are seen in teaching of few subjects. For evaluation purpose examinations in majority colleges are designed once in a year which only test the memory rather than understanding.

There are no adequate books in the library, no computer facility, no audio-visual aids in the institutions. At the same time insufficient staff quarters, inadequate laboratory and lack of teaching-learning materials as a whole obstruct the progress. There is very little ICT enabled teaching, possibly due to resource crunch. As a whole, infrastructure in many institutions is not adequate and maintenance is very poor.

NAAC has revealed that research is the weakest link in the quality of higher education in Odisha. Academic and industry linkage is very limited. Community outreach activities are ad-hoc and have virtually no positive impact on society.

It was found that ten per cent of the institutions have no formal and informal arrangements for counseling. There is limited provision for students' welfare.

Different types of institutions have also developed their own system of financing. The state government in many cases does not follow the UGC rules and norms. On the one hand it gives permission for mushrooming growth of colleges, on the other it does not take any responsibility for funding in lines or the quality of institutions. Unequal salary, for equal work in colleges creates confusion, frustration, and a kind of inertia in the minds of the teachers.

Quality of Higher education in Odisha has been disrupted by commercialization of education, coming of poor quality of students for general education, low salary, service insecurity, lack of scope for professional growth of faculty and healthy practices.

CONCLUSION

It is evident from the focus group discussion and observation of quality assessment organizations like NAAC that the following strategic step to be taken to ensure and ascertain the quality education in Odisha.

In the rapidly changing scenario of higher education, every college needs to explore the possibility of introducing more need-based diversified courses supplemented with career-oriented professional subjects and quality infrastructure. It will be more effective in maintaining flexibility in curriculum design.

The institution needs to recruit adequate number of competent, talented and meritorious faculty members so as to make the teaching-learning process more effective and student-centric. It may be more productive if the faculty will adopt modern innovative techniques and technologies at the time of teaching.

Research activity needs to be strengthened and the faculty members be encouraged to publish more research papers/books and take up, M.Phil./Ph.D. programmes. To update their knowledge, the government as well as the institutions need take step to organize orientation and refresher courses as well as seminars, workshops, conferences and other academic programmes from time to time.

Reformation in examination system is to be need by introducing internal and semester system for promotion of students to higher classes. Students' evaluation of teachers' performance through structured formats in the institutes of higher education is to be introduced.

Along with these, infrastructure and quality as well as position of faculty member are to be monitored and evaluated periodically by universities/ government agencies other than UGC, AICTE.

For augmenting financial resources in higher education institutions there are the need of consultancy by the faculty members, more linkages with the industries, running of some need-based certificate courses, and so on. The management of private institutes having professional and technical education need to ensure that the faculty members continue to gain experience in their institutions.

A beginning towards quality assurance in higher education may be made by paying attention to deficiencies in infrastructure facilities and members of faculty in different academic departments. A certain minimum level of such inputs is be ensured in every institution.

Our higher education has been facing great challenges. They are related to finance, accessibility, equality, enhancement and preservation of quality in teaching, research and extension, and governance of institutions. Therefore, higher education is usually meant for developing the professional excellence and intellectual integrity of every institution. As a result of which every institution will get a boost for creating and sustaining quality relevance in respect of all the emerging needs.

In considering the above factors, the Government of Odisha along with related bodies and stakeholders of higher education need to take appropriate steps with positive attitudes to bring quality development in higher education. This can enable to produce expected enlighten generations in future for both individual up-liftment and national development.

Thus, analyzing the available data, findings and the paper is designed to focus on some positive feedbacks on quality education which appear to be the key factors in higher education. Universal accessibility to quality education is considered essential for charging the mind of individuals and emerging society with trained, efficient and accountable manpower to build a strong nation. However, the rapid expansion of higher education institutions in India in general and Odisha in particular, the role of the quality assurance organizations like NAAC is unchallenged one.

REFERENCES

Aruchcami, M. (2004). Quality Imperative in Higher Education. New Delhi: *University News.*

Bhatanagar, S. and Saxena, A. (2006). *Modern Indian Education and Its Problem.* Meerut: Surya Publication.

Bhuyan, Sindhu, ed. (2010). *A Souvenir on Assurance for Bringing Quality Development of Higher Education.* Department of Education, Alaka Mahabidyalaya, Jagatsinghpur: Radhakanta Press.

Coling, C. and Harvey, L. (1995). Quality Control Assurance and Assessment in the link to Continuous Improvement, Quality Assurance in Education, 3 (4),

Crosby, Philip B. (1984). *Quality Without Tears*. Singapore: McGraw Hill.

Harvey, L. and Green, D. (1993). Defining 'Quality' Assessment and Evaluation in Higher Education. 18 (A).

Juran, J. (1989). *Leadership for Quality: An Executive Handbook.* New York: Free Press.

NAAC (2003). *Total Quality Management for Tertiary Education.* Bangalore: NAAC.

NAAC (2004). *Guidelines for Re-Accreditation.* Bangalore: NAAC.

NAAC (2005). *NAAC: A Profile*. Bangalore: NAAC.

NAAC (2006). *NAAC year of Student Participation.* Bangalore: NAAC, 6 (1).

Nigvekar, A.S. (1996). Quality Assurance in Higher Education: An Indian Dilemma. *Journal of Higher Education.* 19 (3),

Pathan, S.N. (2005). Quality Improvement Programme in Higher Education Through NAAC. Bhopal: Intellectual Book Bureau.

Pilai, C.R. (2006). Understanding Quality in Higher Education. Personal Communication to NAAC.

Planning and Co-ordination Department (2011-12), *Economic Survey.* Bhubaneswar: Govt. of Odisha.

Prasad, V.S. (2005). Value Framework for Assessment of Higher Education Institutions. Bangalore: NAAC.

Stella, A. and Gnanam, A. (2003). *Foundation of External Quality as soon as in Indian Higher Education.* New Delhi: Concept Publishing Company.

Saha, Beena. (1988). New Technologies, Lecture Tradition in Higher Education, *University News*. New Delhi: AIU, 25 (49)

29

Changing Trends on Governance of Higher Education – Collegiate Education

Buela Johnson

COLLABORATION OF GOVERNMENT AND REGULATORY BODIES AND EDUCATION INDUSTRY IN TRANSFORMING HIGHER EDUCATION AS A HOLISTIC INDUSTRY

On 25th July 2012, Shri Pranab Mukherjee said, "Education is the true alchemy that can bring India its next golden age. Our motto is unambiguous: All for knowledge, and knowledge for all".

The Government has taken strong steps in the 11th Five Year Plan to increase opportunities in higher education, relieve skill shortages in the economy, and increase competitiveness. The goal for the 11th Five Year Plan for 2007-2012 is an increase of five per cent in the enrolment rate of higher education equivalent to the creation of approximately 8 million new seats in Indian higher and technical education. Some of the steps are: (i) establishment of a central autonomous university in each state, (ii) higher education institutions in each district of the countries, (iii) private institutions to be granted deemed university status, (iv) creation of more Inter-University Centers, and (v) funding of up to 150 new polytechnics autonomous colleges. Further, all institutions are asked to make higher education more inclusive, more responsive to economic needs, and raise quality. Therefore, the public and the government are likely to increase investment into higher education, and in return demand accelerated change in the higher education sector. The governance of the Indian Higher education sector is changing. Like the Indian economy underwent a liberalizing in the 1990s, the education system is gradually being opened up for change and decentralization. In particular, the federal and state governments are gradually giving higher education institutions more decision and spending power. This represents a move away from detailed government control over spending, teaching, and curriculum decisions, which required frequent approval from federal or state government.

The University Grants Commission which came into existence on 28.12.1953 became a statutory body of Government of India by an Act of Parliament in 1956. The Section 12 of the UGC Act provides that the Commission shall in consultation with the concerned universities, take all such steps as it may think fit for the promotion and coordination of university education and for the maintenance of standards in teaching, examination and research. For teaching and research, extension was added as the third dimension of education by the Commission. The UGC serves as a vital link between the Union and State Governments and the institutions of higher learning. In addition to its role of giving grants to universities and colleges, the University Grants Commission also advises Central and State Governments on the measures necessary for the improvement of university education. It also frames regulations such as those on the minimum standards of instruction and qualifications of teachers on the advice of subject specialists and academicians with whom it frequently interacts in connection with the formulation, evaluation and monitoring of programmes. Higher Education in India has evolved in distinct and divergent streams with each stream monitored by an apex body, indirectly controlled by the Ministry of Human Resource Development. The 550 universities/institutions, are mostly funded by the state governments. However, there are 40 important universities called Central universities, which are maintained by the Union Government and because of relatively large funding, they have an edge over the others. The engineering education and business schools are monitored and accredited by the All India Council for Technical Education (AICTE) while medical education is monitored and accredited by the Medical Council of India (MCI). Like-wise, agriculture education and research is monitored by the Indian Council for Agriculture Research. Apart from these, National Council for Teacher Education (NCTE) controls all the teacher training institutions in the country. The country has some ace engineering, management and medical education institutions which are directly funded by the Ministry of Human Resource Development of the Union Government. Admission to all professional education colleges is done through all-India common admission tests of which the IIT-JEE, AIEEE, CAT and CPMT are the most popular ones. Most of the institutions reserve a small percentage of seats for foreign students. On January 3, 2011 the President Mr. Pranab Mukherjee stressed on evolving an educational system that imbibes scientific culture and focuses on innovation to compete in a globalised economy. He also called upon the scientific fraternity to work in a "time bound manner" to help India win a Noble Prize in science, as he noted that its over 83 years since C.V. Raman won the Noble Prize for Physics at an International Conference at Kolkata.

Ownership, Management and Administration – Current Trends, Coordination and Code of Conduct

Governance in higher education refers to the means by which higher educational (also tertiary or postsecondary) institutions are formally organized and managed, though often there is a distinction between definitions of management and governance. Simply, university governance is the way in which universities are operated. Governing structures for higher education are highly differentiated throughout the world. Noted by Altbach (2005: 16-18) the different models for higher education throughout the world nonetheless do share a common heritage. Coldrake, Stedman, and Little (2003: 5) also discuss the shared traditions and history of higher education worldwide. Internationally, tertiary education includes private not-for-profit, private for-profit, and public institutions governed by differentiated structures of management. Governance and management of postsecondary institutions becomes even more diverse with the differences in defining the relationships between higher and tertiary education (university education), postsecondary education, technical and vocational education, and community college models of education. The issues are complicated by current debates over collegial and shared forms of governance contrasted to corporate and business forms of institutional governance.

The concept of governance for post-secondary education predominantly refers to the internal structure, organization and management of autonomous institutions. The organization of internal governance is generally composed of a governing board (board of regents, board of directors), the university president (executive head, CEO) with a team of administrative chancellors and staff, faculty senates, academic deans, department chairs, and usually some form of organization for student representation. In the United States, state institution governing boards often emphasize the concept of citizen governance in recognizing that board members serve a civic role for the institution. Managing structures themselves have become increasingly complex to establish a means of organizing an equally complicated system of intraorganizational, interorganizational and governmental relationships. Whether college and university education, adult education, technical and vocational education, the complexities of managing education in today's world proves true at all levels of private and public education (for even the interdependence with primary and elementary education to the management of secondary education).

Higher education in India is going through a transitory phase with rapid changes in a sector used to stagnation. However, the changes are not uniform; two contrasting trends are emerging in higher education with a rapidly expanding private sector at one end, and a public sector at the other in terminal decline. The regulatory system has failed to hold new private institutions to standards while erecting formidable barriers to competition and quality. The sector is tightly controlled by the government and as a result, regulatory bodies are poor at enforcement. In effect, the University Grants Commission (UGC), professional councils, a few research councils and state governments are the main regulators of the higher education sector. In addition, there are almost fifteen ministries/departments in the Government of India that establish, finance, or regulate higher education institutions and hence interfere in their working." The government has not armed regulatory bodies with the powers mandated by the Constitution. The regulatory bodies have also failed to devise a mechanism at their own level and have not framed appropriate rules and regulations; they have also not developed a system of supervision and control over the institutions they are required to deal with.

These bodies have been hampered by low levels of independence, both functional and financial, in discharging their functions. For example, the UGC is vested with the responsibility of coordination and provision of funds and, determination and maintenance of standards in higher educational institutions. The UGC does not have the means to control the quality of teaching and recruitment of faculty, ensure minimum infrastructure for all institutions and engage in the monitoring and promotion of research." In all, the higher education institutions and regulatory bodies are maintained and funded by the government and key appointments are also made by the government.

This enables the government to have a final say on major issues:

To improve the regulatory environment in this sector, the National Knowledge Commission (NKC), an expert group, has recommended the establishment of an Independent Regulatory Authority for Higher Education (IRAHE) that would be an umbrella organisation founded under a separate statutory act. The IRAHE is expected to foster competition as well as accountability in institutions. The IRAHE would be the only agency to accord degree granting power to higher educational institutions and monitor standards, settle disputes, and license accreditation agencies. IRAHE would provide single window clearance and replace multiple existing regulatory agencies which have often been inconsistent in their adherence to principles. To sum up, regulatory reforms are important for attracting investment to creation of infrastructure and promoting consumer satisfaction to the extent possible. In India, (so called) independent regulators have been established in certain sectors but the government has continued to encroach on the domains of various regulators in the name of achieving policy objectives. A clear distinction between policy and regulation and its use in practice is required.

SOUND EDUCATIONAL SYSTEMS AND SET UP IN DEVELOPING ECONOMY

Cases and Models with Reference to Philosophy, Politics and Professionalism

CASE 1

Madras Christian College established in 1835. It was named after the supreme governing body of the Church of Scotland and aimed at attracting students from the Hindu higher castes with the aim of "conveying as great as an amount of truth as possible through the channel of a good education especially of Bible truth". The college grew from the school into a 375-acre (1.52 km^2) wooded campus under the leadership of educationalist Dr. William Miller, who created hostels and several academic and cultural associations, which shaped MCC into a premier educational institution in South Asia. The rapid expansion of the college and the paucity of the space necessitated moving the campus to a more spacious location. Accordingly, the college under the leadership of Rev. William Skinner (principal 1909–1921) initiated the Tambaram Project in 1919. Rev. Gordon Matthew as the town planning secretary negotiated with the government, which set aside 390 acres (1.6 km^2) of the former Selaiyur forest land in Tambaram. While Mrs. and Prof. Edward

Barnes meticulously planted rare tress and worked out the physical landscape, the Swiss architect Henry Schaetti, then based in Kodiakanal, India, designed the buildings. After 100 years in the heart of the city, the college moved to the sprawling, green campus in Tambaram on the outskirts of Madras in 1937.

On 30 January 1937, the governor of Madras, Lord John Erskine declared open the first campus buildings. The hostel gave way to three halls of residence – Selaiyur, Thomas' and Heber – active today as semi-autonomous student communities. Women students were admitted on a regular basis from 1939, and a hostel for them came up in Guindy, Madras in 1950. This too evolved into an on-campus hall of residence for women, Martin Hall, named after Agnes Martin, in 1968.

Governance and Leadership

MCC's leadership in governance and education has arguably evolved its familial culture and values-driven education. The Rev. Dr. A.J. Boyd led the college for 18 years (1938–56). General Krishnaswamy Sundarji's autobiography reveals that Boyd knew each student personally. Sundarji relates in his book that when he expressed his intention to join the army, discontinuing his studies, Boyd advised him against it as he believed Sundarji would make a good doctor rather than a good soldier.

After Boyd, Prof MacPhail became principal, who was then succeeded by the first Indian principal of the college, Dr. Chandran Devanesan in 1962. A man of Gandhian principles, Devanesan involved the faculty and students in working with the neighbouring community in Tambaram. This period (1962-72) is affectionately referred to by MCCians as "The Devanesan Decade". Several principals of MCC have been appointed vice-chancellors of universities across India and have distinguished themselves as successful educationalists and administrators.

The college was one of the first in India to be granted Autonomy in 1978 and the first batch of Autonomous graduates passed out in 1981. The year 2006 marked the Silver Jubilee of Autonomy for Madras Christian College.

The college offers over 30 regular courses in undergraduate and postgraduate programmes in Arts, Sciences, and Commerce, besides undergraduate programmes in vocational streams of Archaeology, Musicology and Industrial Fish and Fisheries; and post graduate programmes in Social Work (MSW) and Computer Applications (MCA). A number of departments at the college offer M. Phil. and Ph.D. programmes.

Besides the regular programmes, MCC offers undergraduate programmes and post graduate programmes in the self-financed stream, including courses in Journalism, Geography, Tourism, Travel Management, Microbiology, Physical Education, Visual Communication, Marine studies and Coastal Resource Management, Computer Oriented Business Applications and Social Work (BSW), besides regular course in Arts, Commerce and Sciences.

MCC has 38 departments including day and evening streams, with over 10,000 students. Half the student body are women and several faculty members are women teachers. The institution has about 220 faculty members, over half of whom are doctorate-holders.

CASE 2

The University of Delhi is the premier university of the country and is known for its high standards in teaching and research and attracts eminent scholars to its faculty. It was established in 1922 as a unitary, teaching and residential university by an Act of the then Central Legislative Assembly. The President of India is the Visitor, the Vice President is the Chancellor and the Chief Justice of the Supreme Court of India is the Pro-Chancellor of the University.

Ever since its inception, a strong commitment to excellence in teaching and research has made the University of Delhi a role-model and path-setter for other universities in the country. Its rich academic tradition has always attracted the most talented students who later on went on to make important contributions to their society.

When the University took birth, only three colleges existed in Delhi then: St. Stephen's College founded in 1881, Hindu College founded in 1899 and Ramjas College founded in 1917, which were subsequently affiliated to it. The University thus had a modest beginning with just three colleges, two faculties (Arts and Science) and about 750 students. In October 1933, the University offices and the Library shifted to the Viceregal Lodge Estate, and till today this site houses the offices of the main functionaries of the University. The University has grown into one of the largest universities in India. At present, there are 16 faculties, 86 academic departments, 77 colleges and 5 other recognised institutes spread all over the city, with 132435 regular students (UG:114494, PG:17941) and 261169 students (UG:258831, PG:2338) in non-formal education programme.

CASE 3

Bangalore University is located in the Garden City of Bangalore aptly hailed as the "IT Capital of India", was established in July 1964 as an off shoot of the University of Mysore, primarily to include institutions of higher learning located in the metropolitan city of Bangalore and the districts of Bangalore, Kolar and Tumkur, which eventually became a separate university. Initially, the two premier colleges of the city, the Central College (CC) and the University Visvesvaraya College of Engineering (UVCE) formed the nucleus of Bangalore University. Soon after the establishment of Bangalore University, as a first step in the re-organization of courses instructions, the University introduced Honours Courses in the year 1965-66.

Bangalore University has completed forty seven years of fruitful existence and has come to be hailed as one of the largest universities of Asia. Though originally intended to be a federal university, it has eventually emerged as an affiliating University. The University was first accredited in 2002 by NAAC with Five Star Status and was re-accredited in the year 2008 with 'A' Grade. According to *India Today* – Nielsen survey of May 31st 2010, Bangalore University ranks 13th in the list of 50 top Universities in the Country. Academically, the University is structured into six faculties – Arts, Science, Commerce and Management, Education, Law and Engineering. It has 43 Post Graduate Departments, One post graduate Centre at Kolar, (Started during 1994-95), three constituent colleges, 665 affiliated colleges (of which 115 have PG Courses) and several other Centres and Directorates of higher learning and research under its purview. At present, the University offers 50 Post Graduate Courses and Employment Oriented Diploma and Certificate Courses. The University has launched the Five years Integrated Courses in Biological Sciences, Social Sciences, Earth and Atmospheric Sciences and Business Studies and the Four-Years B.S. Programme and will be starting a course in Criminology and Rehabilitation from this academic year.

The Bangalore University has achieved milestones by establishing MOUs with Universities and Institutions of national and international repute.

To cater to a student population of over three lakhs, the University is striving to provide access, expansion and excellence in higher education. The vision of the University is to make distinctive and significant contributions to the cause of higher education in Humanities, Social Science Law, Commerce, Science and Technology.

COMMODITATION vs. CUSTOMIZATION OF HIGHER EDUCATION IN INDIA

Students Aren't Customers; Education is not a Commodity

By only viewing education as a way to a higher-paying job we're giving a free pass to the prevailing machinery of power. At so many of today's so-called institutions of higher learning, students are offered a straightforward answer: For a better job, higher salary, more marketable skills, and more impressive credentials. All the more so in today's collapsing job market. It's simply not enough to prepare students for a job: We need to prepare them for life, while challenging them to think beyond the confines of their often parochial and provincial upbringings. (As a child of the working class from a provincial background, I speak from experience.) And here's one compelling lesson all of us, students and teachers alike, need to relearn constantly: If you view education in purely instrumental terms as a way to a higher-paying job – if it's merely a mechanism for mass customization within a marketplace of ephemeral consumer goods – you've effectively given a free pass to the prevailing machinery of power and those who run it.

Customization should be towards: The development of information and communication technologies (ICT); The marketization in HE (including changing roles of national governments); Globalization, internationalization and regionalization; The advance of the network society or economy (consortia, public private partnerships, transnational cooperation); The advance of the knowledge (driven) society or economy; Socio-cultural trends; Demographic trends. Vincent-Lancrin, of the OECD's Centre for Educational

Research and Innovation de la OECD develops a similar list and according to this study, the driving forces that will affect higher education in the future are: demographic changes; funding difficulties; internationalization; technology; liberalization; new public governance; knowledge economy; increasing partnerships; diversity of providers; lifelong learning; intellectual property issues.

Marketization – Origin and effects: Among these trends, it is useful to begin with marketization. This is a term which is part of the vocabulary of New Public Management (NPM) and can be understood as the use of markets, or market type mechanisms (MTM), with the (explicit or implicit) aim of improving public sector activities, including the production of public goods. "New public management is conventionally understood as a recipe for correcting the perceived failings of traditional public bureaucracies over efficiency, quality, customer-responsiveness and effective leadership. Public-management reform is often presented as a functional response to such shortcoming. When considering the implementation of these reforms, the term "managerialism" is frequently used.

Is Education a Commodity?

Some have questioned whether, or not education is a commodity. The unfortunate fact is that in the age of globalization and a technology based economy education is a commodity. What you know, and how much you know determines, largely where you will go in your life. Shubert (2004) declares, "One area in which we can quickly do damage to our universities' reputation is the question of the extent to which we will treat higher education as a commodity no different from the raw materials and manufactured goods we export." (Shubert, 2005, Para 5) The damage has already been done, the perception of education as a commodity that arose with globalization and de-industrialization has led to a situation in the United Kingdom and the United States where a university education today is worth less (dependent on one's field of study) than A and O levels or a high school diploma was twenty years ago.

This perception of education as a commodity has worked very well in fact, to change education into a commodity. Unfortunately, this has only worked to increase the competition to get into schools where the education is considered to be worth the student's or their parent's money, and to increased costs to cover the cost of marketing one's school in the education market. Shubert (2004) states that, "Critics say British schools are charging exorbitant fees, in the range of seven times what domestic students pay, to make up for low domestic fees and inadequate public support" (Shubert, 2004, Para 8). This is not just true in the United Kingdom. Research on the Internet indicated that many schools in the United States charge exorbitant tuition and fees to international students in order to cover the costs of marketing their schools.

Moore (2000) argues, "Investing in education pays off just as investing in the stock market does, provided you wait long enough. Attending a better school gets you a better job and a better income. In other words, a certified level of education is a commodity-something that is useful and can be turned to commercial advantage." Much like with other investments however, one must have the patience to wait and watch the value of one's education grow, before one receives a payoff. Wahlberg (2003) states that, "the reality that schools are institutions imbued with social meaning does not contradict the reality that schooling is also a commodity that can be bought and sold, one whose supply responds to cost and demand and other rules of economics." (Wahlberg, 2003, p. 216)

Education in the era of globalization is a commodity and as such, it is labeled, branded, marketed and sold to eager young consumers, anxious to provide themselves with the best education that money can buy, figuring that the more expensive one's education is, the more payoffs the investment will have in the end. Unfortunately, the value of an education is subjective and in many cases, the investment never pays off.

The Marketing of Education

Recruitment and Marketing of Schools: In the era of globalization, education has become an increasingly competitive field; Schools at every level compete for the best athletes, the best academic achievers, the most creative students, and the most alumni donations. This occurs at all levels of education and has caused the public to look at education as a commodity that can be bought and sold just like everything else. Shannon (2005), states that, "who would have imagined even 15 years ago that students attention at schools could be sold to advertisers over Channel One" (Shannon, 2005, p. 51)

Education is marketed, sold and purchased in much the same way that other commodities are. Schools spend significant amounts of their budgets on marketing and according to Shannon (2005), many schools have turned to corporate sponsorship so that they can offer improved computer labs, new and technologically up to date gymnasiums complete with Olympic sized swimming pools, and all of the latest textbooks to appease the students and their parents. This begins in elementary school and continues throughout the college years. This marketing of education and as a by-product schools themselves is no longer a phenomenon of Western nations such as the United Kingdom and the United States however, recently nations as diverse as the nations of the former U.S.S.R., as well as Australia and New Zealand have begun marketing their schools as products to be consumed rather than as a resource for bright young minds.

GLOBAL REFORMS AND RENAISSANCE IN INDIAN HE ON GLOBAL STANDARDS AS THE FUTURE OF GOVERNANCE

Globalization as "the seemingly relentless integration of economies, societies and cultures into a borderless worldwide communications [technology] and supply network [is] a world-transforming process…not all which is pleasant," (Morrison, 2010, p. 32). Although globalization is, and will probably remain for some time, one of "the most nebulous and misunderstood" concepts

(Beck, 2001, p. 19), there is some common ground to be found among all the confusion. That is the idea of connections and relationships that go beyond the immediate, local environment (Gray, 1999). "Globalization is the process by which all peoples and communities come to experience an increasingly common economic, social and cultural environment; but globalization as a theory, deals with the compression of the world and intensification of consciousness of the world as a whole" (Robertson, 1992, p. 8).One critical issue that emerges from all of these restructuring processes is the central role of knowledge, education and learning for the success of the Global Information Society (GIS) and global information economy. Globalization impacts all aspects of society. Higher education may be one of the most affected by global trends, and economics and business contents seem particularly influenced by them. Otherwise, these fields, as social sciences, are framed by the culture of each region. The globalization of the economy and its concomitant demands on the workforce requires a different education that enhances the ability of learners to access, assess, adopt, and apply knowledge, to think independently to exercise appropriate judgment and to collaborate with others to make sense of new situations. Globalization is not the only factor behind the changes that are affecting education, and likewise it is not the only factor that motivates the local interest groups that formulate policy. Nevertheless globalization has posed challenges of a hitherto unknown nature to nation states, and much of the seemingly recent, never-ending change in education is a corollary of these challenges. The nature and complexity of the forces involved in globalization that any discussion of its impact upon education raises fundamental issues and should be a matter of considerable debate among educationists, researchers, and policy makers.

India is one of the largest higher education system in the world facing the crisis of, university of the poor, with continued expansion, deteriorating standards, limited resources, and political involvement (Swar & Panday, 2008). In this regard, it is important to note that recently, the Indian government has approved the Foreign Education Providers (Regulatory) Bill (2010) that will allow foreign universities to open branches in India. When this bill becomes a law after approval in the parliament, foreign universities will be able to enter the education market. However, this raises some concerns among Indian politicians as many believe that there would be no control, over export and import of higher education, and the private institutions, from overseas would open branches in India, exchange of degrees and certificates that would go on without any restrictions. Some of politicians argue that Indian Universities are already at loss as more than 50,000 students of our country are studying abroad in U.S., Australia and U.K., where as a very small number of foreign students are seeking admissions in Indian Universities.

On the other hand, some politicians argue that the presence of foreign universities, within India would also undermine task of creation of knowledge and services for the community and for nation building, as Indian Universities have their special mission to provide traditional educational values, which perpetuate the caste system which severely impacts women along with teaching, learning and research. The vedic values of gurukul, are embedded in the higher education of India, to preserve the cultural heritage to keep our customs, rituals and spiritual touch of divinity alive (Swar & Pandey, 2008). The suggestion is that for higher education faculty and administrators, our university policies can greatly impact our international and national students to help them explore innovative perspectives to educate humankind for future global citizenship. Education toward a future where global cooperation is the social norm and the notion of universal citizenship is the foundation of a globalized world. Universities, though pressured by market forces can and must lead in framing education policies to ensure that the common good of the world is our focus.

The objective of education is no longer simply to convey a body of knowledge, but to teach how to learn, problem-solve and synthesize the old with the new. The emphasis is less on community and equity, and rather more on individual advancement and the need to satisfy investors and influential consumers. Education has come to resemble a private, rather than public, good. Only focused aware actions by those in higher education can ensure the role of universities in the promise of a better life. Thus, there is an urgent need for setting up new agendas and curricula issues to address the challenges of higher education in a globalized world. It is important to note that global processes are putting immense pressure on educational practices world-wide. Spring (2009) not only underscores the emergence of the global superstructures and multi-national corporations in the education sectors but also reminds us that that we cannot simply ignore global processes in the evaluations of educational (including higher education) policies, practices, discourses, and curriculum in local contexts.

We propose that higher education institutions consider in their strategic planning the world-wide forces from economic and social perspectives. First, the challenge that most global educators are facing is to design visionary and new agendas to cultivate a re-vision of humankind with the view of generating the learners' intellect necessary to cope with the complexity of globalization as an evolving new reality. The emergence of globalization is making educators' task more challenging than ever it was. Second, it must be the utmost priority of the higher institutes to cater the needs and demands of diverse population of the global world. Third, higher education institutions need to look for all possible avenues and to foster their quality of education.

FINDINGS

1. Government plays major role in Legitimizing, Reforming and Regulating HE in order to depict Uniformity, Equity and Access, also Quality.
2. Government is Liberalizing HE more in the form of Change and Decentralization unlike the Economy in Instrumentalization of Education Policies, Investments also Infrastructure accordingly.

3. Governance changes and gets updated as the time and technology changes, so government also supports in India.
4. Issues, Changing roles and responsibility, Systems and Structures of HE gave new approaches to the Governance in order to be at the most flexible.
5. Stake holders of HE Governance are Nation at large, Government, Universities, Institutional Owners and Management, Teachers and Students, Society and Markets etc.
6. Three cases that were analyzed in the study depicts that, Universities and Colleges change face of society at large as they are potential to generate Human Capital to the Employment or Entrepreneurial activity in turn Empowering the Youth through their effective Governance in regulating He reforms as well as imparting education the Masses.
7. Education is neither commodity nor a thing to be marketed, it is considered so due other factors like Utility of Time, Application of Technology and Techniques of imparting education.
8. Education should be customized not commoditized, since the needs of masses are changing invariably.
9. Globalization has affected the Economy on all grounds. Education can only solve and supply the complete support to the society as well as the nation at large to accept effects and impact of globalization
10. Global standards and reforms are part of Nation since centuries, it is not new, HE is the most affected segment.

Contributors

Agarwal, Rajesh, Department of Sociology, K.R. [PG] College, Mathura, Uttar Pradesh.

Ahmad, Jasim, Assistant Professor, IASE, Faculty of Education, Jamia Millia Islamia, New Delhi.

Altaf, Faiza, Research Scholar, Jamia Millia Islamia, New Delhi.

Bafila, Gaurav Singh, Research Scholar, Jamia Millia Islamia, New Delhi.

Bohet, Ajit Kumar, Assistant Professor, IASE, Faculty of Education, Jamia Millia Islamia, New Delhi.

Chaudhary, Deepti Rani, Assistant Professor, Khalsa College of Education, Amritsar.

Gupta, Ankur, Asst. Professor, Department of B.Ed., Hashmi Girls PG College, Amroha, U.P.

Gupta, Savita, Assistant Professor, BIT, Rajasthan.

Johnson, Buela, Lecturer Sambhram Academy of Management Studies, Bangalore.

Juyal, Megha, Research Scholar, Education Department, Hemwati Nandan Bahuguna Garhwal (Central) University Srinagar, Pauri Garhwal, Uttarakhand.

Kamal, Peeyush, UGC Senior Research Fellow, Department of TT & NFE (IASE), Faculty of Education, Jamia Millia Islamia, New Delhi.

Kamble, B.N., Professor and Director, Center for Educational Studies, Indian Institute of Education, Pune, Maharashtra.

Keshari, Rakesh Kumar, Asst. Professor-in-Education, Dewan Institute of Management Studies, Meerut.

Khan, Fauzia, Associate Professor, Jamia Millia Islamia, New Delhi.

Kumar, Kawendra, Asst. Professor, Department of Education, Bhagwant College of Education, Muzaffarnagar, U.P.

Kumar, Sushil, Asst. Professor-in-Education CAEHS, Meerut.

Mishra, L., Principal, Vivek College of Education, Bijnor, Uttar Pradesh.

Pandey, Dheeraj Kumar, Research Scholar, Faculty of Education (Kamachha), BHU, Varanasi.

Parveen, Naushaba, Principal, Hashmi Girls PG College, Amroha (U.P.).

Raft, Zakiya, Associate Professor, Sociology Department, R.B.D. PG College, Bijnor.

Rajput, Shalini, Research Scholar, Vivek College of Education, Bijnor.

Ray, Biswajet, Asst. Professor, Alaka College, Puri, Odisha.

Rout, Gyanendra Kumar, Assistant Professor (Education), Government Degree College, Rikhnikhal Pauri Garhwal, Uttarakhand.

Shukla, Brajesh Kumar, Assistant Professor, Institute of Education, SHEPA, Varanasi.

Shukla, C.S., Head, Department of Teacher Education, Vardhaman (PG) College, Bijnor.

Siddique, Ismat Jahan, Faculty of Education, Jamia Millia Islamia, New Delhi.

Siddiqui, Mohammad Shaheer, Assistant Professor, Department of Education, Visva-Bharati, Santiniketan, West Bengal.

Singh, Kartar, IASE, Faculty of Education, Jamia Millia Islamia, New Delhi.

Singh, Vidhi, Asst. Professor, Department of Education, Bhagwant College of Education, Muzaffarnagar, U.P.

Sinha, Bipasha, Assistant Professor, Department of Education, S.S. Galen Girls' College, West Bengal.

Sur, Shyamasree, Research Scholar, University of Kalyani, West Bengal.

Swain, S.K., Faculty of Education, Banarus Hindu University, Varanasi.

Titrek, Osman, Associate Professor, Dr. Sakarya University Educational Science Department, Turkey.

Topal, Mithilesh, Research Scholar, Education Department, Kumaun University, Almora, Uttarakhand.

Tripathi, Lokpati, Research Scholar, Faculty of Education (Kamachha), BHU, Varanasi.

Tulika, Assistant Professor, Institute of Education, SHEPA, Varanasi.

Verma, J.S., Associate Professor, PG Department of Education, Hindu College, Moradabad.

Yusoof, Mohammad, Assistant Professor, Faculty of Education, Institute of Advanced Studies in Education, Jamia Millia Islamia, New Delhi.